"Modern art? What is it?"

"Scandalous! Shocking! Fanatical! Ugly! Insane!" were the early answers, from critics and public alike.

The answers are different now. Modern art is the art of our century. It has won its battle with time.

Here at last is a much-needed, popular and authoritative book on modern French art and the men who made it:

Manet	Seurat	Léger
Degas	Gauguin	Miro
Monet	Lautrec	Modigliani
Renoir	Rousseau	Rouault
Cézanne	Matisse	Mathieu
Van Gogh	Braque	Picasso

and thirty-two others

About the Author:

Sam Hunter is Lecturer in Fine Arts at Barnard College. A former art critic for the *New York Times,* he has written extensively on modern art for publications in America and Europe. He is the author of the monographs, *Toulouse-Lautrec, Raoul Dufy* and *Henri Matisse,* and is presently engaged writing a history of modern American painting and sculpture.

Modern French Painting

1855 — 1956

by Sam Hunter

A Dell First Edition

FOR MY WIFE, EDYS

Author's Note

The author wishes to acknowledge his appreciation for the many courtesies extended him by the museums, galleries and private collectors who have permitted their paintings to be reproduced in this book. Special thanks for their generous cooperation in putting materials at his disposal are owed to Miss Frances Pernas of the Museum of Modern Art, to Huntington Cairns of the National Gallery of Art, acting on behalf of Mr. Chester Dale, and to Marshall Davidson of the Metropolitan Museum of Art; the author also wishes to thank Henry Clifford of the Philadelphia Museum of Art, William S. Lieberman of the Museum of Modern Art and Frederick Sweet of the Art Institute of Chicago for their assistance in assembling photographic material. Mr. Bernard Karpel and the staff of the Museum of Modern Art Library have been most generous with their time.

The author wishes to thank Edward Parone for his enthusiasm and support throughout the project.

Without the original encouragement and interest of Karl Weston and S. Lane Faison it is not likely this volume would have seen the light of day; to them the author wishes to express a very particular gratitude.

Published by DELL PUBLISHING COMPANY, INC.
261 Fifth Avenue, New York 16, N. Y.

Designed and produced by Western Printing & Lithographing Company

Library of Congress Catalog Card Number 55-7514

Cover and book design by Jerome Kuhl

Printed in U. S. A.

Contents

Illustrations

Part I:

The Modern Spirit
1855 — 1895

"Modern times find themselves with an immense system of institutions, established facts, accredited dogmas, customs, rules, which have come to them from times not modern. In this system their life has to be carried forward; yet they have a sense that this system is not of their own creation, that it by no means corresponds exactly with the wants of their actual life, that, for them, it is customary, not rational. The awakening of this sense is the awakening of the modern spirit. The modern spirit is now awake almost everywhere. . . ."

Matthew Arnold, *Essays in Criticism* (1865)

Line Drawing: Edouard Manet. Portrait of Baudelaire. Etching, 1862
Second plate, first state, Bibliotheque Nationale, Paris

1

Salon of the Rejected

"He will be truly a painter, *the* painter, who will know how to draw out of our daily life its epic aspects, and will make us see and understand in color and design, how we are great and poetic in our neckties and polished boots."
—Charles Baudelaire, *Review of the Salon of 1845*

It is convenient to begin the story of modern painting in France with the so-called *Salon des Refusés* (Salon of the Rejected) in 1863, where Edouard Manet exhibited his revolutionary painting, *The Luncheon on the Grass* (see plate 5). The Salon represented the first organized protest by artists of progressive tendency against official art, and it was the rudimentary beginning of those exhibitions by "independents" that soon afterward punctuated the history of modern painting. In Manet's three works exhibited at the Salon, and especially in the very controversial *Luncheon,* the public received its most convincing demonstration of the boldest new techniques of painting.

The Salon had been initiated by decree of Emperor Napoleon III, after numerous complaints about the official biennial Salon's severe admissions policy were brought to his attention; in 1863 alone more than four thousand paintings had been turned down by the ultra-conservative jury. The "rejected" artists were now to be given their day in court, and the more vigorous and uncompromising among them welcomed this unique opportunity to appeal to the public over the heads of the parochial, Academy-dominated jury. The *Refusés* were certain to become marked men for subsequent Salon juries, but only a relatively small number of artists elected not to enter the counter-exhibition out of fear of future reprisals.

The exhibition was a huge public failure just as the established artists had hoped; ridicule and abuse were heaped on the participating artists in the press, and the public came to scoff. Even the Emperor found the exhibition a source of embarrassment and revoked the privilege the following year. Despite its poor reception, however, the Salon made significant history. It robbed official art institutions of their sanctity and created the schism between progressive and academic art that a decade later was to become open rebellion when the Impressionists established their independent group exhibitions. Perhaps most significantly, it focused public attention on Manet's radical technical innovations.

The Luncheon on the Grass soon became the scandal of the new Salon and the particular whipping boy of the most violent critics of modern painting. Manet had upset the public by taking a classical theme of figures in a landscape, based on a Renaissance engraving by Marcantonio Raimondi, and putting it in modern dress—and undress. He had posed a nude young woman in the company of two fully dressed gentlemen; the convincing naturalness of the figures and their setting left no classical allusions to hide behind. Accustomed to a convention of the nude based on vapid Greco-Roman idealizations, the public found Manet's charming realism and candor indecent, and critics in the leading journals of the day said as much. (When Cabanel that same year, however, had exhibited at the official Salon a Venus which was far more suggestive than Manet's figure and which was described by one observer as "wanton and lascivious," there was little reaction. The slick academicism of the work was widely admired, and it brought its creator public honors.) People were probably as offended by Manet's *peinture claire* methods as they were by his subject matter. Instead of following the prevailing academic practice of modeling with many value gradations from light to dark, Manet set down limpid and relatively unmodeled color in dramatic, flat tonal contrasts.

Manet's blithe defiance of contemporary taste at the *Salon des Refusés* conveniently and distinctly marks a great moment in the evolution of modern painting. His radical innovations, however, were possible only in an atmosphere that had been created by three leading spirits of his own and the immediately preceding generations: the painters Delacroix and Courbet and the poet-critic Baudelaire. They were the catalyzing agents that released the revolutionary forces of the modern spirit; and in the context of their time, their individual contributions take on a heroic dimension and significance.

In the middle of the nineteenth century French painting was ruled with an iron hand by the Academy of Fine Arts, which was composed of the various teachers in the Ecole des Beaux-Arts, in whose studios young artists received their education. The members of this august body controlled the juries of the biennial Salons, which, in the absence of private art galleries as we know them, were the only means of public recognition for the artist. They were influential in placing public commissions and also advised on museum purchasing policy. The style of their painting was some fifty years out of date and generally based on the neo-Roman recipes of David or the more supple but equally doctrinaire classicism of his most celebrated pupil, Ingres. Both David and Ingres were men of genius, but in the hands of their followers their artistic formulas were reduced to uninspired pedantry and a vulgar eclecticism. The Academy banned realistic subjects taken directly from contemporary life; these were considered unworthy of the high vocation of art. The ideal forms and linear mannerisms of Ingres were universally admired, and for Ingres such forms could exist only if paint were kept to an enamel smoothness, color restrained to a tint, and expression of personal emotion suppressed.

It was against the sterile rules and procedures of the Academy that the "romantic" painters Delacroix and Géricault had revolted. At the age of twenty-seven, and just five years before his death, Géricault exhibited at the Salon of 1819 a painting

that became a center of controversy: *The Raft of the Medusa.*
This painting was a history piece, a genre much favored by
academicians, but it was based on contemporary history, the
actual ordeal of a shipwrecked crew after their frigate had
sunk. It not only dealt with tangible realities, but it became a
vehicle for the expression of powerful emotions; its figuration
and mood of terror were quite consciously based on Michelangelo's Vatican frescoes, *The Last Judgment.* Géricault's subject was neither easy nor attractive, and he spared the public
few details of human suffering in the realistic, if slightly melodramatic, bodies of his desperate sailors. He portrayed death
not with the cold, marble presence of David's *Marat* but with
an intense physical reality. The painting also gave Géricault an
opportunity to exercise his personal interests in anatomy, human psychology, and the drama of human conflict.

Eugene Delacroix was profoundly affected by *The Raft of
the Medusa,* and it released new energies in him. Three years
later he painted his *Bark of Dante,* a work whose freedom and
emotional power were comparable to those of Géricault, and
in 1824 he exhibited at the Salon the even more significant and
ambitious composition, *Massacre at Chios.* This painting, like
Géricault's, was inspired by contemporary history, an incident
in the Greek wars of independence. (Lord Byron, another romantic apostle of human liberty, had celebrated Chios in poetry
and fought and died in Greece.) In Delacroix's art we find the
themes so characteristic of what is loosely called the romantic
movement: scenes of violent physical action and emotional
conflict; the struggle for liberty; moments of great psychological
drama, often extracted from the literature of Shakespeare,
Dante, or Sir Walter Scott. Later in his career, after a trip to
North Africa, Delacroix introduced a new exoticism of color
and subject in his art. In fact, his later technique and his subjects represented a much more personal expression based on
the most vivid color orchestrations.

By mid-century the tempo of romanticism had slackened,
and Delacroix alone carried it on, in the face of intense official
disapproval. The Academy refused Delacroix admission six
times and only grudgingly took him in six years before his
death in 1863. In his last years he became a solitary and remote

figure. A man of superior civilization and intelligence, as his remarkable journal amply demonstrates, he moved in a fashionable and refined intellectual milieu, but it rarely included other artists of the period. He was something of an artistic anomaly in his stubborn individualism, and his greatness was by no means apparent to the world of art or to the public at large. In his own period his genius, with its incalculable influence on modern art, had to be "smuggled through," as the French critic Georges Duthuit has aptly phrased it. Later in the century van Gogh was to copy from Delacroix and call him the pioneer of modern painting; Cézanne was to dream of painting an *Apotheosis of Delacroix* in which the figures of Monet, Pissarro, and himself would appear, and Seurat was to declare that he based his color theories directly on Delacroix's discoveries.

What did this artist who now seems to us to have worked in an obsolete rhetorical style, whose manner owes so much to Rubens, contribute to modern painting? There was first his general sensibility. He was perhaps the first modern artist *of* sensibility; this quality is abundantly revealed in his journal, which is so often concerned with the analysis of his most intimate thought and feeling. And there were his actual technical discoveries in color, which helped to free the next generation from the bitumenums and opaque shadows of prevailing pictorial styles. The full implications of these discoveries were not realized by Delacroix, but the Neo-Impressionists, led by Seurat, later systematized his method of modeling form with broad touches of juxtaposed color and found new possibilities of luminosity in the splendors of his palette.

It was Baudelaire, a gifted art critic as well as a poet, who first discerned in Delacroix the prototype of the modern artist. From 1845 to 1859 Baudelaire reviewed a number of the Salons and the World's Fair Exhibition of 1855 and his estimates of the greater artists of his period, Delacroix among them, are rather like notes for the new chapter of modern art. His most considered evaluation of Delacroix came in a lengthy eulogy published in 1863.

To Baudelaire, Delacroix represented a tension of passion and order, of romantic disgust and heroic aspiration, of interest in life and an aristocratic detachment from it. Delacroix's name, he wrote, conjured up vague ideas of "misdirected ardor, turbulence, daring, inspiration and even disorder." These ideas, in turn, he took as indications of the new freedom of artistic imagination, a freedom which expressed the sensitive and superior individual's bitter opposition to the restraints of the social order and the vulgar mediocrity of bourgeois society. In Baudelaire's view the artist as typified by Delacroix was a member of an intellectual elite with its own moral code, a "dandy" who belonged to an aristocracy of the spirit. The dandy cultivated his own sensations and feelings but never betrayed them to the mob, against whose vulgar tastes he was ever on guard. As a dandy, Delacroix "was passionately in love with passion and coldly determined to find ways of expressing passion in the most visible manner."

The intense intellectual pride reflected in Baudelaire's cult of Dandyism and his public hostility in time became open warfare with society. His *Fleurs du Mal* had been a *succès de scandale,* and many of his poems were suppressed for lubricity; Baudelaire retaliated with an icy contempt, repeatedly expressed in his writing, for the detested middle class. In some degree his isolation and feeling of isolation led him to exaggerate his belief in the privileged status of the artist. And some of his insistence on the artist's martyred role and the extreme morbidity of his point of view were also the posturing of a "romantic" of the period.

As a result, perhaps, Baudelaire responded to Delacroix's art too often in terms of its violence and pessimism (although the painters of the following generation found Delacroix a different, more affirmative symbol). "Everything in his work," wrote the poet, "is only desolation, massacres, conflagration. Everything bears witness to man's eternal and incorrigible barbarism." Baudelaire's erotic sensibility was gratified by the artist's voluptuous color; his violent romantic palate by exotic imagery drawn from the East and scenes of frenzied action, disorder, and strife. Delacroix painted history convulsively and with free dramatic imagination, as if, in Baudelaire's view, it were a series of episodes from Dante's Inferno which the artist was observing from the vantage point of one of the "damned." To

Baudelaire, who saw modern life as a brightly illuminated Hell and himself as its *poète maudit* (poet under a curse), such artistic aims were altogether sympathetic.

While the poet may have romantically exaggerated the violence and pessimism of Delacroix's art, he did appreciate its importance as an expression of individual freedom. He also saw in Delacroix an artist in conflict with or ahead of his age. If Baudelaire read Delacroix's violent romantic disorders as a vague, inchoate indictment of the times, in his own poetry and other writing he left no doubt that he, too, was an enemy of the century of progress. The new urban civilization which the industrial revolution had created offended both his esthetic and his religious sensibilities. T. S. Eliot has indicated that Baudelaire's criticisms of his age were a rudimentary expression of a longing for the spiritual life. "In the middle of the nineteenth century," Eliot writes bleakly and perhaps smugly, "in an age of bustle, programs, platforms, scientific progress, humanitarianism and revolutions which improved nothing, in an age of progressive degradation, Baudelaire perceived that what really matters is sin and redemption. . . . The possibility of damnation itself is an immediate form of salvation—of salvation from the ennui of modern life, because it at last gives some significance to living."

Whatever its spiritual significance, Baudelaire's romantic susceptibility, which was echoed in the person and art of Delacroix, anticipates certain distinctly modern attitudes of protest against a too trusting belief in scientific rationalism and materialism. Such attitudes as well as some of the romantic techniques of unlocking the mysteries of artistic creation have inspired Surrealist painters and poets. As a point of view, these attitudes were fundamentally opposed to the century of Jean Jacques Rousseau with its faith in natural man. They introduced a counter-current in the flow of artistic feeling, a negative and disenchanted reaction to the age of progress. That reaction later took a variety of forms in painting as different as the romantic mood of the early Manet, the "Symbolism" of Gauguin, Lautrec's astringent ironies, and the "metaphysical" ambiguities of Cubism and the Cubist collage. It is a paradox of the modern age and an indication of the strong contradictions within it that the same artist or a single movement may embrace both a Baudelairean mood of extreme romantic scepticism and also invent modern forms in a spirit of free inquiry and experimentation to which the atmosphere of scientific enlightment has contributed so much. The artificial sensibility of romanticism, nevertheless, defines one of the constant tendencies in modern art—lost and found, submerged during the period of Impressionism, revived with modifications in the painting of the Post-Impressionists and in some twentieth-century art.

The meaning of Delacroix's contribution to modern painters, as they understand it, is far simpler and is more a matter of technical procedure. Their interest in him can be associated with his statement that "light, shade, reflections and atmosphere cannot be substituted by line and style." This remark implied a new approach to painting based on natural observation and is at variance with the romantic principles which Baudelaire in 1846 discerned in his art. The poet had written that a picture "should above all reflect the artist's intimate thought, which must dominate the subject in the same way as a creator dominates his creation."

Delacroix's interest in the luminous possibilities of "light, shade, reflections and atmosphere" actually began, in practice, in 1824, when he was deeply impressed by a Constable landscape exhibited in Paris. After seeing it, he retired to his studio in a state of great excitement and repainted the landscape background of his *Massacre at Chios,* giving it more distance and fresh color. He later described Constable and Turner as "real reformers" and acknowledged his debt to them: "Our school, which now abounds in men of talent similar to theirs, has greatly benefited by their example." In his journal he was soon to note from direct observation that nature was full of color and that her most luminous effects could be analyzed as the strongest oppositions of contrasting color. "[At noonday] the gray of the evening clouds turns into blue; the part of the sky which is clear is bright yellow or orange. The general law is: the more the contrast, the more the brilliancy."

At the very end of his life Delacroix applied these radical theories of brilliance through contrast when he was called on to decorate the Chapel of Saint-Sulpice, in Paris. Since the paintings were to be seen at some distance and were to be large, he dramatized his effects by setting down many small, broken areas of contrasting color, to be blended by the eye. The results were more lively than premixed color would have been. He thus anticipated the divided color and optical mixtures of the Impressionists. His methods astonished Signac, who later wrote: "Delacroix proved the advantage of an informed technique. . . . He revealed the secret laws which govern color: the accord of like colors, the analogies between contrasting colors. . . . He indicated the potentialities of optical mixtures which make possible the creation of new tints." The generation of the Neo-Impressionists carried forward and "scientized" Delacroix's discoveries.

At the same time Delacroix also exerted on future generations a tremendous emotional appeal for his resistance to the Academy and his insistence on the artist's freedom to paint as he wished. For example, his allegory, *Liberty at the Barricades,* intended as a symbol of political liberty, in time became a symbol of artistic emancipation instead. When the twentieth-century critic Florent Fels was asked by Matisse to name the single painting that best stood for modernism, he chose it for the following reasons: ". . . Delacroix was not afraid to represent in a sublime image a humanity of all time, and make it topical, mingling citizens in their stovepipe hats with students in blouses and laborers in working clothes, against a background of the towers of Paris painted like a primitive's dream-landscape; with a half-nude woman splashed in with pure vermilions and cobalts . . . Liberty who rises epically from the center of the canvas is less a political than an esthetic symbol."

Despite his denial of classicism and his technical discoveries, however, Delacroix does not provide the direct link to modern painting. His art was still bound by epic themes and heroic subject matter, projecting, as Baudelaire wrote, "a kind of remembrance of the greatness and native passions of Universal man." He was in a sense imprisoned by this grand inspiration and by his own sense of greatness, so that he could not lower his sights to include contemporary life. Delacroix's journal makes clear his feeling of kinship with the exalted artistic spirits

of the past, with Rubens and the great Venetians, and his indifference to the spectacle of actual life.

To redirect the course of modern art a new artist had to re-
discover his own age in terms of its own particular look, line,
and physical environment. Delacroix was in many ways an
advanced modern spirit, as Baudelaire perceived, but he could
not address himself to contemporary life at the level of the
nerves and sensations. The age required a different artist, one
responsive to particularities, to the texture and character of
"modernity." With his uncanny prophetic gifts Baudelaire
also anticipated this new type of artist and prescribed what his
program must be. By doing so he helped create and understand
his age before its pattern was complete.

Baudelaire's prescient and persuasive image of modernity
emerges, curiously enough, in an essay on the minor artist
Constantin Guys. The observations he made in this distinguished critique, however, will illuminate the art of Manet and
Degas as brilliantly as they did the infinitely smaller style
of Guys. The summary of Guys's art may be taken as one of
the first hints of the revolution in painting that Manet and the
artists that soon grouped themselves around him were to carry
out.

The Guys essay, *Le Peintre de la vie moderne,* came out in
1863, the year of the *Salon des Refusés.* Guys attracted Baudelaire for exactly the opposite reasons Delacroix had attracted
him: for the particularity of his imagery, for his observation of
life around him, and for his interest in manners. Guys was a
scintillating water-colorist and draftsman who recorded in a
rapid, improvisatory style vivacious impressions of the spectacle
of Second Empire Paris. He was an inspired artist-journalist
with a feeling for atmosphere and a keen knowledge of certain
milieus: the military life, fashionable worlds of pleasure, the
swarming streets of Paris. His elegant little ladies of the demimonde (see plate 8) turn up again on the beaches of Trouville,
Deauville, and Le Havre in the paintings of Boudin, Degas,
Manet, and Monet. And some of his glimpses into nocturnal
Parisian life are revived with a more sinister inflection in the
brothels painted by Degas and Lautrec.

In his essay Baudelaire charged the classical *pasticheurs* of the period with laziness and indifference to modern beauty. "It is much more convenient," he wrote, "to declare that everything is ugly in the garb of an epoch than to apply oneself to extract from it the mysterious beauty that may be contained in it, be it ever so trifling or slight. Modernity is the transitory, the fugitive, the contingent half of art of which the other half is the eternal and the immutable." He pointed out that every age has its costume, look, and carriage, and that it was the responsibility of the authentic contemporary artist to record them faithfully.

The artist who merely imitated the past would be neither of his time nor convincing. Baudelaire took the example of a painter who wished to depict a courtesan of his own day but proceeded to do so by meticulously following the example of Titian or Raphael. "The study of a masterpiece of that time and genre," he noted, "will teach him neither the attitude, the regard, the grimace nor the vital aspect of one of those creatures whom the contemporary vernacular would class under the gross or playful titles of lost creatures, kept women, gay ladies or love birds." It is fascinating to think that in the year these irreverent remarks were published Edouard Manet was painting a very convincing contemporary courtesan, his *Olympia,* and demonstrating her respectable artistic genealogy by posing her in an attitude which was an ironic allusion to Titian's *Venus of Urbino.*

In Guys, Baudelaire discerned not only the true "painter of modernity" but another refinement in modern artistic sensibility, the concept of the "artist-convalescent." Guys's most congenial milieu was the crowd; his sensibility focused on the passing show, and he recorded his chosen themes with the liveliest interest and curiosity. His curiosity, in fact, was so avid that Baudelaire compared it with that of a convalescent. The sick man who has been invalided out of life sees it freshly upon his return and finds it a new source of stimulation, wonder, and ecstasy. The imaginary malady of the artist-convalescent destroys his capacity for active participation in life, but it "leaves his spiritual faculties intact."

As an artistic type, Guys is related to Delacroix more than may at first be imagined. The delicate convalescent is protected from life by his imaginary indisposition just as the intellectually exquisite dandy is protected by his personal moral code and his pride. They are both detached spectators rather than participants. In setting forth this view of the artist Baudelaire was not simply embracing an ivory-tower preciousness. He had quite literally discovered for himself the importance of artistic detachment and come to its defense long before it became part of any conscious esthetic program, and at a time when artistic freedom sorely needed a champion.

In a passage that is a haunting anticipation of the career and literary method of the novelist Marcel Proust, and of the conscious infantilism of some twentieth-century painting, Baudelaire compares the "virginal impressions" of the convalescent to those of the child. "The child sees everything as a *novelty;* it is always *intoxicated.* Nothing resembles inspiration more than the joy with which the child absorbs form and color . . . genius is only childhood recovered at will, childhood summoned up, in order that [the mature adult] may express himself with the virile organs and in the analytical spirit which permits him to order the sum of material involuntarily amassed. I beg you to consider M. Guys as an eternal convalescent; to complete your conception take him also as an adult-child, a man possessing at every moment the genius of childhood, that is, the genius for which no aspect of life has gone stale."

While Baudelaire was forming his specialized view of artistic sensibility and dramatizing by his eloquent writing the necessary relationship of art to contemporary life, a new spirit of realism had already seized painting. The revolt against the pompous, empty rhetoric of Academy styles and against the suppression of subject matter drawn from life was initiated seriously by Gustave Courbet shortly after the abortive political revolutions of 1848. The same social forces which in that year precipitated democratic revolutions throughout Europe were responsible for the emergence of Courbet, an artist who elected to paint "democratic" subjects such as peasant themes and laborers in a provincial country setting.

Today we think of Courbet's peasants and indeed of his landscape as romanticized. To the academicians of the period they seemed grossly and insolently realistic, at least by comparison with their own repertory of idealized shepherds, nymphs, classical and mythological figures, and the Arcadian groves in which they sported. Not only did Courbet find heroism and grandeur in ordinary people, but he painted his commonplace subjects with a vigor and a *materialism,* a delight in the manipulation of pure paint matter, that was directly opposed to the licked and enameled surfaces of the academicians. The evidence of materialism both in painting and in scientific and philosophic thought at this time was logical and natural; science and the technological application of science in the industrial revolution had begun radically to change the circumstances of life and modes of feeling. It was not by accident that Courbet's curiosity was stimulated by his physical environment, by the world of natural appearances, and by the materiality of medium.

At the Salon of 1850, Courbet made his debut with one of the century's revolutionary works, his *Burial at Ornans.* The subject was an ordinary burial in the artist's native village with the figures of the clergy and the peasantry starkly outlined against a rugged Jura Mountains landscape. Every figure had been taken from life, was treated simply and energetically with little esthetic elaboration. This painting and another of his peasant themes included at the Salon, *The Stone Breakers* (see plate 4), were violently assailed in the press. Critics charged the artist with ineptness, vulgarity, or worse, and one described his *Burial,* certainly the noblest portrayal of the peasantry since Louis le Nain, as "an ignoble and impious caricature." These subjects were held to be a sign of the artist's socialism, and from that date his work became for his enemies the symbol of a political philosophy feared and hated by contemporary authority.

Courbet's vigorous technique startled the public as much as his commonplace incident and the democratic spirit of his themes. His canvases had a distinction in color, indeed at times a silken elegance of hue and tone, and a richness of surface that should have roused the sleeping hedonist in anyone. Unfortunately, the public had been bred on slick-surface, smooth-form classicism and was at a loss before paintings in which every brush stroke was forced up into prominence. While even Delacroix found Courbet's subjects banal and vacant of noble thought, he nevertheless expressed astonishment at the "vigor and relief" of his handling. He had an opportunity to study Courbet at the Paris World's Fair of 1855 and came away after an hour convinced that his painting *The Studio* was a "masterpiece." In a magnificent gesture of defiance after his rejection by the official Salon, Courbet had set up at his own expense a *Pavillon du Réalisme* at the fair and exhibited fifty of his paintings. The new generation of painters, among them Pissarro, Manet, and Degas, were at least as deeply impressed as Delacroix. From that date "realism" became a slogan word and the most vital force in French painting; the most interesting young painters rallied round the banner raised by Courbet.

Few of these young painters, however, were directly influenced by Courbet then. It was not until the late sixties that his style affected the Impressionists and Cézanne, and then only for a brief period. Perhaps his indifference to urban experience, to the surfaces and sensations of contemporary life, and his emphasis on rustic subjects betrayed too narrow interests and isolated him from the new generation. Courbet was a man of the countryside, and his art celebrated, sometimes brazenly so, the rude and homely virtues of the country almost as a challenge and criticism of cosmopolitan urbanity. Perhaps, too, his technique, which still had a strong flavor of romanticism, had no opportunity to be properly assimilated by younger artists, since it was almost immediately superseded by Manet's innovations. And Courbet was by temperament too aggressively independent to encourage disciples. When at the insistence of a group of young painters he opened a studio in 1862, the experiment of teaching soon proved tiresome, and he abandoned it.

However, for his example of free selection of subject matter and his insistence that the artist's proper frame of reference was the visible world, he proved a pillar of strength for the young. His brusqueness and singleness of purpose, his undisguised contempt for official art, and his energy gave real substance to the growing spirit of independence in painting. Courbet was a free spirit, and he encouraged other and perhaps more historically significant artists to be no less. "I have simply wanted to draw from a thorough knowledge of tradition," he wrote, "the reasoned and free sense of my own individuality." Courbet's realism and the climate of freedom he brought to painting prepared the way for the first great painter of "modernity," Edouard Manet.

2

A Detached Observer

"Courbet is still tradition. Manet is a new epoch in painting."
—Renoir

"Manet is the first painter who made the immediate translation of his sensations, thus freeing instinct."
—Matisse

Edouard Manet was born in Paris in 1832, the son of a prominent magistrate who belonged to the prosperous bourgeoisie that flourished during the reign of Louis-Philippe. All his life Manet enjoyed financial independence and a secure social position which enabled him to move in circles which his more *déclassé* artist friends either did not or could not aspire to. He was entirely free from the economic frustrations and anxieties that bedeviled Monet, Sisley, Renoir, and others of the original band of Impressionists. He also cut quite a different figure, with his urbane manners, *boulevardier* air, and impeccable dress. Manet was a familiar sight at fashionable Paris rendezvous like the Café Tortoni and was never completely at ease away from the cosmopolitan atmosphere of Paris. His early paintings gave him much notoriety and apparently conjured up in the public mind a wild Bohemian of the unwashed hands variety. Emile Zola, his first great defender, was at pains to point out that Manet was something quite different, a reserved and distinguished man of the world.

Manet's conservative character and urbanity seem scarcely the stuff of which revolutions are made; yet he was also a man of passion and force. Independence and conviction came through immediately in his conversation, as so many of his critics and cronies have attested. His sense of social caste, however, may indicate why he insisted year after year in sending his paintings to the official salon, where he was rejected as often as not. Perhaps as a result of his bitter experience at the *Salon des Refusés* Manet refused to participate in the independent exhibitions of the Impressionists and thus link himself again with open revolt. After 1863 he tried only once more to appeal directly to the public when in 1867 he built his own pavilion at the World's Fair, as Courbet had done twelve years before, and exhibited fifty paintings. The response was disappointing, however. He persisted ever after in attempts to achieve public honor through existing art institutions and only at the end of his life did he wonder whether it had been worth the trouble. When, the year before his death, he finally received an academy medal permitting him automatic entry into the Salons and was also awarded the Legion of Honor, he had already become bitterly disillusioned. "It is too late," he remarked, "to compensate for twenty years' lack of success."

Manet's independence and spiritual intransigence were expressed at an early age, when he announced to his family the intention of becoming an artist. His father sent him to sea as a merchant marine cadet at the age of sixteen, hoping to divert his son's interests to an equally adventurous but more respectable profession. When some Dutch cheeses spoiled on the voyage and became discolored, Manet was given the task of reddening them—and thus, as he later told his friend Duret, got in "his first bit of painting." By 1850 his father had given up any hope of deferring his son's art career, and Manet was allowed to enter the studio of Thomas Couture. Couture, a teacher at the Ecole des Beaux-Arts, like many other painter-teachers maintained and derived income from a studio of his own. Despite a general lack of sympathy with Couture's academic methods, Manet stayed six years with this conservative artist whose main claim to fame was a historical "machine," *Romans of the Decadence;* painted in an artificial classical style, it had achieved a degree of success at the Salon.

Couture took every possible opportunity to depress the growing reputation of the "realists." At one time he even painted a satirical allegory that caricatured their preoccupation with the common things of life by showing a painter sitting on a plaster bust of the Olympian Jupiter copying a pig's head. Manet's stubborn insistence on going his own way and posing models in contemporary dress so distressed the master that he once reproved his young student with the words, "You will never be anything more than the Daumier of your time." And Manet's friend and fellow-pupil, Antonin Proust, recorded Manet's intense discouragement and impatience with academic methods in his remarks: "I don't know why I am here. Everything we see around us is ridiculous. The light is false. The shadows are false. When I come to the studio, it seems to me that I am entering a tomb." But Manet stayed on in the Ecole de Beaux-Arts studio, and for a much longer period than most of his progressive contemporaries were to do. He thus showed his determination at the very inception of his career to realize his ambitions within the framework of existing art institutions. In even the most revolutionary of his early work, there is a discernible influence of Couture, too, in the strong feeling for black and white values, in the sharp contrast of light and dark, and in the thickness of the paint paste.

Manet's first sizable work on a contemporary theme was the *Absinthe Drinker*, painted in 1859. The subject was quite daring: a dilapidated ragpicker whom Manet had noticed wandering around the Louvre in a picturesque, ragged cape and topper. And the manner was curious, since it so clearly suggested the influence of Velásquez. Of it Manet said, "I painted a Parisian character whom I had studied in Paris, and I executed it with the technical simplicity I had discovered in Velásquez." The figure recedes into a gloomy cavern of space; he is shrouded by his cape and by an air of somber mystery. In the foreground is an empty bottle. There is more than a little of a Baudelairean mood of romantic melancholy and moral ambiguity about this figure. When Couture saw the painting, he exclaimed, "An absinthe drinker! And they paint abominations like that! My poor friend, you are the absinthe drinker. It is you who have lost your moral faculty." Manet submitted the painting to the Salon of 1859, and in due course it was rejected, the first of a long series of official rebukes his art received. There is a reprise of this figure in the more ambitious group composition *The Old Musician* (see plate 2) which is even more clearly based on Velásquez's celebrated work, *The Topers*.

In Velásquez Manet found not only a "technical simplicity" suitable to his artistic aims but also a remarkably unsentimental and direct observation of life. He must have been struck by the flat and almost abstract shapes by which Velásquez organized his compositions, for Manet exploited similar formal devices, as he did, somewhat, the Spaniard's practice of employing silvery grays relieved by touches of color. Velásquez's aristocratic detachment, the "cruel charm" with which, in Manet's words, he observed life, also jibed somehow with the Parisian's own temperament. In these early years Manet was bent on assimilating Velásquez, Goya, and also Hals, another master of grays, whose work he could have studied first hand on a trip to Holland in his student days. Oddly enough, he did not go to Spain until 1865, after his mature style had already been formed.

Manet first came before the public eye in 1861 when the Salon accepted two of his paintings, *Portrait of the Artist's Parents* and *Spanish Guitar Player*. These were far less somber in mood than the *Absinthe Drinker* and more personal in expression. Their dramatic realism immediately drew attention to the young artist but earned him an almost entirely unfavorable press. The guitarist, in particular, put the public's back up because of the strange new fashion in which it was painted. The critics complained bitterly because Manet had picked a commonplace and ignoble subject (he had taken his motif from a Spanish ballet troupe that was just then all the rage in Paris), and they were even more offended by his technique. It was described in the following manner: "The fine brush strokes, each separately visible, caked and plastered on, are like mortar on top of mortar."

The originality of the painting, however, immediately struck

the group of young artists led by Fantin-Latour who had been
working under the inspiration of Courbet's realism; they went
as a deputation to Manet to pay their respects. This was Manet's
introduction to the serious new "realist" artists of Paris; and
he soon met through them their literary champions, Astruc,
Castagnary, Duranty, and Champfleury. In 1862, Baudelaire
warmly praised Manet's "decided taste for modern truth" and
his "vivid and ample, sensitive, daring imagination" in print.

That year there was no official Salon, and the following year
the Emperor instituted the celebrated *Salon des Refusés*. Among
those who participated were Manet, Jongkind, Pissarro, Whistler, Fantin-Latour, and Cézanne. *The Luncheon on the Grass,*
which immediately became a center of dispute, was one of
three paintings that Manet showed. Like his previous work, it
was reviled in the press as much in terms of its unfamiliar technique as its subject. Overnight it brought Manet an enormous
prestige, the prestige of ridicule. But Manet's great innovations
and his embattled position rallied the vital painters to his side.
He was soon something of an artistic hero for them. It was the
beginning of his widely acknowledged leadership of the vanguard of art.

By renouncing the Academy's licked surfaces and chiaro-
scuro (the modeling of volumes by light and shade distribution),
and by placing real-life figures in natural light, Manet set off a
major explosion. With a certain cheek, he had based his composition on a fifteenth-century engraving. For the Arcadian
figures of pastoral tradition Manet substituted real Parisians:
his favorite female model, Victorine Meurend, and the man
who was soon to become his brother-in-law, among others. Had
his undressed female been a conventional, idealized nude, there
would have been no public dismay, but she was "naked" rather
than nude. Manet had, moreover, painted his figures with
abrupt transitions from light to dark, setting one tone directly
against another flatly and skipping the customary gradations
of modeling. The flat, bright, shadowless effect thus obtained
was perhaps the least acceptable aspect of his work. Manet
proved himself an exquisite colorist, combining refinement and
a wonderfully sensuous verve; one of the finest things in the
Luncheon is the still life in the left foreground, but it was lost

on a public bewildered by his novel techniques. Even Manet's blacks and grays were emphasized as distinct colors and as positive esthetic quantities.

With Manet's great new work art emerged from the studio into a more brilliant daylight, and the senses of artists were awakened. In the pre-Impressionist painting which Boudin, Jongkind, and Monet were developing independently around Le Havre and along the Seine Estuary at the same time, a similar freshness had entered art. This group had actually begun to paint out-of-doors directly, unlike Manet, who painted his work in his studio, from memory and from preliminary sketches made on the spot. There are, indeed, certain inconsistencies in Manet's handling that suggest either memory lapses or an incomplete solution to the problem of painting real-life figures out-of-doors in natural light. The main group of picnickers and the still life in the foreground are given a full plastic inflection while the landscape and the young lady bathing in the background are much more summarily treated. The wood-glade setting is flat and in the background has the two-dimensional character of a stage-set. These diverse effects are unified by virtuoso brushwork and style.

Whatever its artificialities, which became more bald when the Impressionists brought their technique to maturity ten years later, Manet's *Luncheon* was the most important work of the period. It takes its place in the company of the great revolutionary masterpieces of the nineteenth century, such works as Géricault's *Raft of the Medusa,* Delacroix's *Massacre at Chios,* and Courbet's *Burial at Ornans.* It summed up a wholly new tendency and put it squarely before the public in a major work. The *Luncheon* also challenged public preconceptions about tradition, for Manet showed that the past *could* be modernized and brought up to date. By recapitulating a traditional Renaissance composition he demonstrated that a modern painter might invoke the past to celebrate the present.

In 1865, Manet exhibited in the Salon his *Olympia,* which was a kind of indoor complement to the *Luncheon.* The painting was if anything even more offensive to general morality since it showed a quite realistic nude lady of the demimonde reclining on her couch with a Negress holding a bouquet of

flowers in attendance. An arched, very Baudelairean cat curled
its tail at the foot of the bed. Such exotic touches as the little
black cat, the Negress, and the gorgeous pictorial accessories
of Indian shawl and bouquet of flowers now appear innocent
enough pieces of romancing. At the time they were held altogether immoral for their too frank declaration of the lady's
vocation. Baudelaire had already been pilloried for his poems.
Now Manet had not only re-created his mood but used some
of the very same stage props. Even such romantic suggestions
of the more sordid aspects of sexual life in the great city were
not permissible in the period before "naturalism" won its
battle for truth. And the atmosphere of picturesque "wickedness" scandalized the public.

There was also an especially annoying candor in the way the
young lady's cool and impudent regard was directed at the spectator, engaging him directly in the scene. Manet seemed to be
inviting the public to become an accomplice to his immoral
scene. In the general howl that went up over the artist's lack
of propriety no one paid much attention to his mastery of form
and color, but Manet had set down with even more distinction
his now characteristic color chords of salmon pinks, claret
reds, cool blues, and oyster grays. As in the *Luncheon*, his composition alluded to art of the past, in this case to a Titian composition of a courtesan and her maid. The painting seemed to
fulfill exactly Baudelaire's program for depicting a contemporary woman of the demimonde in the modern spirit.

Manet's career after 1865 was punctuated by alternate rejec-
tions and acceptances by the Salon; when he did manage to
get his paintings accepted, he was rewarded by violent attacks
from the more influential critics. His notoriety grew, it seems,
in exact proportion to the number of innovations he made.
Each new departure in color and form was greeted by more
public derision, and he bore so much abuse that he began to
develop a feeling of persecution. At a restaurant in Spain in
1865 he was convinced that a gentleman seated at a table
beside him, who was obviously relishing the courses of the meal
which Manet had repeatedly sent back with the waiter, had
been mocking him deliberately. Manet, in great heat, confronted the stranger and accused him of pretending to enjoy

the vile food simply to offend him. He was sure he had been recognized as the notorious Parisian artist and was once more being taunted. He was quite wrong, and as it turned out the stranger was the critic Théodore Duret, who became a lifelong friend and one of Manet's most vocal defenders.

Manet's trip to Spain cured him of his Spanish mannerisms, even though he learned to admire Velásquez all the more. As early as 1862 he had painted subjects taken directly from contemporary life, such as his *Concert in the Tuileries Garden;* but it was only after his return from Spain that he actually began to work out of doors and test his observations against nature. He painted the race meetings at Longchamps, beach scenes and harbor views on the Channel coast, at Folkestone and Boulogne, all with much freer and more vivacious brushwork. His new and more improvisatory manner stemmed mainly from his contact with the Impressionists, or rather, those younger artists who were soon to be known by that label.

After 1866, Manet became the center of a group of young intellectuals who foregathered with him at the Café Guerbois and freely discussed the new painting: the critics Duret, Zola, Astruc, Duranty, and the painters Bazille, Renoir, Degas, Monet, Cézanne, Pissarro, Sisley, and Constantin Guys. Monet later described the effect on the participants of these meetings. "Nothing could be more interesting," he declared, "than these *causeries* with their perpetual clash of opinions. They kept our wits sharpened, they encouraged us with stores of enthusiasm that for weeks and weeks kept us up, until the final shaping of the idea was accomplished. From them we emerged tempered more highly, with a firmer will, with our thoughts clearer and more distinct." In 1870 one of the young artists, Fantin-Latour, painted some of the group in his *Studio in the Batignolles Quarter;* Manet is seated at an easel in the center of the painting surrounded by Monet, Bazille, Astruc, Zola, Renoir, and others.

Under Impressionist influence Manet painted a large outdoor composition, *The Railroad*, in 1872. His palette was brighter, although still lower in key than Monet's or Renoir's, and his brushwork more vivacious than ever; Manet's distinction as a stylist never left him even when he followed the rather

impersonal methods of his younger colleagues. The painting
was exhibited at the Salon of 1874 and drew especially vehement criticism for its lack of finish, for its brilliant color,
indeed, for all the qualities that make it a distinguished, fresh,
and original work of art. In it a young mother in fashionable
dress sits on a bench against an iron fence while a child, with
her back turned, looks through the bars at the curling plumes
of smoke rising from a locomotive in the distance. To call a
painting *The Railroad* when all visible evidence of the subject
was confined to a cloud of steam and all the interest focused on
two figures made a certain demand on the audience's imagination, too great a demand for the period.

The public could not understand that the painting was not a
picture of a railroad except by suggestion but was primarily a
pretext for Manet's enchanting new combinations of form and
color as perceived under natural light. Showing only the back
of the little girl who had turned away from her mother and
the action was considered rude, and the mechanical character
of her pose led critics to compare her with a "trained seal."
The critics had here hit on a very important point. Monet and
Sisley were to abolish figures entirely from their canvases so
that their study of nature would not be affected by any evidence
of human participation; Manet similarly played down the response of one of his figures to the scene and made her little
more than a puppet, so as not to distract attention from esthetic
values. As painting per se became more expressive, human emotions were played down and subsidiary human figures were
often reduced to a suggestive shape or silhouette. A process of
abstraction had begun which in the twentieth century was to
result in a denial of subject altogether.

Manet's position had been immeasurably strengthened in
1871 when the dealer Durand-Ruel bought twenty-three of his
paintings for 35,000 francs. Yet he continued to seek approval
in the Salon and avoided isolating himself with the vanguard
painters. When the Impressionist group held its first joint
exhibition in 1874, Manet held aloof. The next year he exhibited at the Salon his *Boating at Argenteuil,* which was even
more transparently Impressionist in technique than *The Railroad.* He was again singled out for special attention, and the

painting was dismissed with another catchword. A critic referred to the river against which the artist had posed his subjects, a man and woman, as "indigo." It summed up the general
conviction that Manet and the Impressionists used color never
before beheld on land or sea.

In 1877 he painted *Nana,* which shows a half-dressed, vivacious young lady in her boudoir about to powder her nose; cut
off by the picture frame is the figure of a gentleman in top hat
and evening dress. The painting was attacked for its "frankness." In a similar fashion, his outdoor café scene, *Chez le
Père Lathuille,* painted in 1879, was considered too raffish in
subject matter. His only painting of this period that achieved
popular success was his *Le Bon Bock* of 1872, a portrait of an
opulent gentleman holding a glass of beer, painted somewhat
in the manner of one of Franz Hals's jolly cavaliers. The public
appreciated the more cozy sentiment of the painting and was
relieved that Manet had used mainly grays rather than the
sensational colors of the Impressionists. His return in paintings of the next years to a more vivid palette estranged popular
opinion once again.

In the last years of the decade Manet came closer and closer
to the broken color and scintillating light effects of Monet and
his other friends. Impressionism freed him from the artificiality and somber tonalities of his earlier style; at times, at the end
of his life, however, it also threatened to submerge his own distinct qualities as a stylist. Manet was never completely at ease
in the pure Impressionist landscape exercise. His talent found
its most satisfying expression in the treatment of the human
figure.

In 1882, the year before his death, he exhibited one of his
most enchanting figure compositions at the Salon, *A Bar
at the Folies-Bergère* (plate 9), his last significant oil. A maid
stands before a veined marble bar with a gorgeous array of wine
bottles, a dish of fruit and flowers before her; in the background,
reflected in a mirror, are her back, the face of a man in evening
dress with whom she is talking, and a mass of figures and light
globes representing the interior of the cabaret. The reflection of
the otherwise invisible gentleman seems purely arbitrary and a
little mystifying until we realize that he stands where we, the

observers, stand. Manet has again put the spectator in the painting, just as he did with the *Olympia*.

This provides a clue to the curious atmosphere his paintings
often create. With their scintillation of light and their expression of a particular moment in time, they engage the spectator directly as no previous paintings do. And yet Manet's
painted reality is all impression and suggestion, a mysterious
and insubstantial envelope of living, sensible atmosphere. We
are invited to complete his pictures, but if we step too close, the
bubble of illusion breaks, and we see nothing but a lively
jumble of color on a surface. The elusive quality of his vision
is implemented by the detached mood of his figures. As Zola
put it, they seem "to look down at us with solemn and proud
disdain." The enigmatic central figure in *A Bar at the Folies-
Bergère* is a Mona Lisa of barmaids. The painter puts us in
close physical proximity to the action and thereby in the position of an intimate observer; but the girl's extraordinary *savoir-
faire* and imperious air keep us at a distance.

Manet's humanity often has a certain mysterious unreality,
so much so that a critic once accused him of painting people
as if they were still life. Manet never characterized his human
beings sharply, as Degas, for example, liked to do. He saw
them as types, at best as embodiments of such abstract qualities as young manhood, young womanhood, charm or grace.
They participate in a great unfolding tableau of modern life
and take their place in scenes where action has been frozen.
Their expressions have a curious blankness, and even a mystery, as in the *Folies-Bergère* barmaid; but this air of mystery
has little to do with their individual psyches. The barmaid is,
in Oscar Wilde's phrase, a sphinx without a riddle. If she presents an enigma, it is the riddle of Manet's genius and not her
own. Indeed, she is a pictorial metaphor for his secret artistic
life as a detached observer, a vehicle for the expression of pure
esthetic sensibility.

Manet reduced subject matter to a motif or an arrangement
in order to emphasize certain purely pictorial values. He saw
life through a particular repertory of shapes, silhouettes, and
color chords. There is no question that he also responded to
the line and elegance of the period; his paintings evoke all

the piquant freshness of *la vie Parisienne* in its springtide. It is the paradox of Manet's painting that while he was the first great painter of modern life, he was also the first artist who felt compelled to deny subject matter its traditional role in order not to compromise his artistic taste.

3

The Image of Contemporary Life

"... I bought it only a few days ago; a drawing of a female hand by Ingres; look at those fingernails; that's my idea of a genius, a man who finds a hand so lovely that he will shut himself up all his life, content to do nothing else but indicate fingernails."

—Degas to George Moore in conversation

Degas was one of the animators of the Impressionist movement and took an active part in organizing the eight exhibitions that took place between 1874 and 1886; yet he was never in the strictest sense an Impressionist. He respected classical draftsmanship, and he was never particularly interested in landscape as a motif. Degas preferred human images and all his life painted figures in their surroundings, in the environment or particular vocational attitudes that defined their lives. The orthodox Impressionists were Monet, Renoir, Sisley, Pissarro, and, after 1872, perhaps Manet; they were all primarily concerned with optical sensation and the movement of light. Monet, Pissarro, and Sisley virtually abolished figures from their landscapes in their concentration on optics and color. Degas expressed his sympathy with their aims by exploring the more spontaneous effects possible in the medium of pastel. He expressed the movement of forms, rather than of light, and showed a sensitive awareness to the mobility of human moods. He was, indeed, more a "psychological" Impressionist than anything else. He could claim a leading place in the vanguard for his new formulation of a contemporary subject matter, a vision of things inspired by the broader movement of realism and based on the truth of nature. For Degas nature necessarily included human nature.

Degas was perhaps neither so great an innovator nor so important to the evolution of modern art as was Manet, and in his lifetime he never enjoyed Manet's prestige. On the other hand, he carried forward Manet's urbane and cosmopolitan spirit and sometimes found even more daring contemporary subjects to render. And his nimble mind added to the Impressionists' pastoral mood tension, irony, and wit; above all, he steadfastly maintained the focus of art on human beings. In this, and in his artistic methods as well, he directly influenced Henri de Toulouse-Lautrec. Degas's art stands halfway between the health, sanity, and youthful vigor of the impressionist period and the exacerbated disenchantment of turn-of-the-century painting.

Through Manet, two years his senior, Degas was introduced to the most progressive artists of his day. The two painters met around 1861, when Degas was copying in the Louvre and Manet stopped in his rounds to admire an artist who had the audacity to draw directly on a copper plate from Velásquez' *Infanta.* Degas was already aware of and had been deeply impressed by Manet's technical innovations; his own interest in new possibilities for contemporary painting had originally been stimulated by Courbet's *Pavillon du Réalisme,* which he had seen at the Paris World's Fair of 1855. Degas was soon a member of Manet's brilliant circle at the Café Guerbois where he acquired a rather formidable reputation for his mordant wit and general refractoriness. No one was safe from his sallies. To Whistler, who took his artistic role seriously and accordingly dressed in flamboyant Bohemian costume, Degas is supposed to have said: "You behave, my friend, as though you had no talent."

When he first encountered Manet, Degas was still working under the spell of Ingres's neo-classicism which he had learned

to respect at the Ecole des Beaux-Arts studio of Louis La-
mothe, an Ingres pupil. On visits to relatives of his Italian-
born mother in Naples he had studied the masters of the early
Renaissance. And in the Louvre he diligently copied from
the drawings and prints of Dürer, Mantegna, and Holbein,
demonstrating what was to be a lifelong preoccupation with
draftsmanship. The fact that Degas had been executing historical "machines" in a dry, classical manner when Manet met
him was apparently a source of satisfaction to the older artist
in later years, for Manet always felt a certain rivalry with Degas.
Degas, in turn, never acknowledged any personal debt to Manet;
though in his early years he often expressed admiration for
Manet's talent, he was proud to have painted such contemporary subjects as horse races long before Manet discovered them.
The son of a prosperous banker with an aristocratic background, Degas was one of the few members of the Batignolles
group whose social credentials were up to Manet's, and he
shared with him many temperamental affinities, a reserve and
a patrician disdain for the vulgar crowd. However, their friendship was stormy and rent by quarrels, as were most of Degas's
relationships with the artists of his period; in later years Degas
ungenerously accused Manet of not being able to "do a brush
stroke without the masters in mind."

While Degas was undoubtedly influenced by the example
of Manet, he had before their meeting quite independently begun to paint informal portraits which were radically different
from the general studio portraiture of the period. As early as
1856 he made realistic sketches of the family of an aunt, the
Baroness Bellelli, in Naples. He completed the painting in 1862.
Though dark in tone and meticulous in draftsmanship, it
shows unusual powers of psychological penetration into the
contrasting moods of the mother, the prim little daughters,
and the rather withdrawn father, whose head is turned away
and blurred. The characterization is vital and truthful, and the
figures are caught in familiar and natural attitudes, as the camera might have fixed them. They are shown at home in their
natural setting rather than among the customary studio props.
Here was a "modern" genre scene, full of delicate perception
and conceived in terms of the individual's surroundings. Degas's

approach was in line with the program of the naturalistic and realistic writing of his contemporaries, Zola, Flaubert, and de Maupassant. For the early apostles of realism, the critics Edmond Duranty and the Goncourt brothers, it was Degas rather than Manet who became the best example of the artistic commentator on modern life.

Even in the Bellelli portrait, one must add that Degas's classical preoccupations also made themselves felt in the rather severe composition and the clean edges of his forms. About the same period Degas had painted one of a number of historical scenes, *Spartan Boys and Girls Exercising,* a composition of two groups of young boys and girls in a landscape suffused by a golden, Arcadian light. The bodies of the figures, however, are of a stringy toughness and are characterized sharply; they are modeled more on the *gamins* of Montmartre than the bland idealizations of antique figuration. Degas's injection of modern content into traditional themes in his early painting at times bears a curious similarity to what Manet was doing, but, unlike Manet, he never succumbed to Impressionist methods; he couldn't abide *plein air* (out-of-door) painting. Before a roomful of Monets he once complained that all the strong "light reflections" hurt his eyes and turned up his collar before the landscapes with an involuntary shiver.

After 1870, Degas drew exclusively on contemporary life for his themes. He quite consciously set himself the task of interpreting modern life and presenting it in a novel and arresting style. Just as Manet had been affected by Baudelaire's views on "modernity" and even by the stock of contemporary imagery in his poetry, so now Degas was deeply impressed with the program set forth by the Goncourt brothers in their novel *Manette Salomon,* published in 1866. Through one of the artist-characters in the book, they demanded a more refined and poetic realism and by implication attacked the heavy-handed naturalism of Courbet. The Goncourts wrote: ". . . It is possible that the Beauty of today may be covered, buried, concentrated . . . to find it, there is perhaps need of analysis, a magnifying glass, near-sighted vision, new psychological processes . . . The question of what is modern is considered exhausted, because there was that caricature of truth in our time, some-

thing to stun the bourgeois: *realism!* . . . because one gentleman created a religion out of the stupidly ugly, of the vulgar
ill-assembled and without selection, of the modern . . . but
common, without character, without expression, lacking what
is the beauty and the life of the ugly in nature and in art:
style! . . . The feeling, the intuition for the contemporary, for
the scene that rubs shoulders with you, for the present in which
you sense the trembling of your emotions and something of
yourself . . . everything is there for the artist . . . There must
be found a line that will precisely render life, embrace from
close at hand the individual, the particular, a living, human,
inward line. . . ."

As John Rewald, who is the most rewarding historian of
the period, has demonstrated in his *The History of Impressionism,* Degas fulfilled almost exactly the esthetic requirements
set by the Goncourts. He painted what he saw with a cool objectivity but redeemed from ugliness whatever was gross in
life and nature by exquisite style. His selection of subjects and
the intimacy and naturalness of his presentation expressed
admirably "the intuition for the contemporary, for the scene
that rubs shoulders with you." According to Rewald, Degas independently set himself a program for catching the spirit of
modern life when he wrote in his notebooks: "Do expressive
heads (in the academic style), a study of modern feeling. Do
every kind of object in use, placed, associated in such a way that
they take on the life of the man or woman, corsets that have
just been removed, for instance, and that retain, as it were, the
shape of the body, etc!" And he listed for himself various contemporary subjects that might be fruitfully explored: a series
on musicians and their instruments; another on bakeries seen
from a variety of angles; a series on smoke, of cigarettes, locomotives, chimneys, steamboats; on dancers, their naked legs
only, observed in action, or the hands of their hairdressers;
and endless impressions, cafés at night with the "different values
of the lamps reflected in the mirrors . . ." etc.

The way in which Degas felt the imagery of contemporary
life as *material* for art and his concern with artistic method
invite comparison with Flaubert's vision and artistic strategies.
Both were great note-takers and compiled exhaustive dossiers

on their subjects as a preliminary step, drawings or word pictures which were incorporated in their final works. Both had a passion for detail, naturalistic detail that was, however, highly selective and expressive of a conscious esthetic program. And, of course, each was above all a superb stylist. Art was an affair of intellect, built up mentally through patient observation and expressed by style. Degas's notebooks and his vital, on-the-spot drawings recall Flaubert's meticulous notations of all the little visual impressions that would finally make up as a composite image the character of Madame Bovary: how she ate her food, what she wore, the furniture she sat on. Out of a careful mosaic of detail, environmental and psychological, they each constructed artistic monuments of modern life, finding a new form suitable to the world of the bourgeoisie. After Degas and Flaubert, this kind of realism expired; it had said all it had to say consummately in their art. At the end of his life, Degas, like Flaubert, yielded to a new inspiration, seeking a more baroque and barbaric style.

But before he did that he first created a series of inimitable scenes and characters drawn from *la vie Parisienne:* café incident, ballet dancers, prostitutes, race track scenes, milliners, laundresses, circus performers, music hall stars, and the fashionable gentlemen and ladies of the Paris boulevards. Along with Manet and Renoir, he was responsible for fixing in art the image of modern woman, one that still sets the style for models in the pages of our fashion magazines: the slim, chic *Parisienne,* vivid, dainty, with impudent good looks. He registered the elegance and squalor, the glamor and disenchantment, the charm and the *longueurs* of Parisian low life and high life with an impartial brush. He was the first modern artist, in his *Absinthe Drinkers* of 1876, to paint human derelicts, and he thus anticipated Lautrec. (Although he had carefully posed a model and a friend for this café scene and executed it with his customary classical restraint, the unidealized subject of two dissipated individuals brooding over their Pernods scandalized the public.) And he did not hesitate to paint boredom, the boredom of a ballerina exhausted after rehearsal or waiting apathetically for her cues.

Degas's intention was to take art behind the scenes in life

and show human behavior and motivation as it actually is. Sometimes he seemed to catch his models off guard, with an almost cruel calculation, showing them in an awkward pose, in a moment of strain or mental funk. His merciless realism, however, is best understood as a bracing antidote to the vapid generalities and sentimental falsifications of the artificial history and genre painting of the period. When Degas remarked during a visit to his brothers' home in New Orleans that American women there had "even amidst their charms that touch of ugliness without which, no salvation," he spoke as an artist for whom prettification was an outrage against natural truth. He insisted at one time on repeatedly accompanying a fashionable woman friend to her dressmaker for fittings. When she asked him what proved so fascinating, he replied, "the red hands of the little girl who holds the pins." Degas's awareness of human wretchedness was less heartless perhaps than the complacency that could ignore it.

If Degas rubbed the luster off life, he also elevated life into a new order of beauty. In 1884 he painted *Two Laundresses;* one of the girls is shown straining over an iron, the other stifling a yawn, but their arms make a weaving pattern of movement as in the most exquisite of ballets. And the colors create an atmosphere of refinement and utter enchantment. In his innumerable paintings and pastels of dancers, on stage, backstage, and in the rehearsal room, there is the same mixture of realistic observation and elegant style. To an American collector who asked Degas why he concentrated on the ballet, the artist replied: "Because I find there, Madame, the combined movements of the Greeks."

Many critics have felt that when Degas rendered his ballerinas in strained and contorted poses he was projecting his misogyny, venting a bachelor's spleen on womanhood. There is much evidence to the contrary. He showed the ballerina as a work-horse, but he also caught all her grace, immateriality, and power to create poetic theatrical illusion. As a man and an artist, Degas is, indeed, extremely complex. He was a grumbler, a misanthrope, a severe disciplinarian, as hard on himself as on his friends and models. He often confessed that women mystified and disconcerted him; in his art he stripped them of their vanities and fripperies, yet those were exactly the qualities about them that entranced and diverted him. He loved illusion, theater and artifice in any form, and yet he ruthlessly exposed the human truths of weariness and effort behind the theater's façade of glamor. His art was at once intensely calculated and full of fine nerve and fire. This sour, loveless, cranky old male spinster was capable of painting passages that challenge Watteau's dewy elegance.

To project his vision of contemporary life freshly Degas adopted new formal devices, as had Manet and the Impressionists. Unlike them, he retained until the period of his last pastels the convention of local color and kept his forms for the most part separate and intact, defined by line. He used color in subtle touches as a kind of compositional counterpoint to the play of line and arabesques of movement. Influenced by the Japanese prints which his friend the engraver Bracquemond had brought to his attention in 1859 and which soon became all the rage in Paris, he introduced a more exciting, non-Western perspective into his art. His compositions were often made on the diagonal, with a high horizon line, thus creating a more shallow space and one in which decorative elements of design, the play of color and flat shape, could be expressed in more striking patterns. Such devices also dramatized and concentrated action, just as the abrupt cutting off of a figure with the picture frame or the overlapping of figures served to heighten movement and the impression of actual life.

Degas showed his subjects episodically, employing the "close-ups" and angle lighting of the modern camera to give a more intense and immediate sense of reality. Daniel Catton Rich has observed in his penetrating study of the artist that Degas used his canvas as a cameraman uses his "finder" to frame significant slices of life. His effort to capture action corresponded to contemporary discoveries in photography. In the seventies the American photographer Muybridge had published high-speed photographs which showed for the first time the true dynamics of the figure in motion and revealed all the intermediate positions of the body as it moved.

Degas may not have seen these photographs, but his art expressed a similar concern with a sequence of poses of the human figure in motion. He showed movement in progress by catching the body (and, indeed, the inner mood of his subjects) poised between one point of balance and another. This was radically different from the movement, for example, in Poussin and in classical art where figures are frozen into certain conventional poses. In Poussin the element of time is rigidly excluded; in Degas, who was the child of an age preoccupied with time, movement implies the existence of time. His figures, caught off-balance in passage from one position to another, suggest a past and a future as well as a present. This time sense was different from that of Manet, who rarely showed figures in motion in such a pointed manner, stepping in or out of the picture or caught as they involuntarily turned their heads away from the observer. And the orthodox Impressionists fixed their "moment in time" strictly in terms of the movement of light; they presented nature under a variety of conditions, but conditions of atmosphere and light that existed at some particular hour of the day.

To register his sensations directly and rapidly Degas often painted in essence, squeezing the oil out of his pigment and using a volatile, quick-drying medium. Rather than model forms from dark to light to give them volume in the traditional fashion, he set them down as flat color masses, somewhat as Manet had done. As his art progressed, he freed himself from the tightness of form and the darkish palette of his early compositions. After 1874 he used pastel more frequently and more freely, finally abandoning oils altogether at the end of his life. From 1872 he had been troubled by failing eyesight and in his last years he was literally half-blind; capable of distinguishing form only in its broadest masses, he was compelled to work on huge sheets of paper in brilliant pastel or to model sculpture with his hands, more by touch than by sight. Yet these years produced perhaps his most vital creations, for it was only then that Degas entirely put aside the classical rigors of his early art and arrived at passion.

At the eighth and last Impressionist exhibition in 1886 he exhibited ten pastels described in the catalogue as "a series of nudes of women bathing, washing, drying, rubbing down, combing their hair," etc. With this exhibition Degas began to focus exclusively on the single female form. To catch the truth of the female body in motion he had a tin bathtub and wash basins installed in his studio and made his models take every conceivable attitude, compelling them to turn and twist their torsos. He recorded their poses from a variety of angles. To a visitor he explained that he wished to give an intimate and candid view of the female figure, "as though you looked through a keyhole."

The pastels of Degas's last years grew progressively more free, as did the inspired little sculptures which complemented them. These pastels are animated by a new and remarkable energy. They are broader in mass and more luminous in tone; color is electric and fused with drawing. There is a fiery, baroque exuberance in the rhythms of these expressive compositions, and plastic invention is inexhaustible. Degas made out of the unpromising naturalistic data of the female ablutions something quite grand and heroic. At last he freed himself from his perfectionism, from the restraints imposed by rationalism and intellect. No artist in his career had better illustrated the characteristically French qualities of intelligence and taste; yet in these final years Degas threw all caution to the winds in a burst of inspiration, curiously fulfilling David Hume's quixotic epigram: "Reason is, and ought only to be, the slave of the passions."

At the end of his life Degas forsook society almost completely and shut himself up in his studio, a captive of his obsession with the female form. The few friends who were able to coax him out took care to indulge his black humors, knowing that his irritability was the defense of a sensitive and proud man. He alarmed them by his compulsive wanderings about the streets of Paris; half-blind, he was in constant danger of being run down by taxis. There was a curious mixture of pathos and nobility about this angry, unkempt old man—an old-fashioned figure, completely out of touch with his age, feeling nothing but contempt for a world he no longer comprehended.

Degas died in 1917, in the midst of the war. He had told his friend Forain there should be no funeral oration. "If there has to be one, you, Forain, get up and say, 'He greatly loved drawing. So do I,' and then go home." It would have been a most appropriate epitaph. For Degas could have well been described as the octogenarian printmaker Hokusai had pictured himself, "an old man mad on drawing."

4

Analysis of Shadow

"I have indeed a dream, a picture of bathing at La Grenouil-lère, for which I've made some bad sketches, but it's a dream. Renoir, who has been spending two months here, also wants to do this picture."

—Monet in a letter to Bazille, 1869

In their interpretations of modern life both Degas and Manet were constrained by their respect for tradition from completely repudiating the past. Degas painted on a dark or brown ground as the old masters had done, and his realism in the sixties was tempered by a deference to classical draftsmanship. He never showed more than a patronizing interest in the more empirical methods of the new group of landscape artists that he began to meet at the Café Guerbois after 1866, the group that was to be known later as the Impressionists and with whom he would in time exhibit. A firm believer in studio painting, Degas did not approve the "tyranny which nature exerts" on artists who sought only passive optical sensation. To Walter Sickert, the English painter, he later confided, "I always tried to urge my colleagues to seek for new combinations along the path of draftsmanship, which I considered a more fruitful field than color."

And Manet, after pointing the way so brilliantly, had in the late sixties fallen behind as the painter of "the living figure of human society." For the interest in Velásquez and the Spanish masters which his canvases through 1865 evinced he was now castigated by realist critics as a painter of "museum souvenirs." Manet had, in fact, always shown a curious dependence on others for inspiration particularly in terms of themes; he borrowed motifs from his juniors and compositions from the old masters. He never failed to re-create borrowed themes into something distinctly his own, because his talent was so enormous that it could transmute any influence into a vital, personal creation, but only in 1869, during his stay in Normandy, did he begin to observe life directly and set it down in the spontaneous, improvisatory manner adopted by the Impressionists.

At the core of the new group of painters who had begun to irritate Degas and to influence the great Manet were Monet, Renoir, and Pissarro. Soon they would be bearing a large share of the public animus formerly reserved exclusively for Manet. A critic, impressed and not completely convinced by their fresh but somewhat crude approach to painting, had described them as "the primitives of a great artistic renaissance." Unlike Manet's and Degas's art, that of the Impressionists was rooted in landscape and in the out-of-doors. Yet their inventions in color were a direct and logical consequence of Manet's *peinture claire* methods and part of the great continuing revolution in modern painting procedures.

When Manet painted his *Olympia* he had adopted a proto-Impressionist manner. The nude was felt as one flat tone mass, rather high in key; the Negress as a darker shape; the cat, as a still darker tone. These forms registered as flat shapes and silhouettes which a strong light robbed of cast shadows or much internal modeling. The effect was much the same as when one comes from the dark into a well-lighted room and momentarily perceives only the main outlines and masses of forms. Manet picked out salient, expressive shapes much as the eye would register them in the first moment of vision. We are therefore aware that he has painted an *instant* of time, a moment that implies a before and after. He revolutionized painting precisely by capturing in his art significant aspects of the flow and the appearance of actual life as it is lived and felt. The Impressionists carried the process a step further by showing, as we have pointed out earlier, the movement of light in nature and by abandoning entirely the convention of local color.

They insisted on the "scientific" nature of their discoveries of divided color and always spoke of the "truth" of what to many seemed most arbitrary inventions. Such terminology linked them to the century of progress and to a period preoccupied with scientific law and method. Monet, Pissarro, Renoir, Sisley, Bazille, and Berthe Morisot understood that they were fashioning a new pragmatic painting procedure based on pure optical sensation. They doted on the scientific rationalism of their method much as the early masters of the Renaissance had thought of their stylistic discoveries in terms of anatomy and "laws" of perspective. In point of fact, the Impressionists were the least intellectual of painters despite all their analysis and theorizing; they experienced life not through the mind but rather through the senses and in a kind of carefree holiday mood that endowed every aspect of nature with tenderness and poetic charm. They created painting of pure sensibility based on a world that was altogether adorable and enchanting to the eye.

The prime mover in the group was Claude Oscar Monet. Son of a grocer and a native of Le Havre, he had made his first vital artistic contact with the painter Eugène Boudin, a fellow-townsman. In 1858, at the age of seventeen, Monet began to paint out-of-doors under Boudin's guidance, working from the same marine motifs and beach scenes that inspired the older painter. Boudin and the Dutchman Jongkind, who later influenced Monet and who frequently painted in Le Havre and along the Normandy coast, were perhaps the first painters who worked out-of-doors in natural light from start to finish. Both painters were interested in capturing delicate atmospheric effects and particularly the play of light on objects.

Their approach to landscape differed from that of the more influential Barbizon painters, Diaz, Daubigny, Théodore Rousseau, and others, who painted in the Fontainebleau forest just outside of Paris. The Barbizon painters proceeded from nature but finished their work in the studio. Although they often achieved fresh and lively passages, their work was on the whole still romantic in character. They envisioned nature as a kind of picturesque, artificial backdrop for Man and as an

emotional projection of their own elevated and rather sentimental moods. They worked more freely than the members of
the seventeenth-century Dutch landscape school or the English-
man Constable, but their premises were equally romantic.

Boudin, Jongkind, and then Monet proceeded empirically on
the other hand, refusing to add any particular personal sentiment to their work; they also used a much bolder, brighter
palette. Boudin often introduced into his paintings contemporary figures, ladies with parasols taking their ease at fashionable seaside resorts. His work had a special lightness of touch,
employing bright spots of color against a foil of silvery gray.
Both his scintillating manner and his subjects often recall the
"little" style and world of Constantin Guys, whom Baudelaire
admired for his "modernity."

The vitality of the new landscape school had been strengthened immeasurably by two other painters of the older generation, Corot and Courbet. Corot's woodland scenes and suburban
landscapes showed a new simplicity, and, indeed, a fresh feeling for light effects, which he dramatized in his early work by
sharp contrasts of opaque shadow and brilliant, sun-bathed
areas. Courbet, at the time Monet was painting along the
beaches of Le Havre, was doing forest scenes with a loaded
brush or palette knife, paintings full of his characteristic energy
and of an improvisatory nature. At one time or another in the
mid-sixties all the Impressionists worked directly under his influence.

Courbet had met Boudin on the Normandy coast, and it was
he who brought his work to Baudelaire's attention. Baudelaire
praised its freshness and described Boudin as a "monarch of
skies" in his Salon review of 1859. In the next years Courbet
often painted along the Seine Estuary in the company of Boudin, Jongkind, and Monet. (The painters of the Barbizon
School, as well as Courbet, worked so frequently out of an
outlying area of Honfleur known as the Saint-Siméon farm that
Saint-Siméon was sometimes called the Barbizon of the north.)
Courbet's broad technique and somewhat coarse manner found
a sympathetic response in Monet and was important in freeing
him from Boudin's smaller, tighter style.

Monet's admiration for Courbet was not without strong

reservations, however. He disapproved of Courbet's old-master practice of preparing his canvas with a brown tone and of painting from dark to light. Monet had already discovered that greater luminosity could be achieved by setting bright tones down *directly* on the white canvas. He disposed his dark and light masses independently, giving each a positive value. In this way the whole surface of the canvas began to function, not merely those areas that were bathed in light. Monet discovered that the black bituminous pockets of shadow in the old masters, and in Courbet, were an arbitrary convention and that everything in out-of-door nature is penetrated in some degree by light. And where there is light or reflected light there is also color.

By 1865 and 1866, Monet had begun to paint shadows with purple light streaks in them. The use of complementary blue-violet shadows was found to enhance the predominantly warm, orange-yellow tones of sunlight. He also carried color from individual objects to their neighbors and hence broke down the convention of local color. In the limpid fair-weather light of the Normandy coast he had discovered that nature was full of color. By setting himself the task of repeating some of his favorite summertime motifs around Honfleur in the winter, when there was a blanket of snow, he discovered even more strikingly how luminous with reflected light and color shadows could actually be. These discoveries were the basis of the Impressionist revolution.

Working independently along the same general lines was Camille Pissarro, who had come to Paris from the West Indies in 1855, in time to be struck by Courbet's exhibition at the World's Fair. Pissarro met Monet in 1860, when they both found themselves drawing from a model at an informal Paris atelier, the Suisse Academy. He was at that time painting in the manner of Corot, and his example influenced Monet, who also "found the model [of Corot] excellent." Pissarro was the older and more knowledgeable of the two artists, and Monet began by following his lead. With his more analytical turn of mind, however, Monet soon made his own discoveries about nature. Often the paintings of the Impressionists are remarkably similar in manner and have been painted from the same motifs in the same year, so that it is difficult to say precisely who was most responsible for advances in style at any particular moment. Their work has the coherence of a movement, yet there seems no question that Monet led the way, or at least gave the Impressionists their basic analytical tools.

Soon after meeting Pissarro, Monet met Renoir, Sisley, and Bazille, the three young painters who were to participate with him and with Pissarro in the development of Impressionist style. In 1862, Monet returned to Paris after a two-year interval of military service and enrolled in the Beaux-Arts studio of Gleyre. In a short time he became the ringleader for the three fellow-students who were strongly in opposition to Gleyre's uninspiring academic teaching but had not known where to turn. Renoir, Bazille, and Sisley found in Monet the authority of convictions already formed and tested. Impressed by his broader experience, they looked up to a young artist who could boast of friendship with Pissarro, Boudin, and Jongkind and held forth authoritatively on Courbet and the new "realists." When Gleyre's studio was discontinued in 1865, they joined Monet to paint at Chailly in the forest of Fontainebleau. It was the beginning of a life-long friendship and a long working companionship.

In Fontainebleau the young rebels met some of the Barbizon painters and, most important, Courbet. Renoir in particular felt the impact of the man who was an awesome symbol of independence for all the young painters. Renoir's paintings of 1866 and 1867 are full of vigor, thick in paint paste, and rather dark in tonality, showing a clear Courbet influence. His sympathy with Courbet's painterly sensuality emerges in the broad handling of the nude that is the central figure of his *Diana* of 1867. The next year Renoir painted a charming portrait, *Sisley and His Wife;* he retained some of Courbet's voluptuousness and opaque quality of paint, but his figures are altogether more refined and delicate, permeated by light and air. They are, in fact, more suggestive of Manet than Courbet. Shortly after that, Renoir began to paint landscapes and city views with a charming informality and a scintillation of light quite unlike his early, more somber canvases. Pissarro had also begun to paint in a lighter, brighter palette simple warmly felt landscapes of the rural district around Pontoise, near Paris, where he established himself after 1866.

The year before, both Monet and Renoir had obtained a moderate public success with paintings which had been accepted at the official Salon; now they were welcomed among Manet's brilliant and vocal circle of artists, critics, literary characters and *causeurs* who conducted their forum of ideas at the Café Guerbois. The Impressionists' methods became one of the most animated topics of conversation, with Monet and Pissarro, particularly, staunchly defending their theories against Degas's biting scorn and in the face of Manet's scarcely more encouraging polite disinterest. (It was Degas who later suggested that the police comb the countryside and arrest *plein air* painters for desecrating the landscape with their paints and easels.) Monet's effort to fuse his own feelings about out-of-door painting with Manet's feeling for contemporary subject matter resulted in an ambitious plan for painting a *plein air Luncheon on the Grass* that should challenge Manet's great work. The little band of new painters had already become confident that their emphasis on color had superseded Manet's more tonal painting.

At this period both Monet and Renoir were engaged in a bitter struggle for economic survival. Monet, in a moment of despair with his wife ill and no funds on hand or in prospect, attempted to drown himself; in their correspondence both artists wrote of periods of enforced idleness because they were too poor to buy paints. Yet the paintings in progress at the time are among the most cheerful and enchanting landscapes imaginable; they do not suggest in any way the tragic personal circumstances of the artists.

As the little group of new landscape painters became more secure in their styles, each found certain motifs and locales that appealed to his particular interests. With his love of common humanity Pissarro took his inspiration from the rural farmlands around Pontoise and Auvers and painted them in a manner compounded of earthy force and gentleness. Sisley worked in the Fontainebleau forest at Pontoise and, after 1872, around Marly; his range of effects is more limited than some of his colleagues' but has an exquisite lyrical touch quite its own. Monet alternated between the Fontainebleau area, the boating resorts along the Seine near Paris, and the Normandy coast. His canvases were the most radical in technique, and he became more and more preoccupied with the problems of capturing light and atmosphere by means of "pure" unmodeled color. Renoir at an early date had begun to show his great natural gifts with paint, a bewitching sensuous quality, and his interest in more diversified subjects, including the human figure and portraits.

One of the critical moments in the evolution of the new style came during the summer of 1869 when Renoir joined Monet at La Grenouillère, a park at the Seine resort of Bougival just outside Paris. The Impressionists took to frequenting the cheap middle-class boating places along the Seine, just as the older generation of painters had fancied the more fashionable channel seaside places such as Trouville and Deauville. The interest of Monet and Renoir in the middle rather than the upper classes made itself clear in their Seine paintings. La Grenouillère became one of the prototypes of the out-of-door holiday places that Impressionist art makes so attractive; it was described by de Maupassant in his story, *Paul's Wife,* as "the world's most delightful park." Here Monet and Renoir worked together during the summer; and here their conviction that contemporary subjects should be set out-of-doors crystallized, and they broadened their techniques.

In the river scenes they painted, reflections of light on water (described on page 111, commentary, plate 7) played a large role in loosening their styles. Both artists simultaneously began to paint in vivid, little strokes of pure color, breaking light and light reflections down into a dazzle of spectrum colors; by their touches of color they made the whole atmosphere live and the entire surface of the painting function chromatically. At the same time they added a special poetic charm to their subjects, invariably depicting their picnickers and boating figures in a youthful bloom of good health and in high spirits. Renoir interpreted everything he saw in a melting poetic manner. The shimmering, atmospheric envelope of colored light with which he sheathed his delightful and physically splendid human beings was not so much a product of analysis, as it was with Monet, but an expression of his own intoxication with the good things of life. Monet's researches and pictorial formulations had already begun to express a more contemplative, impersonal approach; human sentiment was suppressed in favor of an almost mystical feeling for light.

The Franco-Prussian War of 1870 drove Monet and Pissarro to seek refuge in London. Here they saw in the museums the landscape paintings of Turner and Constable. They were impressed but not directly influenced, as some critics have held; it is unlikely that the contact was crucial to their subsequent development. They saw confirmed their own feelings that landscape could constitute a noble and serious genre. The English had made a worthy effort along the right path, but their effects were artificial, their methods obsolete and inadequate, not sufficiently natural, as Pissarro put it. The Impressionists were repelled by the romantic sentiment of Turner despite his dazzling, virtuoso handling of light. "Turner and Constable," Pissarro later said, "while they taught us something, showed us in their works that they had no understanding of the *analysis of shadow,* which in Turner's painting is simply used as an effect, a mere absence of light. As far as tone division is concerned, Turner proved the value of this as a method, among methods, although he did not apply it correctly and naturally." Here again we come upon the Impressionists' deep faith in the ways of nature and their conviction that they were actually coming closer to the truth of nature with their mosaics of dancing color spots which at the time seemed most arbitrary to public and critics alike.

After the war Pissarro settled again at Pontoise; Monet traveled in Holland and then established himself at Argenteuil, a Seine town near Bougival, where he was frequently joined by Renoir and Manet. Out of Argenteuil in 1873 and 1874 issued the first great Impressionist canvases. Monet's palette became even brighter and more abstract; his surfaces a formless mass of vibrating flecks of pure color which were set down in contrasts, for he had discovered that the most intense optical sensations were obtained when colors were mixed by the eye. A spot of pure red, for example, set next to a spot of yellow not only creates the optical sensation of orange but does so more

vividly than the actual tube pigment of premixed orange. As
Monet's palette became more brilliant so did Renoir's. Even
Manet submitted up to a point to their experiments of painting out-of-doors, though he never entirely abandoned his more
muted color harmonies.

The general discontent of the Impressionists with existing artistic institutions, their need to exhibit and *sell,* and their sense
of common aims resulted in 1874 in their first group exhibition
under the name of the Society of Artists, Painters, Sculptors,
and Engravers *(Societé Anonyme des Artistes, Peintres, Sculp-
teurs, Graveurs).* Monet was the leading spirit in organizing
the show, and he soon enlisted the enthusiastic efforts of
Degas in recruiting participants. Manet held aloof, still intent
on official recognition and unwilling to compromise himself
as he had done in 1863 by associating himself again with
refusés. A group of painters who admitted by such an independent exhibition their failure to make headway with the official
jury of the Salon, he insisted, were destined to be laughed out
of court entirely and could only hurt their cause. Of the better-
known painters, Monet sent five paintings; Cézanne, three;
Degas, ten; Berthe Morisot, nine; Sisley, five; and Renoir, six,
including his charming little ballerina, *Dancer,* and the *Loge,*
one of his most handsome figure paintings.

The derisive label Impressionist was coined by a journalist,
Louis Leroy, after he saw one of Monet's entries entitled *Impression: Sunrise;* in his review of the exhibition he ungra-
ciously compared the painting with "wallpaper in its embryonic
state." The critical notices were hostile and ridiculing; the
painters were reviled and the public was invited to attend the
exhibition for amusement, and indeed many did come to
laugh. Apparently no furious spectators tried to punch holes
in the canvases as had been done in Manet's early exhibitions,
but the general reaction was if anything more outraged. Any
hopes the Impressionists had entertained of making sales were
soon abandoned.

When their second exhibition was held the following year, the
response was equally unfavorable. The critic of *Figaro* described
the exhibition as a calamity: "After the opera fire," he wrote,
"here is a new disaster overwhelming the district. At Durand-

Ruel's there has just opened an exhibition of so-called painting . . . five or six lunatics—among them a woman [Berthe
Morisot] . . . have met there to exhibit their works. . . . Try
to make M. Pissarro understand that trees are not violet, that
the sky is not the color of fresh butter, that in no country do
we see the things he paints and that no intelligence can accept
such aberrations! Try indeed to make M. Degas see reason;
tell him that in art there are certain qualities called drawing,
color, execution, control, and he will laugh in your face and
treat you as a reactionary. Or try to explain to M. Renoir that
a woman's torso is not a mass of flesh in the process of decom-
position with green and violet spots which denote the state of
complete putrefaction of a corpse! . . . And it is this accumulation of crudities which are shown to the public, with no
thought of the fatal consequences that may result! Yesterday a
poor soul was arrested in the rue le Peletier, who, after having
seen the exhibition, was biting the passers-by."

Only the dedicated champions of realism, such committed
critics as Castagnary and Duret, dared express enthusiasm for
the Impressionists. Few could have predicted that the Impressionist exhibitions were to be the entering wedge in the ultimate route to the Salon or that the prestige of official art institutions was from the date of their inception to decline steadily.
Manet and some of the Impressionists continued to submit to
the Salon in the succeeding years, but only Manet seemed to
do so with any real conviction or enthusiasm. The Salon was
within the space of two decades to become at best a second
choice as a place of exhibition for the most vital artists.
When the Impressionists institutionalized themselves, yesterday's heresy was on the way to becoming today's orthodoxy,
and the days of the Academy's iron rule were numbered.

From 1874 to 1886 the Impressionist group, which included
a potpourri of artists of both radical and conservative tendency, held eight exhibitions. Their various manners went
through many mutations during that period, and in time the
most significant members of the group changed their styles
completely. Degas, as we have seen, increased his repertory of
contemporary subjects to include café scenes and the ballet.
Pissarro continued to work in the rural, idyllic surroundings

of Pontoise, and in Paris, but his manner grew progressively more free. Monet painted Paris railroad stations (such as the *Gare Saint-Lazare*), catching in the blue plumes of an engine's smoke some of the complicated poetry of a big city. And he too depicted countryside surrounding Paris with an ever increasing spontaneity and freshness.

In time, however, his lyricism began to express itself through certain repeated motifs, and he developed almost a monomania about optical experience. As Monet began to take a more and more extreme position, his fellow-Impressionists turned their backs on the fugitive effects he sought. About 1886 another great turning point in modern painting had begun to crystallize: the beginning of the Post-Impressionist period.

Monet alone remained faithful to the original tenets of Impressionism, pushing them as far as they would carry him, almost to the point of pure visual abstraction. In the early nineties his preoccupation with method led him to do a number of consecutive, related paintings, a series of *Hayricks, Poplars,* of the façade of *Rouen Cathedral,* of views of London, and of *Water Lilies* in his garden pool at Giverny. His aim was to give a serial, continuous impression of the most minute transformations of light; by de-emphasizing his subject matter through repetition, he felt he could more readily control the variable of light. In some of these motifs he lost the freshness of his early work and became overemphatic and monotonous. The refulgent color of the Rouen Cathedral façades in the Jeu de Paume, the Museum of Impressionism in Paris, have an oppressive sweetness, and pigment looks distractingly like cake icing. On the other hand, his lily pad motifs, where close-valued, but lower-keyed, color is enhanced by a loose and fluent brushwork, today assumes a remarkable power and originality. Only in our time, and particularly in America where a vital new school of chromatic abstraction has arisen recently, has this abstract writing in color of Monet's last period received due recognition. It now excites wide interest and admiration among vanguard artists.

The formlessness of Monet's very last work was part of a personal and mystical esthetic related to Japanese screen and scroll painting. His *Nymphéas,* a continuous low frieze of water lilies painted to go around the walls of a room, now installed in the Paris Orangerie, was produced in 1909. It represents the logical conclusion in near-abstraction of nineteenth-century naturalism and of Monet's obsessive preoccupation with the visual. The artist declared he had wished to "produce the illusion of an endless whole, a wave without horizon and without shore . . . and for him who would live in it, this room would offer an asylum of peaceful meditation in the midst of a flowering aquarium."

It was Renoir who became the most enchanting and was publicly the most successful of the group working in Impressionist technique. His paintings of the seventies fused Monet's methods with his own delighted interest in life. His rich and varied scenes of *la vie Parisienne* displayed a relish for the substance and texture of things, for the spirit of life itself, that brings him closer to Manet than to either Monet or Degas. Renoir registered his vision in a series of large, inspired scenes of *fête* and outdoor figure compositions as ambitious as those of Manet. Among them are *Le Moulin de la Galette* of 1876, in the Jeu de Paume (there is another version in the John Hay Whitney collection) and *The Luncheon of the Boating Party* of 1881.

In these paintings Renoir achieved a transparency and luminosity of tone even more brilliant and delicate than Monet's; these effects are, in fact, directly related to the shimmering vivacities of Watteau and to the paintings of the great eighteenth-century decorators, Boucher and Fragonard. Dappled by a silky, opalescent light, his magnificent human creatures glow with the miracle of youth and ardent feeling. Handsome men pay gallant court to their beautiful women; all are at their brilliant best, at the top of their physical and spiritual being, enamored of each other and of nature. The passionate moments Renoir registers, most particularly in his women, distill a feeling of the delight and promise of youth than can best be compared with Tolstoi's literary portraits of the radiant, young Natasha standing eagerly on the threshold of life, or of Anna Karenina in the fullness of young womanhood. Unlike Watteau's lyricism, Renoir's is neither artificial nor shadowed by melancholy and indecision. Never in the modern period have youth and natural beauty been paid such extravagant tribute.

In the early eighties Renoir's Impressionist phase drew to a close. As Monet began to push his optical experiments to an extreme of pure light sensation, the tempo of Renoir's work and feeling slackened, and he was assailed by doubts. He wished for something more substantial in pictorial structure than the formless Impressionist color haze, and perhaps he had simply exhausted for himself all the possible charms of natural appearances. On a trip to Italy in 1881 he was deeply moved by the classical form and linear graces of Raphael and by Pompeian wall frescoes. He returned to Paris to begin painting in rather stiff and artificial outlines, consciously suppressing seductive colors and emulating Renaissance draftsmanship and also the linear example of Ingres. Later he said to his dealer Vollard, referring to the period of about 1883: "I had wrung Impressionism dry, and I finally came to the conclusion that I knew neither how to paint nor how to draw. In a word, Impressionism was a blind alley as far as I was concerned." The stiff, linear phase, which has been described as Renoir's *manière aigre,* his sour period, lasted only a few years, and by 1890 Renoir was moving toward an art at once more monumental and free, which preserved all the sensuous enjoyment of nature that was characteristic of his Impressionist period.

His last paintings are of the things he loved: the faces of young people, the female nude in particular, fruit, flowers, the rolling fields of France bathed in sunlight. In these, however, he arrived at a new synthesis of color and massive volumes and a new spirit of grandeur. His heavy nudes, generalized, indeed "universalized," seem to belong to no particular nature but to a paradise on earth; figure groupings are composed and painted with the rhythmic energy and sensuality of a Rubens *Kermess.* Renoir was pre-eminently a painter of the flesh. In his early work he painted it in its first gorgeous bloom; at the end of his life he gave flesh the fullness of ripe fruit.

Renoir's repudiation of Impressionism after 1883 was part of a radical and general change in the art of the time. Degas about this period had begun to focus on the form of the single female figure, adding a more baroque and robust inflection to his art. (Even Monet, who doggedly held to his vision, had pushed it to such an extreme that it had drastically changed in character and become an abstract color lyricism.) There was a pervasive feeling that Impressionist discoveries in color must now be combined with more substantial and permanent effects and must be given solid pictorial form. Pure optical sensation was exhausted, for all but Monet. Along with Renoir and Degas to a lesser degree there were two other artists who particularly reflected the denial of Impressionism. They were the young painter Georges Seurat, who came before the public eye at the first *Salon des Indépendants* of 1884, and Paul Cézanne. Cézanne had briefly joined the Impressionist camp and then in the early 1880's had isolated himself in the south of France. There he pursued formal researches which were in a short time to revolutionize painting of the nineteenth century and form the bridge to our own.

5

Cylinder, Sphere, and Cone

"They see poetry in what I have done. No, I apply my methods, and that is all there is to it."

—Georges Seurat

"I wished to make out of Impressionism something solid and durable like the art of the museums."

—Paul Cézanne

In his book *Modern French Painters*, R. H. Wilenski describes the new tendencies in French painting during the eighties decade as part of a general classical renaissance. According to this simplified recipe, Renoir, Seurat, and Cézanne expressed their dissatisfactions with the superficialities of Impressionism by reverting to classical French tradition and stressing architectural elements of pictorial structure. This is fine so far as it goes, but it is not entirely illuminating, for some of the Post-Impressionist styles also represented an effort to *preserve* naturalism. Renoir did so by enlarging his style and idealizing his figures while still expressing a delight in the substance and texture of things. Seurat preserved naturalism under the aegis of "science"; and Cézanne's most arbitrary inventions were based on the prismatic colors of Impressionism and on his own "sensations" before nature. While these Post-Impressionists rejected the formlessness of the Impressionist picture, they absorbed and now extended the movement's basic values and its spirit of radical empiricism. The individual artist's sensations and intimate feelings, his mistrust of all but the immediately given in experience, were retained even within a more formal pictorial framework. The vital, new tradition of direct painting had assumed a programmatic value.

Opposed to the work of these artists was a growing anti-naturalistic reaction. Van Gogh and Redon in varied ways, and Gauguin and the painters around him who drew support from the literary Symbolists, were interested in using art as a vehicle for more personal emotions, for fantasy, reverie, and dream. Within these two camps were any number of divisions and subdivisions defined by the individual styles of the artist, which might in turn be classical, archaic, effete, or mixtures of all. The common denominator of painting in the Post-Impressionist period was a vigorous reaction to pure optical experience and an effort to deepen the meaning of art by a conceptual rather than perceptual approach. Seurat and Cézanne transcended their "sensations" by creating more abstract and impersonal styles in a new form-language. They included the sensuous, palpable things of nature but reorganized them according to the dictates of a lofty intellectual ideal. That resolute objectivity of both Seurat and Cézanne was opposed by the more emotional approach of Gauguin and van Gogh. Although they were not primarily didactic artists, Gauguin and van Gogh managed to transfigure nature in the image of their own mystical aspiration in styles as imposing and hieratic as the Byzantine. It is well to keep in mind the complex changes of style in this period, and the continuing fecundity of the naturalist impulse even in the austere inventions of Seurat and Cézanne.

In the reaction to Impressionism came the second great revolution in late nineteenth-century painting, a movement toward formal pictorial construction. Yet this change in style, as exemplified in the art of Seurat and Cézanne, did not by any means negate the essentially rationalist and positivist spirit of Impressionism; the new formalizations enlarged it to include intellectual order as well as sense data. Cézanne and Seurat refined and essentialized naturalism.

The first public evidence of defection from Impressionism came with Georges Seurat's exhibition of his *Une Baignade—*

Asnières at the newly formed *Salon des Indépendants* in 1884. (Like the Impressionist exhibitions, the new Salon was founded by progressive artists to combat the reactionary policy of the official Salon; Seurat, Odilon Redon, Henri Edmond Cross, and Paul Signac took the lead in organizing the first exhibition.) Seurat divided his tones in this painting as the Impressionists had done, setting contrasting dabs of pure color side by side, and his canvas similarly presented a speckled, multicolored surface. However, his color dots were tinier, more systematically distributed, and they were built up in concentrated, dense clusters that gave a more solid definition to form. Impressionist forms tended to vanish in a chromatic exhalation, in an amorphous, flowing mass of light and colored air. By using dark and light contrasts Seurat dislodged his forms from their surrounding atmosphere, established them firmly in space, and created a tension between them and the space they inhabited.

In *Une Baignade* a group of clothed and half-clothed gentlemen loll on the banks of the Seine before a broad river view, with sails and a bridge glinting with sunlight in the distance. Each human figure is given a sculptural roundness, though contours are softened so that they merge hazily with a living sundrenched atmosphere. One boy, waist-deep in water, cups his hands to his mouth; another young man sits in profile, his feet dangling over the bank; still another is outstretched on his stomach. All these poses are carefully weighed and balanced against each other in a wonderfully choreographed tableau that summons up the stately, measured movements of Poussin. A cunning play of vertical accents (sails, bridge, piers, and trees) and horizontals (the wide, grassy river bank, the reclining figure) gives the composition a carefully thought out architectural organization.

Just as Seurat has carefully controlled his space and volumes, so he has also established the character of the scene in a calculated fashion. Each figure is sharply typed as a personality by some expressive detail in dress or gesture. With his first major painting Seurat summed up and, in a sense, abstracted a common human activity. His elegantly selective vision and formal cunning fix the scene with the power of myth. Descriptive detail is particular and exact, though all superfluous matter has been suppressed, and yet as stylized as that in an Egyptian wall relief. With his remarkable powers of generalization Seurat extended the Impressionists' swift glimpse of a "moment in time" and made an episode stand for something customary and permanent in human activity. And he found a form that could withstand patient and studied contemplation.

Seurat painted and drew innumerable preliminary sketches for *Une Baignade*. He saturated himself in the atmosphere of the Seine bathing site at Asnières and faithfully observed and recorded pertinent incident on the spot. He made charcoal drawings of a number of the main figures, extraordinarily complete and sensitive to character, and incorporated some of these directly into the final work. He also did many oil studies for color and for light and dark distribution. The final painting was the end result of a process of accumulating and distilling innumerable impressions and visual notes made at the site. As a manner of working, this in itself was entirely contrary to the Impressionists' method of seizing the immediate fragment of vision and setting it down with a minimum of ratiocination. Their free-flowing inspiration was exactly contrary to the way Seurat's neat and tidy mind functioned. Monet, Pissarro, and Renoir, in their boulevard scenes, deliberately recorded random, unrelated visual data and by doing so expressed a kind of first principle of artistic freedom. In their Paris street scenes, building façades, trees, moving figures and other incident are related to each other pictorially only in so far as they have the blurred, psychological rightness of a vision assimilated by the eye at high speed. In fact, the Impressionists wished precisely to give the impression of something entirely natural and unarranged, a chance *trouvé* on which was imposed no unity other than that supplied by the individual artist's sensibility and personal "handwriting." Seurat, on the contrary, deliberately *composed*, leaving nothing to chance. His forms take their place in a preordained scheme of things which obeys certain immutable pictorial conventions. Seurat's methods initiated a whole new expression of artistic will, as did the art of Cézanne.

Seurat's precise mind had been classically disciplined for four years in Paris at the Ecole des Beaux-Arts studio of Henri

Lehmann, a pupil of Ingres. The young artist rebelled against the narrow and parochial academic training, but he continued to express his sympathy with classicism in masterful drawings after Raphael, Holbein, and Ingres. In 1879 he left the studio to do military service at Brest, where he lived facing the sea and soon came to feel a special affection for the broad skies, crystalline air, and wide distances. He later painted frequently along the Normandy coast, and there is always in his art a quality that recalls the trance-like stillness of coastal regions and that feeling of suspension in an eternity of space which they induce.

In 1880 Seurat returned to Paris and began to draw intensively. He blocked out his figures freely and massed darks and lights to give the broadest expression to his forms. He was soon using charcoal in a new way, achieving a velvety richness in his blacks and exquisite nuances of gray and white. He discovered that by lightly graying the roughened surface of his paper he could create an interesting texture grain, an effect that is not unlike the "pointillism" later adopted in his oils. His drawing of an artist and friend, Aman-Jean (see plate 17), drew favorable comment from the critic Claude-Roger Marx when it was exhibited at the Salon of 1883. Seurat's drawings are a rare genre in nineteenth-century art; they are rich in tone, remarkably sensitive to character, informal and yet full of aristocratic grace.

Through the *Salon des Indépendants* of 1884 Seurat met Paul Signac. The following years these artists together formulated the theoretical basis of the new style which had begun to emerge in *Une Baignade* and which Félix Fénéon later called Neo-Impressionism. Camille Pissarro was the only artist of the older generation affected by their painting and for a time he worked in their manner. The new esthetic was presumed to be scientifically foolproof and had been inspired by the color theories of Chevreul, O. N. Rood, and Maxwell. Some of the important scientific discoveries that stimulated the Neo-Impressionists were: Chevreul's color wheel of the primary and intermediate colors which represented the component rainbow colors of white light when it is broken down by a prism; Chevreul's "law of simultaneous contrast of colors"; and Rood's discovery that optical mixtures of color were more intense than premixed color. Actually, Seurat and his friends scientifically rationalized discoveries which the Impressionists for the most part already knew and intuitively applied in painting.

Seurat's intense interest in color theory may be understood as part of the scientific preoccupation of his period and of the belief that everything could be formulated and explained in terms of natural law, even the life of the emotions. (Gauguin found the artist's scientism distasteful and referred to Seurat as "the little green chemist." He later wrote: "In art we have just passed through a period of bewildering wandering caused by physics, chemistry, mechanics and the study of nature.") From Chevreul's researches, Seurat deduced that local color was simply one convention among others. Scientifically, it can be demonstrated that any hue modifies its neighboring color since it must induce an aureole of a tone which is its own complementary. Red set down against yellow (if red is dominant quantitatively) not only produces the sensation of orange, their intermediate color, but also of green, which is red's complementary. Rood's experiments in turn proved that red and yellow create a more intense orange as an optical mixture than the actual tube color of pure orange can do.

Seurat apparently first drew inferences about the possibilities of optical mixtures not from Rood's equations but from Delacroix's late paintings, which he was able to study in the Chapel of Saint-Sulpice. He and Signac in fact developed a cult for Delacroix. Delacroix's expressive palette suggested to Seurat the possibility of the use of color to create certain emotions and states of mind, as it had done also to Baudelaire. The poet had written of Delacroix's colors: "Yellow, orange, red, represent and inspire ideas of joy, riches, glory, and love; but there are thousands of yellow or red atmospheres, and all the other colors will be affected to a degree logically determined by the dominant atmosphere. The art of the colorist is evidently in some respects related to mathematics and music." Seurat in time became convinced that some elementary rules of harmony could be established for painting as they had been in music; for painting, the rules would be based on optical laws. He set forth his theory of optical harmonies and contraries in a letter: the manifold elements of painting could be simplified and codified as "tone, tint, and line"; they were found to inspire "gay, calm, or sad" emotions according to their character, with descending lines, dark tone, and cold tints producing sadness; rising lines, luminous tone and warm color, gayety. Curiously enough, Gauguin, whose approach was so different, later suggested that his painting could be understood as a kind of visual music, and he was profoundly concerned with the emotional suggestion of colors.

In 1884, at the age of twenty-five, Seurat began the methodical application of his theories in an immense painting project of a magnitude almost unknown since the days of David and Ingres. On the Seine island La Grande Jatte he began making preparatory oil sketches and drawings, as he had done for *Une Baignade*. Completed two years later, the final painting measured approximately seven by ten feet and had been preceded by some twenty drawings and two hundred oil sketches. *A Sunday Afternoon on the Island of la Grande Jatte* was shown in the *Salon des Indépendants* in 1886 and again at the eighth and last Impressionist exhibition. The painting was opposed by Degas, and Seurat's "Scientific Impressionism" was belabored by the older "Romantic Impressionists," as Monet, Renoir, and Sisley were now called. These last three artists withdrew from the Impressionist exhibition at least in part because they objected to the inclusion of the Neo-Impressionists.

La Grande Jatte was Seurat's great out-of-doors masterpiece (commentary, plate 18; pp. 121-122). It showed a holiday crowd of Parisians on an outing, relaxing on the grass, promenading, fishing, and frolicking in a park that is framed by a background of trees and water. The atmosphere is brilliant, and contrasting dots of pigment create the effect of sun-dazzle; color is much brighter than formerly; characterizations of the various personages are sharp and witty. As in *Une Baignade*, a common human activity has been distilled and charmingly stylized.

Seurat's unfolding panorama of the middle class at play is as eloquent a commentary on contemporary life and manners as Renoir's great lyrical paintings of his middle period, *Le Moulin de la Galette* and *The Luncheon of the Boating Party*. Whereas Renoir's figures are larger than life, with vitality and energy that spill over and animate nature, Seurat's lyricism is more contained. His people are reduced to delightful little statuettes arranged deftly and with much good humor in obedience to the artist's will. They take their place almost mechanically in the compositional scheme, swelling an arabesque, relieving a splash of sunlight or a mass of shade. Much of the drollness and charm of the work comes from the artist's over-control of forms. His human subjects seem to be mechanically propelled; at the same time, they are natural enough to be convincing. Out of a tension between the natural and the artificial, between sensations based on a living atmosphere and an almost religious dedication to formal problems, Seurat constructed a vital contemporary creation. In its time it was thought rather frivolous and fanciful, however; the novelist George Moore reported that the canvas aroused great curiosity, but mainly for its size, its peculiar color scheme, and "a ring-tailed monkey" whose "tail is said to be three yards long." The famous critic J. K. Huysmans wrote, "Strip his figures of the colored fleas that cover them; underneath you will find nothing, no thought, no soul. . . ."

After *La Grande Jatte* Seurat painted a number of scenes which again brilliantly caught the essential character and movements of some aspect of contemporary life: *Les Poseuses*, a group of models in a room with *La Grande Jatte* in the background; *La Parade*, a row of musicians on a proscenium under flickering gaslight at a fair; *Le Chahut*, a cabaret scene; many marine paintings of the Normandy coast; and *Le Cirque*, a bareback equestrian and a ringmaster performing at the circus. In his last works Seurat's rhythms are more emphatic and flat, decorative accents are played up. His quiet humor is also more pointed. *Le Cirque*, for example, burlesques the action portrayed and the figures verge on the fantastic.

Seurat died in 1891 at the age of thirty-two. He left behind only six major paintings; a number of charming marines; innumerable informal oil studies; and a sizable body of exquisite drawings. His achievement cannot be measured by the relatively small number of oils he produced; if he had painted only *La Grande Jatte* he would take his place as one of the finest artists of the modern period. After his death, Pissarro, who had joined and then in 1890 withdrawn from the Neo-Impressionist group, wrote to his son Lucien: "I believe you are right, pointillism is finished, but I think it will give rise to other effects which later will have great artistic significance. Seurat really brought something." What he brought was, above all, a renewed interest in pictorial structure and design, those major formal considerations which Impressionism ignored. He began tentatively to use color for plastic definition as well as for description and hence his art forms a bridge between Impressionism and the great innovations of Cézanne. Seurat's feeling for flat decorative form, his comic exaggeration, and some of his music hall and circus subject matter also link him to Toulouse-Lautrec.

The new interest in the solid presence of objects and deeper concern with the more permanent and formal aspects of nature are even more dramatically illustrated by the paintings of Paul Cézanne. Because of the importance of Cézanne's innovations and their impact on the twentieth century, he has been called, with justice, "the father of modern art." For continuous creative impulse, Cézanne is one of the major figures of nineteenth-century painting, ranking with Manet and Renoir; his inventions in form were as important as Manet's, and since they are still one of the fundamental points of departure for our own contemporary painting, they will be even more meaningful to us than Manet's. By comparison, Seurat must take his place as a minor figure—a perfection, yet a smaller and less influential talent than Cézanne. Seurat's paintings, however, have conveniently led us to the point where Cézanne's art begins; they do not make quite so abrupt a transition from Impressionism. They illuminate Cézanne's radical solution to pictorial problems from the nineteenth century's point of view and may help balance the sometimes parochial interpretation that twentieth-century sensibility has put on Cézanne's forms.

Cézanne's revolutionary achievement was, in Roger Fry's phrase, the invention of "plastic color." To a much greater degree than Seurat, he used color to establish solid form in space. Unlike the Neo-Impressionists, Cézanne abandoned both the dot-and-dash system of color application and atmospheric perspective. Each dab of color became for him a living paint cell, a significant plane defining the position of an object and all the intermediate layers of space between objects. He was conscious of a discrepancy between forms as one felt them in natural space and forms as they were transposed onto the flat surface of the canvas. This, in fact, became the crux of his pictorial problem: finding a new solution that would violate neither his "sensation" of depth in external reality nor his awareness of the two-dimensional limits of the painting surface.

Now, Seurat had never quite resolved this problem satisfactorily. At one time he spoke of painting as the art of "hollowing out a surface," and he sought to preserve the "illusion" of deep space and traditional Renaissance perspective. At the end of his career, however, he was more aware of a conflict between maintaining the unity of the picture plane and creating the illusion of distance. But he settled the conflict arbitrarily, *not* in terms of his sensations before nature but by emphasizing flat decoration.

Cézanne, instead, found an abbreviatory pictorial form that was "plastic" rather than decorative. He at once projected a vital impression of the solid physical presence of objects and still accepted the limitations imposed by a flat surface.

With little curved strokes of color he was able to create a richness of form which has justifiably been compared to the great sixteenth-century Venetians'. Why these forms penetrate to the deeper levels of our feelings, no one has ever clearly understood. Cézanne's humanity, his apples and Provençal mountains appear disguised as the most rudimentary geometries, reduced to the "cylinder, the sphere, the cone" which he advised Emile Bernard to seek in nature. Nature is reduced to a tense skeleton of form and sinks into a homogeneous color structure every inch of which is in dynamic formal operation. Cézanne's art is at the farthest pole from Degas's exact realism or Renoir's feeling for texture and the palpable surface of things; in his painting we feel a sensuous opulence, which is a richness of the pictorial means. But we have learned to read his complex surfaces as a plenitude of sensation extracted from visible nature. His schematic forms look like the merest ciphers, but they exert force just as solid, material objects do; and they are saturated in a natural atmosphere, even though that atmosphere sometimes seems dense enough to be cut with a knife.

To achieve a balance between external nature and the exigencies of the painting on a flat surface, Cézanne had to be a master juggler. He painfully adjusted and readjusted his color dabs and rhythmic contour lines, insisting on sitting after sitting from his human models, which nearly drove them to distraction. The explicit definition of the edges of forms was always just avoided lest line harden into decoration. He reversed perspective, placing the culminating point of objects in the foreground, and at that point he made color richest. He also distorted the normal pattern of optical perspective by tilting up the horizontal plane of a retreating road or the hole at the mouth of a jug so that they came forward, or by bending the side of a house toward the spectator. Or he might paint a landscape from several different points of view and positions to reveal more of its surface than is normally seen. In short, he painted *conceptually* but still included the perceptual sensuous truth of nature.

In Cézanne we find, too, a quality of tension that can be compared to seventeenth-century "metaphysical" poetry. Lyrical sensations of nature and remarkable powers of abstraction are combined at high pressure. The content of Cézanne's thought and his "plastic" ideas are as concrete and apprehensible as the sensuous data of nature. A delicate pattern that pine branches make against the sea or the evocative immediacy of nature's fresh green are no less *real* for us in the abstract formulation Cézanne gives them. The artist sealed in one stroke the breach of form and content that had ruled painting since the death of Giotto.

Because the life or death of his canvas hinged on an accumulation of minute adjustments of color, Cézanne's paintings sometimes seem either overdeveloped or incomplete. An arabesque freezes, the dynamic operation of the many-faceted surface exhausts the eye, or the iron rule of form and structure becomes oppressive. His towering humility before nature and a chance phrase in a letter to the dealer Vollard, confessing an inability to "realize," have unfortunately exaggerated these failures. Cézanne's anxieties are no measure of his very grand achievement; indeed, his last works are sometimes more rewarding considered in series rather than as intact achievements.

There are certain key canvases—two or three versions of the *Card-players,* bathers in a landscape, a number of still lifes, views of Mont Sainte-Victoire—that sum up his methods in a masterpiece. But their meaning is enlarged if we think of even these paintings as thematic variations in one great fugue on nature's grandeur, and as part of an inexhaustible plastic invention.

Despite his concentration on formal structure and pure pictorial values, Cézanne never relinquished the feeling for light and air that he acquired from Pissarro and the Impressionists. As his art progressed, he thinned his pigment so that the white surface lightened tones as it may do in water colors. During his later years he very often worked in water color directly in a manner that was both suggestive and abstract. Cézanne sought in these tenuous impressions to express not the accidental, shifting iridescence of nature as the Impressionists had done, but its intrinsic color in all its intensity. He chose Provence as a painting locale because the even Mediterranean light gave a sharp, unchanging exposure to his motifs; the placid skies of Provence allowed color to burn with an undiffused brightness. And in the clarity of a southern atmosphere, Cézanne felt the sympathetic presence of the great classical masters, of Poussin and the Italians. In his own phrase, he wished to "redo nature after Poussin."

The rational and classical quality of his art is all the more remarkable in view of Cézanne's early struggles with his own exuberant and undisciplined nature. It took an enormous exercise of will to master a turbulent emotional life. The general picture of the artist is based on his mature personality and is that of a "hyper-bourgeois" of fanatical conservatism; a solitary, entrenched in home and church and darkly suspicious of new ideas. Yet in his youth Cézanne was the most defiant of rebels and the prototype of the romantic bohemian.

He first came to Paris in 1860 at the urging of his boyhood friend, Emile Zola, in full flight from his father's banking business. His early paintings were characterized by violent fantasy and melodrama, and they became the butt of much ridicule. A friend of Pissarro, he soon met Manet and his café circle, but his uncouth meridional manners kept most of them at a respectful distance. Cézanne was also something of a *farceur* and played up his crudeness and romantic defiance of authority; he wrote stinging letters to the officials of the Salons who repeatedly rejected his paintings, and he once refused to offer his hand to Manet because he hadn't bathed for a week. At another time he went down on his knees before Rodin, who had just been decorated (Cézanne never was) and half-mockingly, half-hysterically thanked him for the privilege of allowing him, Cézanne, to shake his hand. The violent forces that raged within created many emotional crises in his life and brought on considerable suffering. Yet the same tremendous drive that made him exaggerate his youthful defiance and, in maturity, his defensiveness, also gave him the strength to put his painting world in order.

Even in the earliest work a refinement in color and a way with *la belle matière* made themselves felt despite the often slapdash handling and an extremely melodramatic subject matter. Influenced in turn by Daumier, Delacroix, Courbet, and Manet, his style went through many mutations in the sixties. As early as 1866 he painted portraits of his father, and of one of his uncles dressed as a monk, with the most expressive and original color harmonies. Then, under Pissarro's guidance, he adopted Impressionist methods for a time in the seventies and worked "violently and with all his might to regulate his temperament and to impose upon it the control of cold science." A typical painting of the Impressionist period, *The Hangman's House,* employs divided tones, is much less gloomy in color than the "black idyls" of the sixties, and is thinner in paint paste. The impasto is still more substantial than Pissarro's and gives more solid definition to form.

By the end of the seventies Cézanne's interest in form, especially as derived from still life objects, became all-absorbing (commentary, plate 14; pp. 117-118). In the midst of the Impressionist period, he turned his back on its first principles. After 1877 he never again exhibited with them, and between that date and 1895 his paintings were unknown in Paris except to the few curious artists who sought them out at Père Tanguy's paint supplies shop. The exhibition at Vollard's in 1895 came as a revelation to his fellow-artists; it had been arranged perhaps as an answer to the Luxembourg Museum, which had turned down some Cézannes among others in the superb Caillebotte Bequest of Impressionist work just offered the state. Pissarro wrote to his son: "My enthusiasm was nothing compared to Renoir's. Degas himself is seduced by the charm of this refined savage, Monet, all of us. . . . As Renoir said so well, these paintings have I do not know what quality like the things of Pompeii, so crude and so admirable!" But the impact of Cézanne's work on the new generation was even stronger. Emile Bernard, Maurice Denis, Pierre Bonnard, Edouard Vuillard, young artists who had been painting under the influence of Gauguin's "Synthetism," saw in Cézanne the ultimate repudiation of Impressionism. Denis later painted a *Homage to Cézanne* and described Cézanne's work as "the final outcome of the classical tradition and the product of the great crisis of liberty and light which had rejuvenated modern art." To the later generation of Picasso and Braque these paintings took on yet another meaning and became the point of departure for a purely formal art which dispensed with recognizable subject matter altogether.

Shortly before his death in 1906, Cézanne had declared: "I am the primitive of a new art." The character of the new art became clear, however, only in the early decades of the twentieth century. Cézanne's profound revolution hung in abeyance for a period of some twenty years between 1886 and his death. In that interval the destiny of painting was in hands of other personalities, and the art scene was dominated by other forces.

6

Mysterious Centers of Thought

"Art is an abstraction; derive it from nature by indulging in dreams in the presence of nature, and think more of creation than of the result."

—Paul Gauguin

". . . the worm-eaten official tradition is still alive, but really impotent and inactive, the new painters alone, poor, treated like madmen and because of this treatment actually becoming so at least as far as their social life is concerned."

—Vincent van Gogh

By 1886, Impressionism had spent its force and the original band of pioneers was rent by personal and esthetic dissension. While Seurat and Cézanne were trying to preserve what was valuable in Impressionism and put it in a new formal framework, another group of artists had turned their backs on nature almost entirely. Three young artists emerged who took their inspiration from discoveries in the realm of the imagination and from a world of pure color and design. By 1890 the novel, diversified painting styles of Gauguin, van Gogh, and Lautrec and, indeed, their attitudes toward life had produced a whole new mood in painting. Their personal lives were as eccentric and unhappy as their forms seemed strange. With these artists the strains of the long skirmish between the creative personality and conventional society began to show through the fabric of the creations. A new tension and excitement entered art, accompanied, however, by the loss of a certain naturalness and of a general sense of well-being. It would be tempting to conclude that the great paintings of the Post-Impressionist period are narrower in appeal than comparable painting of the preceding period, but it would be more accurate to say that no valid comparison is possible. The works of Gauguin, van Gogh, and Lautrec are authentic on their own terms and presume an external world that was rapidly changing, a world which imposed different conditions on the artist and required a new set of strategies of him.

The founders of the Impressionist movement had been without exception men of rude health, vigorous in body, sound in mind, sober in habit. And there was a corresponding simplicity, serenity, and sanity in their paintings despite the bitterest of economic struggles. With Gauguin, van Gogh, and Lautrec the tradition of rugged vigor and physical resistance to hardship finally broke down. The artist became vulnerable to the tensions produced by his estrangement from society. He was compelled to adopt exaggerated and self-destructive attitudes in his role of rebellion. Some sympathetic current connecting the artist to society had dried up; modern industrial civilization had begun to vitiate natural instinct and public hostility to new and vital art forms had finally become intolerable. Fine paintings have been produced in alternately hostile and sympathetic atmospheres, but few artists have managed to live happy and creditable lives in the face of intense public contempt for their works. Too wide a gap between the public's values and the artist's may undermine the artist's personal life.

So it was with the three painting-martyrs of the Post-Impressionist period. Gauguin was driven to exotic and primitive sources for his inspiration and into virtual exile. (Renoir, speaking for another generation, could never fathom *why*, since he was convinced an artist might "paint as well in the Batignolles" as in Tahiti.) With van Gogh new elements in the personality of the artist-rebel appeared even more dramatically: spiritual torment and an evangelizing passion. For him painting was also a form of salvation and a confession. To a blasé modern spirit like Lautrec for whom the simple home truths of Impressionism, the faith in man and nature, were no longer inspiring, the more violent stimulation of music hall life and the fleshpots of Montmartre was an emotional necessity. To his great credit as an artist he left a record not of his own exacerbated sensations nor merely a documentation of a sinister world of pleasure and vices. He managed instead to show the human comedy in general and to make a narrow segment of life stand for people acting in gross character anywhere and everywhere.

Lautrec died of a stroke brought on by alcoholic excess at the age of thirty-seven, the same age at which van Gogh took his own life. And Gauguin died at fifty-five of disease and neglect, not long after an unsuccessful suicide attempt, in voluntary exile on a remote Pacific island. One might say they all attracted suffering almost wilfully; but Renoir and Monet and Pissarro suffered physical and mental hardship and lived at peace with themselves—and painted with a superb disregard for their troubles. They had set up an independent exhibiting organization in revolt against official institutions, but by comparison with the Post-Impressionists', their revolution was tentative. They still intermittently sought public approval at the Salons. The Post-Impressionists could no longer live by such illusions and ignored contemporary authority almost completely.

Their tragedy was that they happened along at the wrong moment in time. The Impressionists belonged to a healthy social organism; they could still find a common ground in society as well as among themselves. The Post-Impressionists lived in a different moral atmosphere. They could not put their trust in common life, and they formed no real community among themselves. They were too early to enjoy the protections of a self-perpetuating international Bohemia, a twentieth-century development which made artistic isolation more tolerable. The pure pursuit of form and color was not a sufficient *raison d'être* for the artist, and he was still compelled to make his peace with society at some level, to find an external reality with which he might identify. The careers of Gauguin, van Gogh, and Lautrec represent a heroic effort to find their places in a world which did the minimum to make the progressive artist welcome.

Their extreme lives also represent the first symptoms of a period of cultural crisis that persists to this day. That continuing crisis has produced a fine flow of brilliant and original paintings even while it has taken a tragic toll in the wretched lives society imposed on their creators.

Paul Gauguin had begun to paint as a gifted amateur in 1873 while pursuing a very successful business career with a Paris brokerage firm. His interest in painting was stimulated by the Impressionists, whom he met soon afterward through his friend and first teacher Pissarro, and he became a modest but discriminating collector of their paintings. One of the canvases he was most attached to was a still life by Cézanne which he kept with him always and even introduced into the background of one of his own works, *Portrait of Mlle Marie Henry*. In 1876, Gauguin had a little landscape accepted by the Salon, and he felt encouraged to give more and more attention to painting until finally in 1883, at the age of thirty-five, he resigned his position on the stock market to devote himself exclusively to art. He took his Danish wife and their children to Rouen, where life was cheaper, but the experiment proved a failure. When he went to Copenhagen to stay with his wife's family and tried his hand at business once again, the results were even more disastrous. He antagonized his wife's relatives by his arrogance, and his efforts to sell tarpaulins to the Danes for a French firm were as unsuccessful as his efforts to find a new market for his paintings. Gauguin left his wife behind and returned to Paris with the understanding that the family would be reunited when better days came along, but the separation became permanent.

In Brittany in 1886, Gauguin for the first time showed his original style after his apprenticeship in a soft, formless Impressionist manner. He was attracted to this remote corner of France by the primitiveness of the life, the savage desolation of the landscape—and because living promised to be cheap. At Pont-Aven, in a little inn frequented by other impecunious artists whose company and talents the morose and egocentric Parisian scorned, Gauguin began to paint with strong expressive outlines and in the bright patterned colors that were to become so characteristic of his later works. The word "Synthetism" soon figured in his conversations and descriptions of his work.

It defined a less imitative approach to nature, a technique of reducing forms to their essential outlines and arranging them with a new simplicity in brightly colored, flat patterns.

By 1888, Gauguin had completely abandoned the amorphous shapes and graduated color of Impressionism for a crisp and more arbitrary definition based on his new theories. He and a young friend, Emile Bernard, who had joined him in Brittany, declared their intention was to "paint like children." Indeed, Gauguin's work of the period has all the quality of "naïve" art or that of children: bright, gay colors, dramatic patterns, an apparent disregard for proportion or natural coloration, and the substitution of lively "ideograms" for natural appearances. Despite their apparently crude simplicity, however, there was a good deal of intellectual sophistication behind these paintings.

On the one hand, Gauguin wished to find a fundamental, simple style of painting, and of living. He felt acutely the desiccation of instinct that has plagued so many overcivilized moderns, and he welcomed the unsophisticated, primitive culture of the pious, superstitious Breton peasants. But he also sought a new expression for the more intangible and mysterious aspects of esthetic experience. His paintings are allied in both theory and practice with the contemporary literary movement of Symbolism; they are suffused with the subtle imaginative shadings and even something of the romantic escapism that characterize the most refined literary creations of the period. Yet for the Symbolists, the new outlook represented a radical liberation. Remy de Gourmont later defined Symbolism thus: "individualism in literature, liberty of art, abandonment of existing forms, a tending toward what is new, strange, and even bizarre; it may also mean idealism, disdain of the social anecdote, anti-naturalism, a tendency to take only the characteristic detail out of life, to pay attention only to the act by which a man distinguishes himself from another man, and to desire only to realize results, essentials. . . ." With the poet Mallarmé, a contemporary and a friend, Gauguin would no doubt have agreed that the artist must proceed obliquely: "To name an object is to do away with three quarters of the enjoyment . . . to suggest it, to evoke it—that is what charms the imagination." Of the Impressionists' direct address to life the painter spoke scornfully: "They look for what is near the eye, and not at the mysterious centers of thought. . . . They are the official painters of tomorrow."

The curious conflict in Gauguin between a genuine primitive style and sophistication, between the urge to get back to fundamentals and a certain romantic enervation, reflects a typically *fin de siècle* mood. In Brittany and Oceania he found and re-created authentic worlds which funneled off his fantasies into reality. For weaker personalities, however, Symbolism, fantasy, and a private dream-world closed in and became an open invitation for literary reveries in a gilded style. The pale religious mysticism of the Rose-Croix group, the hothouse refinements of Gustave Moreau's visions, and Puvis de Chavannes's Pre-Raphaelite Arcadia were symptomatic of the hermetic styles that characterized the dying century. In the ferment of the era bold new affirmations and romanticism's last refinements competed for attention.

One of the most interesting manifestations of the conflict between romanticism and a new, vigorous simplicity was the emergence of *Art Nouveau*. *Art Nouveau* was a style, or perhaps a fashion, of decoration in architecture, furniture, and objects that swept Europe for a decade from the early nineties to 1906. It originated in Belgium, first in the architectural decoration of Victor Horta in 1893 and shortly thereafter in the buildings of Henry van de Velde, who became its chief spokesman and theorist. We now tend to think of *Art Nouveau* as a fanciful and capricious style of decoration, a frivolous bit of *fin de siècle* romanticism that had little to do with the evolution of modern art forms. It is associated with the esoteric convolutions of Aubrey Beardsley drawings, the attenuations of Tiffany glass, the curlicued iron grilles of Guimard's Paris métro sheds.

It may or may not come as a surprise to learn that *Art Nouveau's* stylistic vocabulary was derived from the flat arabesques of Cézanne and Seurat; from the free curves and serpentines of van Gogh, Lautrec, and Gauguin and their decorative derivatives in the North European painting of Munch, Toorop, and Hodler. In France this form of decoration was called the "new" style; in Germany, the "youth style," or *Jungendstil*. The first suggests something new in the sense of novelty and artificiality; the last, something vigorous and just beginning. *Art Nouveau* contained both elements, the artificial and the robust beginnings of an art that hinted at a whole new simplicity and functionalism. It anticipated the invention of utilitarian modern forms in architecture as much as it reflected the last exotic flowering of the romantic decadence.

Gauguin was never directly associated with *Art Nouveau*, but along with Seurat, Cézanne, van Gogh, and Lautrec he was exhibited in Belgium in the late eighties and early nineties by a group of progressive artists known as *Les Vingt. Art Nouveau's* high priest, Henry van de Velde, who began his career as an artist, had been a guiding spirit of *Les Vingt;* thus he had known Post-Impressionist painting and was deeply impressed by its frankness, its new forms and robust expression. His linear esthetic was based on the same natural forms which Gauguin employed. As Gauguin's art developed, he had emphasized flowing arabesques, flat serpentines, and curving shapes not only for their decorative effects but also because they suggested a flowering, organic nature. Gauguin's search for harmony in the bosom of primitive society and primitive nature is expressed metaphorically in these forms. The same nostalgia for a pre-industrial age of innocence and for a more harmonious relationship to nature curiously enough also inspired the artificial decorations of *Art Nouveau.* Yet as Nikolaus Pevsner, the architectural historian, has pointed out, the organic forms of *Art Nouveau,* and indeed of Gauguin's paintings, are reminiscent of stalks of lilies, of insect feelers, of slender flames; they express "an ideal, not of strength and health, but of delicacy and sensitiveness." The general return to nature had then a touch of escapism and malaise about it.

Despite the fragile rococo look and romantic suggestiveness of his curvilinear forms, Henry van de Velde was acutely aware of the need for and actually intended to create an art and architecture that were adapted to the new social environment of modern industrial life. He declared his distaste for eclecticism and revivalism in architecture and insisted on a new respect for the nature of the materials used. The character of the materials, van de Velde wrote, should not be disguised in an effort to imitate the past. Most important, he expressed a belief in the need to integrate construction, interior architecture, and decoration. In short, he set forth in his architectural writing a completely modern-sounding functional esthetic. Yet, since there was still no sound understanding of the machine age on the level of engineering and construction, *Art Nouveau* degenerated into superficial decoration and a flippant, virtuoso exhibitionism. It became little more than a neo-rococo style of inventive, linear detail. Only under such logical, disciplined architects as Behrens in Germany and Olbrich in Austria some years later was the spurious trickery of *Art Nouveau* cut away and modern architecture set on the high road of rational construction.

Gauguin did not engage in *Art Nouveau*'s decorative frivolities but found robust new forms to suit his artistic needs. Yet neither was he a rational constructor of form in the sense that Cézanne was, and his art clearly reflected in some degree the esoteric romanticism of the period. Far more important than the romantic elements in his art, however, was the fact that Gauguin *did* invent a vigorous new expression, particularly in terms of color, and that he simplified art. He had definite Symbolist predilections, but he was far too vigorous an artistic personality to indulge in any escapist "estheticism," as did Beardsley, the English Pre-Raphaelites, Moreau, Puvis, and many others.

There were serious social aims implicit in Gauguin's style of art and living, as there were in the style of *Art Nouveau*. Gauguin registered his protest against industrial society both in a spirit of romantic nostalgia and, in a perhaps more profound and positive sense, by purely plastic means. He dreamed of reviving a primitive, mystical state of unity between man and nature, the unity that industrial civilization so rudely destroyed. Gauguin also deliberately began to create works that went beyond easel painting, works whose frank mural character gave in vital plastic terms a whole new public significance to art. If the artist could not control his actual environment, Gauguin seemed to imply, he could paint works of art that by their very nature created their own ideal environment. His own approach to an art of a more decorative and public nature became the basis for a whole new esthetic expressed repeatedly by his followers, the so-called Nabis, a Hebrew word meaning "prophets."

In 1888 the painter Sérusier had come back from a summer in Brittany with a cigar box lid on which he demonstrated to Bonnard and Vuillard Gauguin's revolutionary principles of flat colors ringed by strong outlines. And the next year the young painters had a chance to see these theories more dramatically demonstrated when Gauguin and his friends and followers, Emile Bernard, Schuffenecker, Laval, Louis Anquetin, and Daniel de Monfreid showed their paintings and lithographs at the Café Volpini. The group called themselves "peintres synthetistes et symbolistes." Gauguin soon tired of his "movement" and disassociated himself from work whose inferiority he felt was compromising. The loose association of Nabis continued, however, and under the leadership of Sérusier grew and attracted more artistic and literary disciples.

Gauguin and Emile Bernard had been influenced by the decorative conventions of medieval stained glass as well as expressive outlines of the Japanese prints. That esthetic interest also jibed with certain romantic hopes of restoring to the artist the role of craftsman which he had enjoyed in the medieval community. Gauguin never carried these ideas very far, but he did at one time express a belief in the possibility of a new, primitive artistic community. He had planned to take a whole group of artists with him to the tropics to begin a "new" life "free from the bondage of money, beyond the reach of the corrupting influence of civilization." Out of a similar urge to revive the role of craftsmanship in art, he began in Brittany to make woodcuts, the first method of printmaking used in the Middle Ages. Here again is a paradox of the period: Gauguin's life and personality seem the ultimate, anarchic expression of individualism, but he also longed for the solidarity of the medieval artistic community.

That paradox was pointed up by the interpretations of his theories of art as decoration which were put forward by the Nabis. Albert Aurier, a spokesman for the literary Symbolists, the Nabis, and Gauguin, wrote that a work of art should be: ". . . *decorative:* for decorative painting, properly speaking, as the Egyptians and probably the Greeks and the Primitives conceived it, is nothing but a manifestation of art at once subjective, synthetist, symbolist. . . . Painting can only have been created to decorate with thoughts, dreams, and ideas the blank walls of human buildings. The easel picture is nothing but an illogical refinement invented to satisfy the fancy or commercial spirit of decadent civilizations." Verkade, a Dutch painter who joined the Nabis, described the new condition in painting at this time in a declaration that has a distinct twentieth-century ring: "In the early part of 1890 the war cry went up from studio to studio: 'No more easel pictures! Away with useless bits of furniture! Painting must not usurp a freedom which cuts it off from the other arts! The painter's work begins where the architect decides that his work is finished! Give us walls and more walls to decorate! Down with perspective! The wall must be kept as a surface, and must not be pierced by the representation of distant horizons. There are no such things as pictures, there is only decoration!"

In this statement we have an important key to all Post-Impressionist styles and to their sequels in our own century. With the Post-Impressionist period begins the decline of traditional easel painting. By stressing internal pictorial structure, Cézanne and Seurat implied a renewed relationship of painting to architecture. Their emphasis on the impersonal aspects of form challenged the intimacy and informality of Impressionist easel painting. And the art of Gauguin, van Gogh, and even Lautrec has a decided mural character. As Gauguin's style matured, it became more simple and monumental, suggesting the grave, hieratic wall decorations of Egyptian and Byzantine art.

Gauguin consciously modeled his style on non-Western cultures. It was drawn from a variety of traditions: Indian, Indonesian, Egyptian. In Paris he was a regular visitor to the newly created Museum of Ethnography and the Guimet Museum, and he made a thorough canvass of decorative objects, sculptures, and paintings from many unfamiliar cultures, including Negro Africa—which, of course, was to inspire directly the later generation of Picasso. To his friend Monfreid he gave the advice to avoid "the Greek" above all and to have always before him "the Persian, the Cambodians, and a little of the Egyptians." Gauguin's primitivism was the result of a socially conditioned aspiration toward a style of monumental decoration and of the wish to rejuvenate art by going to "savage" sources; it was also a product of the encyclopedic museum, a new phenomenon of the late nineteenth century.

His desire to find a new primitive basis for art and for his own life, and his powerful atavism—he had Peruvian and Incan blood on his mother's side—finally took him to Tahiti in 1891. Led by the poet Paul Verlaine and the theatre impresario Lugné-Poë, Gauguin's friends organized a "symbolic" evening to help raise money for the trip. In Tahiti, Gauguin lived, as he put it, on "ecstasy, quiet, and art" in "amorous harmony with the mysterious beings around me." The splendor of tropical color, the touching simplicity and mysticism of the natives impressed and inspired him. His paintings subsequently acquired more brilliance, power, and complexity, and his command of technique grew even though the fundamentals of his style changed little from the days in Brittany. Gauguin returned to Paris in 1893 and held an exhibition which impressed at least Mallarmé, who expressed his wonder that Gauguin could achieve "so much brilliance" with "so much mystery." The show excited almost as much curiosity as the artist's exotic appearance and his style of life did. He now affected an odd combination of Oceanic and bohemian costume, had outfitted his studio with masks, spears, native furniture, and kept there a Javanese mistress and a monkey.

By 1895 he had had his fill of civilization and returned once again to his Oceanic paradise. There he worked steadily, first in Tahiti and then, feeling the encroachment of French colonialism, on the more primitive island of Hiva-Hoa in the nearby Marquesan archipelago. Unnerved by frictions with the island administration, haunted by mounting debts and deteriorating health, he contemplated suicide. Before making the unsuccessful attempt on his life he worked for one intense month in 1897 on a huge canvas entitled *Where Do We Come From? What Are We? Where Are We Going?* (see plate 21), a work which measures approximately four and a half feet by twelve feet. This painting is another extraordinary and original masterpiece in a period notable for novel and major efforts.

It is a complicated composition divided into three main

figure groupings set in a jungle clearing with the sea in the background. In the center a Polynesian Eve reaches up to pick a fruit from a tree branch; at either side are groups of native women and children, apparently representing the various ages of man. In the background an idol glows with an eerie bluish light and two rosy phantom-like figures glide by. Before them, in the words of the artist, "an enormous crouching figure, out of all proportion, and intentionally so, raises its arm and stares in astonishment at these two who dare think of their destiny." The pervading tonality is blue-green; the bodies of the main figures are a darkish golden yellow. (These tonalities and the mannered archaic poses of the figures seem to have influenced Picasso during his so-called "blue" period.)

Gauguin denied the allegory any explicit meaning, and in a letter to André Fontainas stressed the vague and uncertain nature of his creation, and its abstract, musical quality. "My dream is intangible," he wrote, "it comprises no allegory; as Mallarmé said, 'It is a musical poem, it needs no libretto.'" Be that as it may, the imagery suggests certain general meanings: life and a supernatural "Beyond" confront each other and flow together imperceptibly in a primeval setting. Lascivious, curving forms of jungle growth and the languorous, rhythmic undulation of the sea gently envelop living forms. The painting is a meditation on life played out on a darkening stage. Some of the attitudes of the figures and their disposition against the background of a deep wood also suggest a curious relationship to Botticelli's *Primavera*. Gauguin kept a Botticelli reproduction with him in Tahiti; he was attracted by the Italian master's elegant decorative sense and perhaps too by his romantic melancholy and awareness of death.

In 1903, Gauguin died in his little hut in Hiva-Hoa of heart disease, embittered by his economic struggles and his isolation. With characteristic candor he had written to his friend Monfreid what he imagined his main contribution to painting would be: "I have attempted to establish the right to dare everything: my capacities did not give any big results (monetary difficulties were too great), but anyway the thing is started. The public owes me nothing, since my pictorial work is only relatively good, but the painters who now avail themselves of this freedom do owe me something."

One of the painters of his own generation who definitely "owed" something to Gauguin was the Dutchman Vincent van Gogh. Van Gogh had come to Paris in 1886 to study painting after unsuccessful efforts to make himself into a picture salesman, a pastor, and an evangelist preacher in the Belgian mining country. His many early disappointments included a number of unhappy emotional experiences with women, whom he frightened away by his intense need for love and by his religious fervor. Through the efforts of his younger brother Theo, an art dealer, Vincent was brought to Paris and took up painting seriously; he had already begun to make oils and etchings in Holland. In Paris he met the Impressionists, Degas, Seurat, Lautrec, and shared their excitement in color and in the novel conventions of the Japanese print. He worked with Signac, lightening his dark northern palette in favor of bright, sunny colors and employing paint in the pointillist technique.

In 1888, weary of café esthetics, Vincent left Paris for Arles in the south. He dreamed of a new artistic community "created by groups of men combining together to execute an idea held in common," a dream that was never to be satisfied. Vincent's powerful emotions found release, however, under the brilliant southern sun, in a "kingdom of light," as he ecstatically described the new locale. Like Seurat, Cézanne, and Gauguin he declared his new allegiance to Delacroix rather than to the Impressionists. "Instead of trying to reproduce exactly what I have before my eyes, I use color more arbitrarily," he wrote, "so as to express myself forcibly." Influenced by Gauguin, whom he had come to know in Paris and whose Symbolist aims he found sympathetic, Vincent told his brother that he was "trying now to exaggerate the essential and to leave the obvious vague."

At Vincent's behest Gauguin joined him at Arles in the fall of 1888, and for a brief time they worked together. Gauguin was influential in van Gogh's transition from an Impressionist manner to a more personal expression which utilized flat areas of uniform color and aggressive outlines. The intense temperaments of the two artists soon led to violent quarrels, however. "Our arguments," van Gogh wrote to his confidant and pro-

tector, Theo, "are terribly *electric,* we come out of them sometimes with our heads as exhausted as an electric battery after
it is discharged." In the first of his psychotic episodes, van Gogh
attempted to kill Gauguin, and then he cut off his ear and
delivered it as a Christmas present to a prostitute who had once
playfully asked for it. On petition of the alarmed townspeople,
van Gogh was soon afterward hospitalized in the asylum of
nearby Saint-Remy. His illness is now attributed to epilepsy and
was possibly the result of venereal disease attacking the brain.

During his four years of artistic maturity, from 1886 to his
death by suicide in 1890, he spent periods in mental hospitals,
both at Saint-Remy and at the asylum of Dr. Cachet in Auvers.
But with the exception of a few very late canvases, in which a
chilling darkness falls over his ecstatic palette and rhythms become compulsive, his art shows no direct evidence of morbid
self-preoccupation. There is struggle, conflict, and even extreme nervous excitement but neither oppressive introspection
nor despair. His purity and his realism as an artist won through
and subdued his fantasy. It is interesting that van Gogh, with
all his intense need for salvation and his Christian feeling about
human solidarity, should have rejected as unhealthy the nostalgic religious pictures of his friend Emile Bernard, paintings
which were inspired by medieval Christianity. His sincerity
required that he address himself to subjects of contemporary
life, which in his terms meant the peasant folk of the south of
France and their lyrical natural setting. He elaborated on some
of his themes in his ecstatic, poetic letters to Theo, but the
actual paintings often appear less bizarre than he made them
out to be in his own mind.

He painted, for example, a café-poolroom scene in Arles;
figures hunched over absinthe-green tables are illuminated by
brilliantly shining light globes against a decor of red and green
walls and a dazzling yellow floor. The floor goes off in rapidly
converging perspective lines. A dramatic mood is further heightened by a certain strangeness in the color scheme and by the
whole burning brilliance of the impression. Yet was the scene
as sinister as the artist later imagined? Would the unprejudiced
eye of a spectator who knew nothing of van Gogh's inner
drama read a moral message of damnation in the work? Van

Gogh wrote Theo that he had portrayed the café as a place of wickedness, "a place where one can run mad, or commit a crime . . . I have tried to express the terrible passions of humanity by means of red and green," but in the actual work there is no such simple didactic content. If there were, the painting would be only an extended monologue on anxiety. On the other hand, van Gogh's emotion is transparently direct and even child-like. He is a "primitive" of the emotions in the sense in which some of the great lyrical poets have been. Like William Blake or Shelley he can with facility convey, in the midst of lyricism, a sudden, frightening, almost uncivilized awareness of the lonely destiny of the individual. Joy and melancholy, exaltation shadowed by grief, rise unbidden from the deeper levels of his personality.

Whatever the real or imagined symbolism of his art, van Gogh found a non-naturalistic and more emotional use for color, as Gauguin was doing at the same time. Like Gauguin he "simplified" in an effort to get back to fundamentals, to deep common truths. "In a picture," he wrote to Theo, "I want to say something comforting as music is comforting. I want to paint men and women with that something of the eternal which the halo used to symbolize, and which we seek to give by the actual radiance and vibration of our coloring . . ." In style van Gogh combines the innocence of children's art with the flat, decorative monumentality and brilliance of color of early Christian mosaics. He, too, was moving away from easel painting toward a broader style of monumental decoration characteristic of the great archaic periods in art.

It is significant that his art was also extremely personal and charged with subjective meanings. Its drama, emotionalism, and "confessional" mood directly inspired the later Expressionist movement. Here again is the paradox of the period. The painting of both van Gogh and Gauguin seeks a relationship to wall decoration, as if the artists were insisting that a wider public significance be attached to painting. Yet they were driven in on themselves and forced to develop highly personal expressions tinged with mysticism. They were men of genius because of the intensity of their feeling and their success in finding a viable form for their feeling. But there is a discrepancy between their expressive means and what they had to say. In the art of Degas, Manet, and the Impressionists we feel the personal pose, the very "style" of the man. In the work of the Post-Impressionists we feel instead an impersonal and archaic style, a style whose pictorial conventions are more important than the individuality of the artist. In another era Gauguin and van Gogh should have made ideal decorators of public places; they would have been able to "decorate with thoughts, dreams, and ideas the blank walls of human buildings" as Albert Aurier had hoped artists might one day do again. However, the times did not favor their ambitions. Van Gogh and Gauguin were forced into lives of violent, anarchic individualism, lives entirely in conflict with the social and spiritual aims of their art.

In a somewhat similar fashion, the art and life of Henri de Toulouse-Lautrec reflects a new rapprochement with popular art forms and illustrative conventions—and hopeless personal eccentricity. It is no accident that he has been identified with the development of the poster and the color lithograph or that he invented a style in the graphic arts which still guides commercial artists. He expressed himself in drastic silhouettes, bold outlines and original color, a form of dramatic presentation that put over its message in a single statement. The simplicity and economy of his expression is deceptive, however. Lautrec was an uncannily sharp observer of life as well as a brilliantly succinct and expressive draftsman. His resourcefulness in the graphic media allowed him to set down his subjects with a stylized flatness and still to characterize them in the psychological round. He had a genius for reducing the whole style of a personality to a few gestures and capturing it with a bold silhouette or a single line. His figures are full of life and character no matter how schematized and abstract his pictorial means may appear. He held in a wonderful tension the spectacle of life and pure pictorial values. Like Gauguin and van Gogh he wished the spectator to experience his painting directly through the dynamic operation of his surfaces and with a minimum of interference from pictorial illusion. The spectator is invited to participate in the experience of form and color to a much greater degree than he is, for example, in the paintings of Manet, Degas, and the Impressionists. The elementary potencies of medium and the artist's operations take on an almost independent, abstract importance. This is particularly true in the case of Lautrec's nervous, mobile line, which continually stresses the active presence of the creator in the work of art.

To arrive at his novel style, a style that was vitally of its period, Lautrec passed first under the influence of Impressionism and then that of Degas and the Japanese print. His painting was also directly connected with the life that he chose for himself in the pleasure-traps of Montmartre and with his physical appearance, which influenced that decision. Lautrec was born a count in a family of provincial aristocrats; his name was Count Henri-Marie-Raymond de Toulouse-Monfa. He was a delicate, rachitic child, and after two falls in early childhood which broke both his legs he never regained normal growth in them. In maturity he was physically grotesque, with a fully developed torso and head and tiny, shrunken legs. His curious appearance cut him off from a normal social life and probably was the factor which led him to choose the demimonde, an underworld of pleasure and vice, as his social and artistic habitat.

Lautrec came to Paris in 1882 to paint and in the next five years attended a number of studios. He had begun to paint and sketch scenes of sporting life at home at the early age of sixteen: horses in motion, tandems being driven along in the Toulouse region at a great clip. Some of these scenes are reminiscent of Constantin Guys's *reportage*, but they have a greater and, for a young boy, remarkable energy. Then he learned to work in a soft Impressionist manner but, unlike Monet and Pissarro, always fixed on the human figure as a center of interest. He later told his biographer and closest friend, Maurice Joyant, "Nothing exists but the figure. Landscape is nothing, and should be nothing but an accessory. Landscape should be used only to make the character of the figure more intelligible." At Cormon's, the last studio in Paris where he worked, he met such independent spirits as van Gogh and Emile Bernard, and he soon began to seek a more original and vital style. In this he was deeply influenced by the Japanese print, which had already played such an important part in supplying new pictorial conventions for the other Post-Impressionists. And he became an admirer and rapt student of the art of Degas, whom he probably met in 1884. So great was his veneration that he is reported to have led a party of fellow-revelers, as a very special treat, on a dawn excursion to Mlle Dihau's apartment so they could share his rapture over the master's paintings. The elder Dihau was a bassoonist whom Degas had painted in the orchestra pit of the Paris Opéra, and the musician's family collected the artist's work.

Degas supplied Lautrec with forms of composition, which he freely adapted in a simpler and more audacious fashion, and with a whole new repertory of unromantic contemporary subjects. Under the spell of the animated nocturnal life of the Montmartre music halls, cabarets, and brothels Lautrec pushed on even beyond Degas's most controversial subject matter. Degas in his collotypes had depicted inmates of brothels but never with the knowledge and first-hand experience which Lautrec brought to the same themes. Lautrec went to live in the bordellos and became a confidant of prostitutes and pimps, partly no doubt because he wished to defy convention and thereby assuage his own feeling of being socially undesirable. But Lautrec also approached human squalor for the most serious artistic reasons. He refused to be intimidated by taboos on subject matter. For the painter, still working in the spirit of nineteenth-century naturalism, human degradation and the more sordid truths of sexual life in the great city were simply one set of facts among others. Since art had not dealt squarely with them, they were still fair game. Lautrec's unprejudiced observation of sexual matters, neither morally aghast nor sensational in any way, reaffirmed the artist's prerogative to set down the truth of life as he found it.

Sometimes Lautrec, who had a natural instinct for the preposterous, could not help twitting his subjects. In the dress or undress of his models, in their boredom, or in their contrasting characters he found much that lent itself to ironic treatment or outright comedy. Yet his approach was as serious and detached, rather than professionally disenchanted, and as intensely honest as was Degas's attitude towards his little ballet "rats."

While he investigated low life, Lautrec in the early nineties was also developing an expressive style which in song sheet illustrations, posters, and lithographs managed to find public favor. Something of a natural showman, he had a feeling for good visual "copy," as the success of his posters of La Goulue dancing and of various vignettes of cabaret life attested. At the same time he had begun to penetrate the shadier regions of the Paris underworld and to present its subject matter with an uncompromising candor that utterly alienated the public. He was finally as unable to satisfy conventional taste and morality in his own time as were van Gogh and Gauguin.

In his oil paintings Lautrec learned to enrich his surfaces and marry line and color as he mastered technique. Near the end of his career he produced works (they were few, as in the case of Seurat) of remarkable magnitude and power. Perhaps his greatest technical innovations were made in the color lithograph and poster; between 1892 and his death in 1901 he produced some three hundred lithographs and thirty posters which were distinguished by their boldness of attack, freedom of invention, and expressive color. But his precious handful of large paintings were his major effort; they stand with the greatest masterpieces of the modern period.

Among them is the painting, now in the Art Institute of Chicago, *At the Moulin Rouge* (see plate 20). A group of ladies and gentlemen gather around a table; in the right foreground a woman, theatrically illuminated by a greenish light full on her face, is cut off by the picture edge. In the background a figure we recognize as the dancer La Goulue adjusts her hair while nearby pass an incongruous pair, the tall, funereal Dr. Tapié de Céleyran and his cousin, Lautrec himself. The composition burns with electric colors of orange and green; structurally it is organized along the diagonal axis of a handrail, Degas-fashion. The gay-nineties costumes, dresses with leg-of-mutton sleeves, elaborate plumage in the ladies' hats, stovepipes for the gentlemen, have been pushed to the glittering edge of fantasy. The atmosphere is unreal and bizarre; the characterization of personality, brilliantly incisive. Lautrec has endowed a rather shabby music hall setting with barbaric splendor. His figures are described by sinuous, curving contours somewhat in the manner of *Art Nouveau* (although he was openly critical of the new style of decoration which he had had occasion to see first hand on trips to Belgium). While Lautrec's figures are fitted into a decorative ensemble of arabesques and curves, they give an impression of mass and bulk. They break out of their molds and live an intense life of their own both as personages and as vigorous plastic forms.

Lautrec's late lithograph series, called *Elles,* was devoted to women, women who serve sullenly in a world dedicated to carnal pleasures but whose forms have a monumental import and dignity. Like Degas, Lautrec made something legendary and immense out of the stereotypes of naturalistic subject matter. He was perhaps the last modern artist who was able to express a vital interest in life and a curiosity about the human animal without compromising his pictorial values. In the process of doing so he introduced dynamic new elements into his art: irony, fantasy, and an interest in forms and colors as expressive ends in themselves. When he died in 1901 of a stroke produced by alcoholic dissipation, the effort to capture modern life in terms of some realistic convention had been exhausted. The twentieth century took its inspiration instead from Gauguin's advice that "art is an abstraction" and from the formal logic of Cézanne's last compositions.

Commentaries to Color Plates: 2 – 23

PLATE 2

The Old Musician

Edouard Manet

Oil, 1862, 73¼" x 98"
National Gallery of Art (Chester Dale Collection), Washington, D. C.

The critic Champfleury, champion of naturalism and of Courbet, had unwittingly anticipated the character of Manet's early painting when he wrote of Courbet in 1860: ". . . the master, with his rehabilitation of *the modern* and the excellent manner in which he recaptures the presentation of the modern, will perhaps facilitate the arrival of a noble and great Velásquez . . ." Until 1865, when he actually visited Spain for the first time, Manet showed every sign of fulfilling that prophecy. *The Old Musician* is in his early "Spanish" style, which he curiously enough abandoned only after his contact with Spanish painting in Spain. Despite the obvious relationship in composition and technique to Velásquez' early painting, *The Topers*, the painting has moved away from the dark tonalities of Manet's earliest Spanish realism. It anticipates the fresh color and the feeling for natural light and atmosphere of *The Luncheon on the Grass* of 1863.

Baudelaire insisted that Manet had seen almost no Spanish painting during this period and that his new style was a "correspondence" to Velásquez' manner, intuitively arrived at out of some inner necessity. The Spaniard's unadorned realism and technical simplicity directly and consciously occupied Manet's thoughts, however, on his own admission, and it seems almost impossible that he had not seen somewhere in Paris or in his early European travels a copy of *The Topers*. The forms of the

two compositions and even the visages of the figures are remarkably similar. The charming little gypsy waif in the broad-
brimmed hat has an expressive face very much like Velásquez'
Bacchus, though he is, of course, much younger; in the Spanish
painting there is a bearded figure similar in pose and feature to
Manet's musician, a blurred, shadowy figure in the upper right
corner doffing a hat, and many other resemblances. The odd
disparity of the ragged assortment of picturesque types also
recalls the earlier painting.

Manet has loosened the whole composition, however, and
reduced the number of figures, allowing more circulation of
light and air. Although the pigment matter is still substantial
and form is vigorously modeled, the colors are much less
somber and the handling is effervescent by comparison with
Velásquez'. Manet's *peinture claire* period is only a step away,
and his color has already begun to scintillate and burn more
vividly in an out-of-door light.

PLATE 3

Woman with Chrysanthemums

Edgar Degas

Oil, 1865, 36½" x 29"
Metropolitan Museum of Art, New York

Degas was one of the members of the famous Batignolles group that congregated around Manet, so named because they met at the Café Guerbois in the rue de Batignolles. When Degas first encountered Manet in 1861 he was still a *"peintre d'histoire,"* turning out elaborate historical machines based on antique myth and classical figuration. However, he also independently (in his portraits) turned to a vein of realism that was audaciously "modern."

For the influential critics Edmond de Goncourt and Edmond Duranty it was Degas who soon became the commentator par excellence on contemporary life. Degas developed a new repertory of unheroic subject matter that the preceding academic painters with their taste for an imaginary classicism found merely banal: shop girls, laundresses, music hall denizens, ballet dancers, professional entertainers. For his subjects he drew on the world he actually knew. With exquisite perceptions—sometimes tender, often cruelly frank—he characterized his models in terms of their surroundings, always as part of some scene that expressed the substance of their lives.

As early as 1859, Degas had recorded his interest in doing "portraits of people in familiar and typical attitudes, above all in giving to their faces the same choice of expression as one gives to their bodies." His coherent treatment of his models, even to the sharply observed details of costume accessories, is apparent in this vivid characterization.

Woman with Chrysanthemums is a superb example of the controlled tensions of Degas's art. Not the least of the many enchantments of this remarkable work is the triumphant balance between the model's self-absorbed concentration and the gorgeousness of the flower piece. The color in the bouquet is restrained and yet sumptuous enough to provide a lyrical release from the subject's intense mood. Now that we are accustomed to the unexpected angles of the candid camera, Degas's composition, placing the human subject at the far edge of the picture, does not seem so remarkable. In his day, however, it was a bold innovation and attracted a good deal of unfavorable comment. By cutting off his figures with the picture frame, by introducing odd and unexpected angles of vision, Degas restored to painting the actual flavor of real life.

PLATE 6

Terrace at the Seaside near Le Havre

Claude Monet

Oil, 1866, 23½" x 31½"
Collection Rev. T. Pitcairn, Bry-Athyn, Pa.

A native of Le Havre, Claude Monet came under the influence of his fellow-townsman and painter, Eugène Boudin, at the age of seventeen. After his return from military service in 1862, Monet rejoined Boudin and Jongkind to paint on the beaches of Le Havre. These artists were the first to make nature their studio and to dedicate themselves to the business of recording her variety of moods under changing light conditions. In this way they were ahead of the painters of the Barbizon School, who had also begun to paint nature on the spot but invariably finished their canvases in the studio, where muzzy romantic sentiment was allowed to intrude upon direct observation.

Boudin was an Impressionist in spirit but not in method, still using bright local color against a foil of gray—just as Manet had done—for his most effective harmonies. He set the stage for the new generation, taught them, through Monet, to observe nature directly and to open themselves to new impressions. But he himself never carried his researches in luminosity to their logical conclusion. While his oils and watercolors had already achieved a new lightness and transparency at this time, he was far from the radical innovations that the young rebels from Gleyre's studio were soon to introduce under the leadership of Claude Monet.

The first brilliant promise of Impressionism is seen in the vivid *Terrace at the Seaside near Le Havre*. Monet's palette, which heretofore was limited to leaden hues and earth tones, relieved by spots of color, suddenly comes to life. The crimson accents of the flowers are so intense and so prodigally distributed that even in the backdrop of the sea Monet has been forced to abandon the genteel neutral tones he learned from Boudin and introduce fresh, vivid color, simply to maintain a consistent effect. His bold temperament has pushed him into fresh discoveries.

The painting is a transitional one, however, merely suggesting the artist's later fluency. The figures detach themselves stiffly from the background, caught in a bald and glaring light. Local color is respected, and the handling of light is relatively conventional. There is a dazzle of sunlight *on* objects which intensifies their colors but throws shaded areas into sharp relief, even though there is a pale, purplish cast of reflected light in some of the shadows. As Monet's researches later developed, all his forms, light and dark, became so impregnated with direct or reflected light that they seemed to give back a soft radiance of their own. With his discoveries in luminosity and color Monet finally arrived at a method of composing not by incident but exclusively in terms of a continuous color rhythm.

PLATE 7

Basin at Argenteuil

Claude Monet

Oil, 1872, 18⅞" x 28¾"
Rhode Island School of Design, Providence

In the Seine Estuary, at Le Havre, Honfleur, and neighboring towns, Impressionism appropriately received its first impulse, in an environment of sea and brilliant light. Reflections of light on water, in fact, became a *leitmotif* of the new group; the rainbow palette could almost be said to be a result of the observation that light broke down into the prismatic colors in contact with the many-faceted surface of a body of water. Ranking in importance with Monet's activity in the Le Havre region were his frequent painting excursions to the bathing and boating resorts along the Seine near Paris, La Grenouillère, Chatou, and particularly Argenteuil, where he lived after 1872. A turning point in the evolution of the new style was his visit to La Grenouillère with Renoir in 1869. Working together from the same motifs, they found in the mercurial play of sunlight on water direct inspiration for the broken color and division of tones that became the basis of their technique.

It was at Argenteuil, however, that the new vision came to mature expression. In 1874—the year of the first Impressionist exhibition at the photographer Nadar's former studio—Monet was living there and painting nature with a greater luminosity than ever. He was joined by Manet and Renoir. And it was there that Manet painted his first truly Impressionist work, *Boating at Argenteuil,* now in the museum of Tornai, Belgium, as well as a number of charming records of Monet himself working from his studio-boat. Renoir painted many of Monet's favorite Argenteuil motifs in his own distinct manner, with a special lightness of touch. Together, with Monet in the lead, these artists formulated in their work the attitudes of Impressionism. Nature was no longer to be interpreted as picturesque; it was to be rendered rather in terms of an objective optical sensation.

In *Basin at Argenteuil,* Monet's color scheme has become much brighter, and his brush strokes have also changed, forming a vibrating tissue of minute dots and small colored streaks which seem to re-create the very texture of light. Our eye composes the scene and picks out the salient forms of sailboats and the cottage on the river bank, but only at a distance. Seen close, the surface of the canvas registers as a meaningless mosaic of bright orange patches of color swimming in a bluish haze. Monet's scene conveys a certain voluptuous and personal satisfaction, as if he were quite intoxicated with this little summer idyl. The injection of such personal emotion is more characteristic of Renoir; it is impossible to contemplate his perfumed mists and splendid human beings without the feeling that the artist is charmed and enraptured by what he sees. Monet's work is usually more impersonal and analytical, lacking what, for want of a better word, must be called tenderness. As he addressed himself to the repeated motifs of his last years—the lilies, the poplars, the façade of the cathedral of Rouen, which he painted as series—he became exclusively concerned with pure optical sensation; all elements of personal feeling were subordinated to a lofty abstract esthetic.

PLATE 10

Dance at Bougival

Pierre Auguste Renoir

Oil, 1883, 70⅞″ x 38⅝″
Museum of Fine Arts, Boston

Nothing could be further in mood from Degas's tense little dancer (plate 11) than this opulent couple. We usually mistrust artists who identify themselves too completely with their subject, but Renoir's rapturous scene is utterly disarming. He makes us experience intensely all the charm of this lovely moment, and he also demonstrates a remarkable finesse and tact as an observer. How discreetly and gently the rather burly male holds the young lady, crooking his arm in order to avoid putting too much physical pressure on her! That detail makes her seem all the more precious and all the more like the most exquisite of porcelain dolls.

And how well Renoir captures the intense, single-minded concentration of the male on the object of his affection, felt right down to the tip of his nose and beard. Like an arrow his face compels our attention to the open, sweet, and demure countenance of the lady, and there our gaze rests for a long, pleasurable moment. As delightful as all this little expressive detail is, we are not distracted from the equally lovely play of form and color. The soft, silken pinks and blues in the dress of the pair, which has the look of watered silk, make a subtle harmony of colors; it is capped and strengthened by the more vital contrast of forceful yellows and reds in the hats.

At that, Renoir is not at his sensuous best in this painting, even though his human perceptions are altogether exquisite.

The Dance is drier in tone, and colors have more of a tinted character than the chromatic magnificence of such Impressionist masterpieces as *The Luncheon of the Boating Party*, painted in 1881, or *Le Moulin de la Galette* of 1876. By 1883, Renoir had absorbed a trip to Italy during the course of which he was deeply impressed by classical Italian painting that emphasized linear design and restrained color. He was dissatisfied with the superficiality of Impressionist vision and had just begun to move away from it to seek a more solid pictorial structure. In the mid-eighties Renoir's art became emphatically linear and curiously academic as he tried to discipline his exuberant senses. By the nineties, however, he had passed through his crisis and arrived at a new synthesis in a more monumental but lush style that once again sumptuously projected his delight in the substance and sensuous texture of the things of nature.

PLATE 11

Ballerina and Lady with a Fan

Edgar Degas

Pastel, 1885, 25⅛″ x 19¼″
Philadelphia Museum of Art (John G. Johnson Collection)

Degas is quoted as saying to an Impressionist painter, "You seek inspiration in nature . . . I need the artificial life." For a man of Degas's refinement and civilization, art was supremely a matter of artifice and calculation, and he was sympathetically drawn to those milieus dedicated to the creation of illusion. Since he was also a perfectionist with a scrupulous regard for detail, he welcomed a setting where the subjects could be counted on to re-enact, with repeated variations, their movements and poses. In the theatre, and particularly in the ballet, he found the combination of make-believe and intriguing, repeated patterns of movement required by his artistic needs. They provided a controlled environment already set up for him, an ideal artistic laboratory, as it were. The living gesture of the ballerina gave Degas an excuse for working out an endless series of intricate formal patterns in his compositions. In oil, in pastel, in pencil, and in modeled wax he made countless variations on the theme of the dance. Edmond de Goncourt was amazed when he called on the artist to find Degas gesticulating energetically like a ballet master and demonstrating the movements of the dance steps he knew by heart.

Ballerina and Lady with a Fan is one of the most dramatic and concentrated of these subjects. The violent angle lighting on the ballerina, the unexpected diagonal composition, and the delicate, moving frieze of dancers in the background organize the scene in an indelible impression. As in all of Degas there is considerable human content here, though the artist insisted that his "ballet girls were but the pretext for design." The little ballerina's charm and the brilliant "on-stage" atmosphere do not divert Degas from a merciless objectivity. Like a performing puppet's her facial expression mechanically mirrors the will and pleasure of the audience. Her straining effort to please is in contrast to the majestic passivity of the shadowy figure in the box. Aside from the bold design and colors, the painting is fascinating as a complex psychological document. For we actually are experiencing the scene from two points of view, both sides of the footlights. How different is the Renoir dance opposite (plate 10) where everything in the scene, including a lyrical natural setting, contributes to the single rapture of a moment. Degas's vision requires more mental agility of the observer than Renoir's, for we are put in the position of both the actors and the spectators; we appreciate the tense effort of the little dancer, and we are *still* entranced by the brilliant and immaterial illusion she creates.

Degas often introduced into his compositions persons standing outside of the action, like the lady in the loge, and he distinguished sharply between active and passive participants in his little pictorial dramas. He invited his audience to share the view of the spectators within his paintings, and to be "onlookers" at a spectacle. By such devices the artist played down or entirely suppressed sentiment and emotional reactions, for such reactions might disperse or compromise his esthetic effects. Like Manet, Degas was remarkably unsentimental in his art, but not, as many imagined, because he mistrusted emotion or was inhumane. He had to be unsentimental in order to achieve the purity of expression he sought.

PLATE 14

Still Life: Jar, Cup, and Fruit

Paul Cézanne

Oil, 1877, 23⅞" x 29"
Metropolitan Museum of Art, New York

The radical redirection that Cézanne was to give modern painting is already implicit in the structure of this still life of 1877.
Still life had been a congenial theme for Manet, Renoir, and
Monet, but none of them had ever conceived painting it in such
grave and simple architectural terms as Cézanne has done.
Painting was moving in quite the opposite direction, toward
evanescent effects of light and toward formlessness. Cézanne's
stubborn intellectualism and his insistence on the importance
of the felt weight and structure of objects were definitely out
of tune. His deliberately crude simplifications, even at this
early stage of his career, were prophetic of periodic sea changes
in the evolution of modern art which have persisted right into
our time. Time and again, from Cézanne, van Gogh, and Gauguin to Matisse and Picasso, the progressive modern artist has
refreshed and rejuvenated painting by abandoning past refinements for a more primitive directness.

Cézanne's "primitivism" is curiously combined with refinement, with a subtle articulation of form, classical in its order
and clarity. In *Still Life: Jar, Cup, and Fruit* he stresses certain
basic geometric shapes: the ovals of the fruit and the cup; the
rectangle of the table; the triangle of the cloth. These forms
are related to each other in a compositional scheme that is all
traction and tension. And yet the composition has a serene
poise; we feel in it the measured rhythms and solidity of pic-

torial substance that great classical paintings have. We may understand Cézanne's admiration for the seventeenth-century French artist Poussin, whose ordered and lucid compositions he had studied with such intensity at the Louvre.

In order to emphasize the decorative unity of his painting, Cézanne had begun as early as 1877 to "flatten" his picture space by means of distortion and arbitrary color accents. He stresses flatness here by juggling perspective: by tilting the horizontal plane of the sideboard up, thus thrusting the background closer to the foreground; by widening the curved mouths of the jar and the cup, and by color modulation. We are looking at the apples in the foreground at eye level; but the objects behind them are seen from above. Cézanne has taken the liberty of "abstracting" certain aspects of form and color from nature and making a new synthesis, all to the end of discovering unexpected formal relationships which are beautiful in themselves. He uses color—notably in the apples—in tiny, flat planes to stress the plastic structure of the painting as a whole and to define the position of the fruit in the general scheme. The unification in one frontal plane of different visual points of view and the construction of form by means of color was the direct inspiration of twentieth-century Cubism. Cézanne's great innovations shattered with one blow all painting formulas based on traditional Renaissance perspective.

PLATE 15

The Cardplayers

Paul Cezanne

Oil, 1890, 32⅛" x 22⅝"
Collection Stephen C. Clark, New York

After 1877 Cézanne became the forgotten man of French painting; between that date and the great retrospective of his paintings at the Vollard Gallery in 1895 he exhibited only twice in Paris, single Impressionist works at two Salons. After the exhibition of 1895 it was among the new, emerging generation of Nabis, Maurice Denis, Emile Bernard, Edouard Vuillard, and Pierre Bonnard, that the master of Aix aroused the most enthusiasm. The younger painters saw in his work confirmation of their own efforts to go beyond Impressionism.

The Cardplayers is a superb example of Cézanne's mature style. It may have been inspired by a similar composition by one of the brothers Le Nain, French painters of the seventeenth century. The classical poise and gravity which Cézanne admired in their work have been conscientiously preserved in this monumental study. The models are peasants, and the artist has characterized them with a dignity and strength that shows profound respect and understanding. They give an impression of stern impassivity and durability characteristic of those who traditionally work the land. Cézanne did a number of versions of this subject; two other famous ones are in the Louvre and in the American collection of the late Dr. Albert Barnes.

The interplay of a variety of formal elements is inexhaustible. A cluster of repeated rosy color accents on the peasants' hands form the vital hub of the composition. Such particularized de-

tail at the center is in contrast to the voluminous folds of the
blue cloak of the cardplayer seated right and the broad sweep
of the hanging drapery. One of the most remarkable inventions
is the narrow, cylindrical figure of the standing peasant. With
his slim torso and tiny head he appears a relatively indistinct
form, standing at a great distance from the central figures;
yet we *know* that he is close by. The illusion of his remoteness
is contradicted by the fact that his dark cloak is firmly connected at the base with the shadowed areas of the peasant in
brown. Like the chair, which is tilted diagonally, the standing
figure relieves the compact grouping around the table and
opens up the tight composition.

Cézanne had felt the need to revise traditional perspective
in order to bring the spectator into a more immediate relation
with his sensation. Hence the standing figure pushes into the
front plane of the picture, even as he creates distance. The
background merges into the foreground, and the figures in the
painting are projected *toward* the spectator rather than away
from him. The usual front-to-back movement of traditional
perspective has been reversed. All the forms are related to the
rectangular frame of the painting, as well as to the front plane.
By such formalizations Cézanne virtually remade painting.

At the same time, he was anxious to renew contact with classical art of the past. Therefore he has quite consciously emphasized in his figures the ideal, noble beauty and generalization
we find in the finest Hellenic sculpture. The figures occupy a
kind of arched space that stresses elevation, rather in the manner of niche sculpture on a Gothic cathedral front. The slim,
column-like form of the standing figure and the perpendicular
accents of table legs and pipe stems emphasize elevation and
extension.

PLATE 18

A Sunday Afternoon on the Island of La Grande Jatte

Georges Seurat

Oil, 1884-86, 81¼" x 100¼"
Art Institute of Chicago

That exquisite sense of life which animates the whole beautiful painting episode of Impressionism is here formalized and fixed forever. It is well worth analyzing the attractions of this delightful painting. The first thing that strikes us as remarkable is that despite the excessive orderliness of the confetti-like surface, the picture is vividly alive. The body of water is the most sparkling of blues; the air is tonic; the shadows are of a velvety richness, and pregnant with interesting shapes and activities. It would be difficult to think of a contemporary painting more full of life and atmosphere. And yet life and movement are at a complete standstill. The figures at first glance look like tailors' dummies, and nature seems an entirely artificial creation.

This air of contrivance reflected in part Seurat's patient and exact methods. He wished to leave nothing to chance in the construction of his painting and he carefully planned every step of the composition. Despite his passion for scientific method, however, Seurat was an artist of exquisite sensibility. Even his systematic arrangement of forms and his mannered style are turned into positive emotional elements, designed to enhance a serio-comic mood. The general patterning and the immobile, geometric character of his figures add a note of pomp to the Sunday promenade and give it the formality of a stately ritual. There is something wonderfully mechanical and droll about some of the characters, particularly the foreground couple at the right. Their figures are the expression of propriety and dignity, yet they seem to glide along automatically, pulled by invisible wires. If their solemnity were a trifle more exaggerated, the effect would be quite ludicrous.

Exaggerating, or contrasting with, the more formal figures are such fanciful touches as the monkey, whose curled tail echoes his mistress's bustle; the lyrical relief of the child skipping in the middle distance and of the sails on the river; the relaxed pose of the gentleman leaning on his elbow. Quite properly this man, so natural and in harmony with nature, has behind him a mongrel dog of a relaxed and friendly character. The more formal couple, on the other hand, is accompanied by a monkey and a dainty little beribboned toy dog. Throughout the painting the formal and the natural compete as they had begun to do in all the most significant works of the period. The balance of these two elements is worked out with the most genial good humor. Few artists were as keen observers of life as was Seurat or more sophisticated than he in their observation, yet he managed to see the adult world as if it were an entirely marvelous toyland of mechanical marionettes.

This vision, combined with his remarkable ingenuity, might have led the artist astray along frivolous paths had he not been as remarkable a composer as he was an observer of life. His figures are reduced to colored silhouette but retain their essential humanity and convey, where the artist wished it, a real physical presence. There are few figures in French painting of the period more beautiful or convincing than the man who puffs on a pipe and reclines on an elbow in the left foreground of *La Grande Jatte*. He sums up the glowing good health, sanity, and substance of the middle class whose happiest moments the Impressionists celebrated. The solid virtues of his character are echoed by his massive importance in the composition. His body exerts a downward force through the crook of his elbow, anchoring the rest of the busy incident of the painting to the earth. He is firmly planted, as substantial a piece of pictorial architecture as some weighty *repoussoir* in a classical landscape by Poussin.

PLATE 19

Circus Fernando: The Ringmaster

Henri de Toulouse-Lautrec

1888, Oil, 28¾″ x 63½″
Art Institute of Chicago (Gift of Tiffany and Margaret Blake)

This large painting is one of the earliest in Lautrec's mature
style. It is also one of the gayest and most energetic, even
though there are certain inconsistencies in the handling. The
artist's superb gift for characterization—extremely simplified,
close to the preposterous but not quite caricature—is caught in
the tense figure of the ringmaster and in the smart bareback
rider. The massive horse is a marvel of grace and is a solidly
felt form despite its almost schematic simplicity. Lautrec's feeling for the moment of action and his ability to set it down precisely with a minimum of waste motion are splendidly demonstrated. The ringmaster with his outthrust arm acts as a pivot
for the rest of the composition, driving it along a controlled
arc. That drastic, knife-edge silhouette is in contrast to the
fluffy skirt of the rider and the horse's bushy tail.

With his acute theatrical sense, Lautrec felt related to
figures of temperament and enjoyed showing them performing, whether they were circus characters, music hall prima
donnas, athletes, great surgeons in the operating amphitheater,
or famous trial lawyers. The common link between these varied
subjects was the grace and skill of the actors and the moment
of action that called forth their typical efforts. Like Degas,
Lautrec spotlighted his main protagonists in these little dramas
with a more intense illumination or a flash of color, giving
them a rich pictorial life. In contrast to the more animated

and fully developed figures are set the spectators or those who merely support the action. Hence the puppet-like subsidiary figures of the "onlookers," and the clowns who are cut off by the frame in this painting. This combination of full and merely suggestive treatment concentrates and intensifies the moment of action.

Here Lautrec is also trying to reconcile deep space and surface unity, one of the central plastic problems of modern painting from Manet to Matisse. To bring the action closer to the viewer and to emphasize the pure pictorial values of his work, Lautrec has adopted the conventions of the Japanese print, using the high horizon of the seat tiers to make the space more shallow, creating diagonal movement, and squeezing a host of impressions into expressive and compact, flat shapes. There is some discrepancy between the bulk of the horses and the flatness of treatment given the rest of the forms. Similarly, Lautrec has settled on a draftsman's expedient of using linear hatching to model form but still keep it flat. The effect is postery, and of course anticipates the even more simplified conventions of the posters and lithographs Lautrec produced so prodigally after 1892. In later years, in his paintings, however, Lautrec was able to give a richer physical and psychological presence to his forms through splendidly orchestrated color as well as expressive, "colored-in" shapes, and thus avoid the flat, decorative effect of *Circus Fernando*. This painting is nevertheless very remarkable, and far ahead of its time in its bold simplicity of design, if we compare it to Seurat's or Degas's work of the period.

PLATE 22

Old Women of Arles

Paul Gauguin

Oil, 1888, 28¾" x 36"
Art Institute of Chicago

In 1886, Gauguin went off to paint in the seclusion of the Breton town of Pont-Aven. There he began to formulate the theories and the novel style which became the basis for the Synthetist-Symbolist movement. What he sought was contrary to Impressionist realism; he wanted a radically simplified design and a more forceful statement of line and pure color. And he was no longer interested in representing the truth of natural appearances so much as in inventing a new formal language that would capture the truth of his innermost feelings. As a "Symbolist" painter he sought a plastic formula for his mental images, emotions, and ideas, not the literal facts of visual experience alone.

To clear himself of Impressionist realism Gauguin drastically simplified form and color. (In doing so he was also consciously trying to hark back to a more primitive state of being and to imitate works of earlier traditions, such as that of medieval stained glass.) By the time Gauguin joined Vincent van Gogh briefly in Arles in the fall of 1888, he had established his new style and felt secure in it. *Old Women of Arles* shows these new interests in brilliant, unmodeled color and flat forms starkly silhouetted or outlined. The deliberate crudeness in Gauguin's *Arlesiennes* is in line with his announced intention to "paint like children." This was, again, a reaction to Impressionist refinements.

Out of his figures and picket fence Gauguin has made a dramatically effective flat pattern which is both intensely expressive and effective decoration. His women have somewhat the harshness and force of some of Vincent's images of the craggy-faced, stolid local peasantry, and the sharp relief which the brighter background has given their dark and somber forms suggests some of van Gogh's icon-like portraits. Bright color areas float on the surface like concentrated and more homogeneous pools of dazzling Impressionist light. In fact, even with these abstract shapes (which are ancestors of the amorphous pure-color masses of twentieth-century "free-form" abstraction) Gauguin manages to create space, albeit a very shallow space; his warm colors come forward and cool colors recede. Cézanne complained of Gauguin that he never understood "the planes" and "produced nothing but Chinese pictures." Gauguin was not a rational constructor of form and space as was Cézanne, but within his decorative formula he nevertheless managed, particularly in his early paintings, to transpose relationships of form he had observed in nature.

By a strange twist of history, however, in his own time it was Gauguin rather than Cézanne who was thought to have been the more radical and generative force. The Nabis misunderstood Cézanne, interpreting him not as a supreme, rational architect of space but as a Symbolist painter in the primitive state. Maurice Denis credited him with originating the Symbolist "doctrine of equivalents," the program of translating nature into a language of visual symbols which corresponded to certain subjective emotions experienced in the presence of nature. Denis took as a prophecy and justification of his own methods Cézanne's statement: "I have discovered that the sun is a thing that one cannot reproduce but that one can represent." For Denis and the Nabis-Symbolist generation it was Gauguin who "clarified" and most fully realized Cézanne's symbolizing intention, thus restoring to painting its magical and incantatory powers.

PLATE 23

Public Garden at Arles

Vincent van Gogh

Oil, 1888, 28" x 35"
Collection Jakob Goldschmidt, New York

This charming, intimate, vigorously handled little scene was painted at Arles in October, 1888, not many months after van Gogh had come from Paris. It was done just before Gauguin joined him briefly in the south, and before his first attack of insanity. The highly charged colors reflect van Gogh's sense of release when he came in contact with the powerful sunlight of the Midi.

Van Gogh has to a remarkable degree intensified and simplified his palette. Instead of indulging in the almost infinite range of multi-colored touches the Impressionists favored, and which he himself for a time employed, he has limited himself to a striking polarity of blue and yellow. (In his Provençal landscapes, yellow became the equivalent of sunlight, of pagan joyousness; blue represented an infinity like the night sky.) He has strengthened his expression by troweling paint on the canvas until it stands out in low relief. The surface has a rhythmic life of its own organized by the emphatic, parallel strokes of a loaded palette knife. The energy of the technique and the dramatic foreshortening recall the artist's description of one of his drawings: "The lines of the roofs and gutters shoot away in the distance like arrows from a bow; they are drawn without hesitation."

How charming are the two tiny figures strolling beneath the shade of the magnificent pine, and how novel the particular view the artist has selected. It seems clear that Vincent is still under the spell of the Impressionists' holiday mood, even though his painting methods have changed. Yet what a singular version of their mood this is. Everything in nature is activated; his pigment is volcanically energetic; the focus is on neither the sunny weather nor the plain folk enjoying their promenade, but rather on the great spreading canopy of the pine branches. The pine is really a symbol for the artist, a giant of the earth blotting out the sky, anticipating his later obsession with cypresses.

There is also something a little sinister about the rapidly diminishing perspective of the band of the road. In the middle distance walk the couple, forlornly small, shot away, as it were, from the body of humanity. These unstable forms—too big or too small, caught up in the rush of van Gogh's pigment—reflect the artist's inner pattern of conflict. All of van Gogh's art poignantly projects his sense of being trapped and his wild, elated rush for union with some symbol of love or human solidarity, which may be real people like the peasant folk of Arles or symbols of God's bounty in nature.

Van Gogh is a sublime artist not for his mysticism and torment alone, but because he was also a painter who could come to grips with physical nature. His most transcendent effects would fail to move us were they not anchored in solid observation. The mystical aspiration of some of his last works go far beyond sensory data and the visual. Imagery takes on preternatural meanings, and the phenomena of nature are charged with cosmic drama. Had he not first learned to master the things of nature in tangible, painterly terms, however, he would have failed to convey his exalted mood.

Plate 1. Edouard Manet (1832-1883)
SPRINGTIME
Pen and wash drawing, 1881
Fogg Museum, Harvard University

Plate 2. Edouard Manet (1832-1883)
THE OLD MUSICIAN
Oil, 1862, 73¼" x 98"
National Gallery of Art (Chester Dale Collection), Washington, D. C.

Plate 3. Edgar Degas (1834-1917)
WOMAN WITH CHRYSANTHEMUMS
Oil, 1865, 36½″ x 29″
Metropolitan Museum of Art, New York

Plate 4. Gustave Courbet (1819-1877) THE STONE BREAKERS
Oil, 1850   Formerly Kunstmuseum, Dresden

**Plate 5. Edouard Manet (1832-1883)
THE LUNCHEON ON THE GRASS**
*Oil, 1863
Louvre, Paris*

Plate 6. Claude Monet (1840-1926)   TERRACE AT THE SEASIDE NEAR LE HAVRE

Oil, 1866, 23½" x 31½"   *Collection Rev. T. Pitcairn, Bry-Athyn, Pa.*

Plate 7. Claude Monet (1840-1926)   BASIN AT ARGENTEUIL

Oil, 1872, 18⅞ x 28¾"   *Rhode Island School of Design, Providence*

Plate 8. Constantin Guys (1802-1892)
TWO LADIES IN A CARRIAGE
Wash drawing, about 1860
Metropolitan Museum of Art, New York

Plate 9. Edouard Manet (1832-1883)
A BAR AT THE FOLIES-BERGÈRE
Oil, 1881
Courtauld Institute of Art, London

Plate 10. Pierre Auguste Renoir (1841-1919)   DANCE AT BOUGIVAL
Oil, 1883, 70⅞" x 38⅝"
Museum of Fine Arts, Boston

Plate 11. Edgar Degas (1834-1917) BALLERINA AND LADY WITH A FAN
Pastel, 1885, 25⅛″ x 19¼″
Philadelphia Museum of Art (John G. Johnson Collection)

Plate 12. Edgar Degas (1834-1917)
WOMAN BATHING
Pastel, 1885
Metropolitan Museum of Art
(H. O. Havemeyer Collection), New York

Plate 13. Pierre Auguste Renoir (1841-1919)
BATHERS
Red chalk, about 1885
Fogg Museum
(Maurice Wertheim Collection), Harvard University

Plate 14. Paul Cézanne (1839-1906)
STILL LIFE: JAR, CUP, AND FRUIT
Oil, 1877, 23⅞" x 29"
Metropolitan Museum of Art, New York

Plate 15: Paul Cézanne (1839-1906)
THE CARDPLAYERS
Oil, 1890, 32⅛" x 22⅝"
Collection Stephen C. Clark, New York

Plate 16. Odilon Redon (1840-1916)
THE GNOME
Charcoal drawing, 1880
Art Institute of Chicago (David Adler Collection)

Plate 17. Georges Seurat (1859-1891)
PORTRAIT OF AMAN-JEAN
Conté crayon, 1882
Collection Stephen C. Clark, New York

Plate 18. Georges Seurat (1859-1891)   A SUNDAY AFTERNOON ON THE ISLAND OF LA GRANDE JATTE
Oil, 1884-86, 81¼" x 100¼"   *Art Institute of Chicago*

Plate 19. Henri de Toulouse-Lautrec (1864-1901)   CIRCUS FERNANDO: THE RINGMASTER
1888, Oil, 28¾" x 63½"   *Art Institute of Chicago (Gift of Tiffany and Margaret Blake)*

Plate 20. Henri de Toulouse-Lautrec (1864-1901)
AT THE MOULIN ROUGE
Oil, 1892   *Art Institute of Chicago*

Plate 21. Paul Gauguin (1848-1903)
WHERE DO WE COME FROM? WHAT ARE WE? WHERE ARE WE GOING?
Oil, 1897   Museum of Fine Arts, Boston

Plate 22. Paul Gauguin (1848-1903)
OLD WOMEN OF ARLES
Oil, 1888, 28¾" x 36"
Art Institute of Chicago

Plate 23. Vincent van Gogh (1853-1890)
PUBLIC GARDEN AT ARLES
Oil, 1888, 28" x 35"
Collection Jakob Goldschmidt, New York

Plate 24. Paul Cézanne (1839-1906)
WOMEN BATHERS
Oil, 1898-1906
Philadelphia Museum of Art (Wilstach Collection)

Plate 25. Pablo Picasso (1881-
LES DEMOISELLES D'AVIGNON
Oil, 1907
Museum of Modern Art (Lillie P. Bliss Bequest), New York

Plate 26. André Derain (1880-1954)   BLACKFRIARS BRIDGE, LONDON
Oil, 1906, 26" x 39"
Museum of Modern Art, New York

Plate 27. Henri Rousseau (1844-1910)   THE DREAM
Oil, 1910, 80" x 118½"
Museum of Modern Art (Gift of Nelson A. Rockefeller), New York

Plate 28. Henri Matisse (1869-1954)
JOY OF LIFE
Oil, 1906
The Barnes Foundation, Merion, Pennsylvania

Plate 29. Henri Matisse (1869-1954)
THE RED STUDIO
Oil, 1911
Museum of Modern Art
(Mrs. Simon Guggenheim Fund), New York

Plate 30. Henri Matisse (1869-1954) WOMAN WITH THE HAT *Oil, 1905*
32" x 23½" *Collection Mr. and Mrs. Walter A. Haas, San Francisco*

Plate 31. Georges Braque (1882-   ) MAN WITH A GUITAR   *Oil, 1911*
45¼" x 31⅞"   Museum of Modern Art (Lillie P. Bliss Bequest), New York

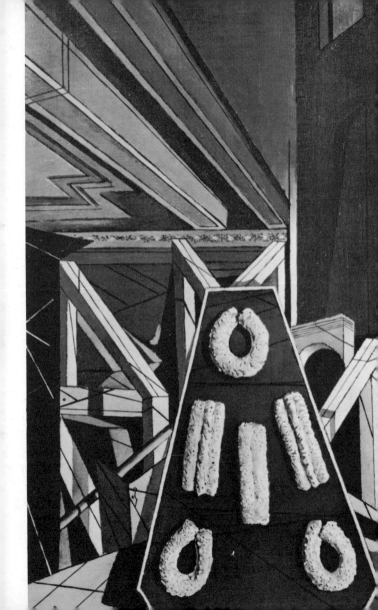

Plate 33. Kurt Schwitters (1887-1948)
M2 430
Crayon and pasted paper, 1922
Courtesy Sidney Janis Gallery, New York

Plate 32. Giorgio de Chirico (1888-   )
THE REGRET
Oil, 1916
Collection Munson-Williams-Proctor Institute, Utica, New York

Plate 34. Fernand Léger (1881-1955)
THE CITY
Oil, 1919, 91″ x 117½″
Philadelphia Museum of Art (A. E. Gallatin Collection)

Plate 35. Joan Miró (1893-   )
PERSON THROWING A STONE AT A BIRD
Oil, 1926, 29" x 36¼"
Museum of Modern Art, New York

Plate 36. Pablo Picasso (1881-   )   TWO PEASANTS
Pencil drawing, 1919
Santa Barbara Museum of Art, Santa Barbara, California

Plate 37. Henri Matisse (1869-1954)   STUDY FOR THE WHITE PLUMES
Pencil drawing, 1919
Collection Henry P. McIlhenny, Philadelphia

Plate 38. Amedeo Modigliani (1884-1920)   WOMAN WITH A NECKLACE
Oil, 1917, 35¾″ x 23½″
(Mr. and Mrs. Charles H. Worcester Collection) Art Institute of Chicago

Plate 39. Henri Matisse (1869-1954)   ODALISQUE WITH RAISED ARMS
Oil, 1923, 25½" x 19¾"
National Gallery of Art (Chester Dale Collection), Washington, D. C.

Plate 40. Marc Chagall (1887-   )
BIRTHDAY
Oil, 1915-1923
Solomon R. Guggenheim Museum, New York

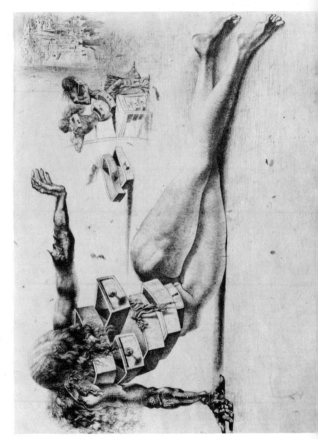

Plate 41. Salvador Dali (1904-   )   CITY OF DRAWERS
Pen and ink drawing, 1936   Collection Edward James, London

Plate 42. Chaim Soutine (1894-1943)
SEATED CHOIR BOY
Oil, 1930, 25¼" x 14¼"
Private collection, Paris

Plate 43. Georges Rouault (1871-   )
THE OLD KING
Oil 1936, 30¼" x 21¼"
Carnegie Institute, Pittsburgh

Plate 44. Pablo Picasso (1881-)   MINOTAUROMACHY
Etching, 1936   Museum of Modern Art, New York

Plate 45. Pablo Picasso (1881-   )
GUERNICA
Oil, 1937
Owned by the artist. Courtesy Museum of Modern Art, New York

Plate 46. Pablo Picasso (1881-   )   NIGHT FISHING AT ANTIBES
Oil, 1939, 86" x 136"
Museum of Modern Art (Mrs. Simon Guggenheim Fund), New York

Plate 47. Georges Mathieu (1921-   )   HOMAGE TO RICHARD I, DUKE OF NORMANDY
Oil, 1954, 38" x 64"
Collection Richard B. Baker, New York

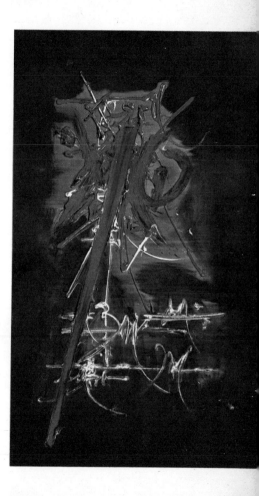

Plate 48. Jean Dubuffet (1901-   )
EYES CLOSED
Oil, 1954
Courtesy Pierre Matisse Gallery, New York

Commentaries to Color Plates: 26 – 47

PLATE 26

Blackfriars Bridge, London

André Derain

Oil, 1906, 26" x 39"
Museum of Modern Art, New York

André Derain had met Matisse in the studio of Eugène Carrière and later introduced Matisse to Vlaminck at a van Gogh exhibition in 1901. In 1905, Derain joined Matisse, Vlaminck, Marquet, and others in the first Fauve exhibition; by the second year of activity as a Fauve, he had, like many of his associates, added a more compact and solid design to the exuberance of his colors. *Blackfriars Bridge, London* is organized by the architectural structure of the bridge, by vertical and horizontal accents of the buildings in the background. The intensity of the color and the particular dissonant color chords of chrome yellow and orange set against deep blue recall the vehement chromatics of van Gogh, who was particularly admired by both Vlaminck and Derain at this time.

Unlike Vlaminck, with whom he was perhaps most closely associated in his early years as a painter, Derain exercised his intelligence to restrain spontaneous emotions. "If you rely on the sheer force of the color as it leaves the tube," he once remarked, "you won't get anywhere. That's a theory for a dyer." Yet he understood perfectly the necessity for the Fauve liberties and explained them with precision. Referring to his Fauve "ordeal by fire," he wrote in retrospect: "It was the era of photography. This may have influenced us, and played a part in our reaction against anything resembling a snapshot of life. No matter how far we moved away from things, in order to observe them and transpose them at our leisure, it was never far enough. Colors became charges of dynamite. They were expected to discharge light. It was a fine idea, in its freshness, that everything could be raised above the real. It was serious, too. With our flat tones, we even preserved a concern for mass, giving, for example, to a spot of sand a heaviness it did not possess, in order to bring out the fluidity of the water, the lightness of the sky."

With the advent of Cubism, Derain's palette darkened, his color schemes became simpler, and he painted in a rather austere "classical" style with considerable distinction and charm. Then around 1919, in the postwar reaction that affected both Picasso and Matisse, he developed a naturalistic manner in a series of solid nudes, harlequins, and landscapes. He was never a great inventor nor a very profound investigator of either color or form. After 1930, Derain was satisfied with pictorial stereotypes, and his facility led him to turn out fashionable potboilers, in portraits, landscapes, and still life. Yet, after Matisse, he was perhaps the most complete, intelligent and satisfying of the Fauves.

PLATE 27

The Dream

Henri Rousseau

Oil, 1910, 80″ x 118½″
Museum of Modern Art (Gift of Nelson A. Rockefeller), New York

Henri Rousseau was a Paris customs official with a taste for
music and painting. He retired from government service in
1885 to live on a modest pension and devote himself entirely
to painting. From 1886 he exhibited regularly at the *Salon des
Indépendants,* much to the astonishment of most critics, who
found his untutored, "naïve" painting utterly ludicrous. The
more discerning partisans of advanced art, such as Gustave
Coquiot and the painter Redon, however, as early as 1888
praised his "noble classical style." And the simple, modest
"Sunday painter" himself was refreshingly convinced of his
own genius. At a later date he told Picasso, "We are the two
greatest painters of our epoch, you in the Egyptian style, I
in the modern style."

Rousseau's fantasy and the atmosphere of dream in his paintings anticipate the work of the Surrealists. Unlike them he
needed neither artificial mental stimulation nor a program to
provoke his remarkable visions. In his own life he apparently
drew no hard and fast line between the real and the supernatural, and the invisible world was as concrete and actual to
him as the visible. He was convinced of the reality of ghosts
and complained often about his own private specter who
followed him about and annoyed him. When some friends
rigged up a ghost and put it before him, the credulous Rousseau
took the apparition quite seriously and politely inquired if it

would care for some wine.

The touching simplicity of Rousseau's character and his complete innocence of art school technique, however, did not prevent him from being an impressive and serious artist. His color sense is distinguished; his forms, elegant and authoritative; his sentiment, lofty. More than anything else, he possessed some profound and pure contact with the primitive, mytho-poetic levels of his own personality. The imagery that wells up in his art comes from the deeper regions of the psyche and is completely convincing.

The Dream was the last painting Rousseau did. He described it thus: "This woman asleep on the couch dreams that she has been transported into the forest, listening to the sounds of the enchanters' instruments." The luxurious tropical scene was perhaps an imaginatively heightened memory of the Mexican jungles he had seen during his participation in Maximilian's campaign, in his youth. There is subtle drama, not without Freudian overtone, in the play back and forth between the gorgeous flora and fauna of this mysterious jungle-Eden, the chaste nude figure, and the vague menace of the moonstruck lions, elephant, and pink serpent. In his youth Rousseau had had an amorous escapade with a Polish woman whom he thenceforth privately referred to by the name of Yadwigha, the same name he gave to the nude in this painting.

PLATE 30

Woman with the Hat

Henri Matisse

Oil, 1905, 32" x 23½"
Collection Mr. and Mrs. Walter A. Haas, San Francisco

For many years after its purchase in 1905 out of the historic Autumn Salon, this painting hung in the apartment of Leo and Gertrude Stein in the rue de Fleurus, Paris. Accounts of the purchase have differed; both Leo and Gertrude claimed credit while Matisse has indicated that Leo and his sister-in-law, Sarah Stein, were the original enthusiasts. In his version of the acquisition Leo Stein also described his first shock at seeing this radically different work: "It was . . . a thing brilliant and powerful, but the nastiest smear of paint I have ever seen."

Such strongly expressed doubts on the part of Matisse's first significant collector were mild by comparison with the opinions of the Paris art press; the painting, in fact, became something of a *cause célèbre,* crystallizing all the antipathy and bewilderment the public felt at the first dramatic exhibition of Fauve painting. For Matisse, the painting represented his first great liberation from modes of the past, from the Neo-Impressionism of Signac and from the preceding inspiration of Manet's "dark Impressionism." Out of this critical work, with its vital handling, freedom and chromatic magnificence, flowed one great line of subsequent twentieth-century painting: free-color abstraction, as later practiced by Kandinsky, Delaunay and others. In *Woman with the Hat* for the first time in the new century the operative elements of painting became the real theme of the work of art: the brush strokes, the rhythmic dis-

position of color accents over the surface, the materiality of
pigment matter—or as Maurice Denis later declared, "the act
of pure painting." Matisse's methods were, however, only an
extension of an evolving process of abstraction that had begun in the art of Manet, and which is perhaps the common denominator of all modern art.

At the same time, Matisse was conscious of his relation to
French tradition; he felt he was renewing a current of art, in
expressing form by color, which stemmed from Cézanne. He
had merely found new methods and insights based on contemporary values with which to extend the aims of Post-Impressionist painting. Actually, such effects as the shocking green
nose shadow and vermilion eyebrows of Matisse's subject and
the use of pure, unmixed tube color, were related to Impressionist practices of seeking the most intense luminosities. Matisse could exercise such strategies with more energy and
boldness (which eventually changed their whole qualitative
character) because he felt able to express life and his own
sensations more directly and more simply than his predeces-
sors had. That sense of emancipation accorded with a new
spirit of hopefulness, experimentation and a growing sentiment
of freedom which characterized the intellectual climate of
the early years of the century. Today his riotous color schemes
and sketchiness no longer shock, but fit securely into the general scheme of French hedonist tradition. It is a measure of
Matisse's mastery of expressive color that after half a century
this early work should still seem compelling and retain its freshness and impact.

PLATE 31

Man with a Guitar

Georges Braque

Oil, 1911, 45¼″ x 31⅞″
Museum of Modern Art (Lillie P. Bliss Bequest), New York

Braque was an original member of the Fauve group, though his Fauvism was perhaps less predatory and more tender than that of Matisse, Derain, or Vlaminck. Then under the influence of Picasso his art began to change, and he helped to originate the style of Cubism. Braque has explained how he came to abandon exuberant Fauve color for the sober discipline of Cubism: "It was impossible to make any further progress with the method adopted at that time. All those who have accomplished anything since, have, to a greater or lesser degree according to their temperament, sought resistances. After Marseilles, what you need is the Congo. . . . You can't remain forever in a state of paroxysm." Braque has also declared himself in favor of "the rule that corrects emotion" and stated that progress in art "does not consist in extending its limits, but in knowing them better."

During his "analytical" Cubist phase, Braque often painted pictures that could easily be confused with Picasso's work of the same period. But on close examination certain fundamental differences emerge. Picasso's paintings of 1910-1911 are in some ways less harmonious, if more intensely felt. He seems to pile up his planes more erratically, the rhythm and coherence of his surfaces are subject to eruptions of formal incident and sudden concentrations of expressive effects. We feel a more powerful, but more artificial, temperament loose in his early

Cubist paintings, a need to discharge emotion even if it means breaking the texture and unity of the work of art. Braque's articulation of form is smoother, the general impression more serene and—there is no other word for it—more beautiful. His "handwriting" is less personal than Picasso's, but he reveals himself an accomplished master of the formal vocabulary of Cubism.

We can discern here, in among the shifting and overlapping planes, the schematized eyes, chin, the fingers, an elbow and a knee of the guitar player; the scrolled neck of the instrument becomes a repeated motif, as does the round aperture of the sound box. Braque has reduced his theme to an abstract arrangement of intersecting lines and planes; all the little elements and small articulations harmoniously and rhythmically swell into one grand, massive effect, a solid but transparent structure of form. By little adjustments of line and direction he tips and then rights the figure, keeping the painting free from monotony and a deadening immobility. In a language of almost pure abstraction, Braque has tackled the problem that so profoundly concerned French painters from Manet to Cézanne: the expression of a three-dimensional physical reality within the limits of a flat surface. He keeps his space fluid and shallow by juggling planes. By welding an accumulation of small accents into a solid, emblematic ensemble—for the structure is still a legible symbol of a guitar player—he avoids the pitfall of mere decoration.

The painting is a great tour de force of intelligence and sensibility. Little planes float and dance on the surface and yet tenaciously grip each other, creating a feeling of resistances and mass. The repeated vertical lines in narrow parallels give a liberating sense of extension. Paint is applied in emphatic touches not only in order to vary texture and enliven the surface, but to give resonance and materiality to the floating, immaterial forms. The mind is stimulated and refreshed by Braque's improvisations and witty variations on his guitarist theme; one feels the esthetic purity of his inspiration, and in the blocky, adumbrated figure there is a solemn majesty. This painting strikingly illustrates the artist's statement: "Nobility grows out of contained emotion."

PLATE 34

The City

Fernand Leger

Oil, 1919, 91" x 117½"
Philadelphia Museum of Art (A. E. Gallatin Collection)

When Picasso and Braque moved away from the "analytical" phase of Cubism and restored color to painting, it was a signal for the other painters of their generation to follow suit. In 1912, Delaunay began to exhibit paintings in a lyrical style of pure color abstraction, compositions with circular motifs and based on spectrum hues, a style which Guillaume Apollinaire promptly dubbed "Orphism." And Léger began to intensify and simplify his color after a period of working under Cubist chromatic restraints. In 1913, Léger had already shown a distinction of color, limited to tints, however, in his Cubist-inspired diagrams. By 1919 he had developed a robust and brilliant color expression whose limited range of primaries anticipates the simplicity of his mature style. As a footnote to Léger's history, it might be added that around 1917 in Holland, Mondrian, van Doesburg, and van der Leck had joined forces in a new purist, architectural style of painting, called *de Stijl*, which utilized only the primary colors.

Léger studied as an architect before settling on a career of painting and worked with and became a lifelong friend of Le Corbusier; his predilection for the clean, efficient forms of modern architecture and engineering are apparent in *The City*, perhaps his first major canvas and one of his most ambitious. In addition, his taste for machine forms was also an important factor (he has said that the sight of a gleaming cannon barrel during the First World War revolutionized his conceptions of painting). This is clear not only in the robot-like figures ascending the stairway in the middle of the composition, but also in the resemblance of almost every decorative area to a variety of machinery parts: tubing, shafts, flywheel, casings, etc. If one can adduce movement or direction to forms in painting, in Léger's they suggest the up-and-down pumping or rotary motions of some smoothly functioning industrial machinery. Léger has animated this abstract arrangement by the rhythmic play of colored shape against shape, and by his subtle, vertical space divisions.

Léger is one of the powerful composers among modern painters and one of the most balanced colorists. Color functions plastically, creating traction and tension, and its strong impact is commensurate with the powerful thrust of the blunt, impersonal forms. *The City* catches Léger emerging from Cubism into a style of breadth and easy articulation which would, in his words, "liberate color in space." He passed through many phases in subsequent years, arriving at a simple monumental style and an even happier balance of form and color; but few of his later paintings are more exciting chromatically than *The City*.

PLATE 35

Person Throwing a Stone at a Bird

Joan Miró

Oil, 1926, 29" x 36¼"
Museum of Modern Art, New York

Miró may have found the original inspiration for much of his
fantasy and expressive color in the romanesque fresco decoration and manuscript illumination of his native Catalonia. In
Paris, where he settled after 1920, he made contact with advanced art modes and learned to give his native tendencies a
modern inflection. Drawing on Cubism, on Surrealism and on
abstract art, he evolved a distinctly individual style which
brilliantly mixes wit and a poetic-symbolic content with powerful plastic form. His contribution to modernism, which is far
from being complete, must be accounted one of the most
original and significant, ranking him with the great artists of
the twentieth century. Curiously enough, during the past decade
Miró's combination of "automatism" and abstract painting
procedures have made him an even more vital influence among
younger artists abroad, and particularly in this country, than
some of the more imposing reputations in Paris.

In his first ventures, Miró painted in a style of crisp, ornate
realism which he schematized somewhat according to Cubist
principles, although with a more decorative effect. A crucial
painting of this period, *The Farm*, 1921-1922, is an accumulation of metallically precise descriptive detail, densely packed
laterally and vertically over a flat surface; its stylized convention and a static piling up of "little" descriptive elements suggest an art both naïve and extremely sophisticated. In the next

two years, perhaps in contact with Dada or proto-Surrealist art, Miró's style changed radically. Realism was replaced by abstraction, and instead of "describing" objects literally, he began to "signify" them through a repertory of abstract shapes and a personal, cursive calligraphy.

Around 1926, Miró's art changed again as he reduced and simplified the number and complexity of his forms for purposes of dramatic emphasis. *Person Throwing a Stone* shows a new movement towards monumentality and is also a wonderful demonstration of the artist's continuing wit and ingenuity as a composer. The painting was executed just after Miró had discovered the slack silhouettes and "biomorphic" forms of Arp, and when he was perhaps aware, too, of the simplified compositional schemes and colors of Mondrian. The painting was also of a period with Picasso's first fantastic anatomies which reduced the human figure to a series of curvilinear, amorphous shapes. Like Picasso, whom he always admired and often adapted to his own more whimsical purposes, Miró creates plastic incident that has curious psychological overtones.

Persons in dreams or under the influence of drugs have often experienced a sense of infinite extension and attenuation. One way to express this disturbing state of mind is as Miró has done, by creating a figure who drags a monumentally large foot and whose head is disproportionately small and remote from this lower appendage. To show such a figure only in profile, as a white silhouette, further compresses symbolic content and removes the situation from rules of logic, one of the central aims of Surrealism. An ambiguous, indeterminate space also supports the evocation of a hypnotic mood. In this strange, floating dream-world the artist draws us up from our drugged inattention with a sharp accent of red on the bird, with the white flash of a stone in flight. Movement and activity are suggested by the dotted trajectory line and the solid black line that is its fulcrum. In this way a sedative landscape reveals unexpected expressions of life and energy.

PLATE 38

Woman with a Necklace

Amedeo Modigliani

Oil, 1917, 35¾″ x 23½″
Art Institute of Chicago
(Mr. and Mrs. Charles H. Worcester Collection)

In a period notable for its originals, Modigliani was one of the most extravagantly individualistic members of Paris's Bohemia. He came to France from Italy in 1906 and very soon acquired a formidable reputation for his flamboyant artistic dress, raffish and disorderly living, and wildness. He was always in dire economic straits, poaching on friends when he was too poor to pay for lodging or board. Towards the end of his life he began almost methodically to destroy his already delicate health by excessive drinking and drugs; he finally died of tuberculosis at the age of thirty-six. When in the course of his funeral—attended by Picasso, Max Jacob, and many of the artistic greats of Montmartre and Montparnasse—his mistress Jeanne Hebuterne committed suicide, his passing was given the stark horror of a Greek tragedy. In a penetrating and elegantly written catalogue for the Museum of Modern Art's Modigliani retrospective of 1951, James Thrall Soby suggests that the artist's fever of self-destructiveness was "integral" to his talent. "It is idle to argue," Mr. Soby writes, "that he might have been a more profound artist had he nursed his energies. Exacerbated nerves were part of his talent's high price."

Modigliani was a traditionalist rather than an innovator, and he perhaps owes more to Post-Impressionism and to his Italian heritage than to contemporary idioms. Cézanne, Fauvism,

Negro sculpture and Cubism touched him, but he utilized these influences not for any very profound investigation of form and color but rather as expedients. He formulated a mannered style whose emphasis on aristocratic line and elongated, columnar forms summons up the refinements of Italian Mannerist painting. Modigliani's sensuality, particularly as exemplified in his splendid nudes, is characteristically Italian in its candor about the female form.

Woman with a Necklace has the linear graces and elegant stylization of a Botticelli. The image of young womanhood has been sublimated into something dreamlike; yet there is a flush in her cheek and an impression of brooding sensuality about her. She does not quite belong to the genre of the ugly or the *femme fatale* of so much twentieth-century portraiture, nor is she idealized, as the exaggeration of her coiffure attests. The figure is posed rather like a Cézanne model and given extreme frontality, but she is more languid and relaxed than his stiffly formalized figures. The shallow space, the emphatic division of the wall, and the blue-green color chords also suggest the influence of the master of Aix.

PLATE 39

Odalisque with Raised Arms

Henri Matisse

Oil, 1923, 25½″ x 19¾″
National Gallery of Art (Chester Dale Collection), Washington, D.C.

After 1917, when he began to winter at Nice, Matisse's painting became more "realistic" and anecdotal, perhaps in obedience to the general postwar reaction that found artists all over
Europe returning to a more conventional and "humanist" vision
of things. Early in the twenties Matisse began to paint the
odalisque themes that were to be a major part of his artistic
production during the next decade. *Odalisque with Raised Arms*
was one of the first, and it is a particularly ingratiating one with
its vivid but lightened colors and thinnish medium. Few of the
painter's tones are fresher than the rosy flesh color of the
nude, which makes a controlled, vibrant harmony with the
cool green striping of the chair and the pale gray-green wall
hanging. The cool colors are admirably balanced against the
warm orange-brown floor tone and the red-flowered print in
the background. Matisse builds up a variety of different run-
ning patterns, a discreet and subtle profusion of stripes and
flower figures, but rests the eye in the blank, rectangular intervals of the ochre wall. In a smiliar fashion small, busy detail is
balanced off against wide stripes, little repeated curves against
broad, sweeping curves. The effect is of a controlled scintillation of color and light within a masterful, coherent design.

The small sienna and burnt orange touches which give definition to the various parts of the lady's face and anatomy are
witty reminders that his model is female; yet these accents

call attention to themselves as mere elements in the design and echo the small notes in the wall hangings. The internal modeling in the figure gives it a shallow relief, but any illusion of depth is discouraged and counteracted by the bold vertical striping of the chair cover, which absorbs and flattens the body. In the same way the raised arms are distorted to emphasize a flat, rectangular frame for the rounded, vaguely shadowed head; this slightly awkward shape is echoed and reinforced by the flat, rectangular wall hangings, again suppressing any effect of depth.

PLATE 42

Seated Choir Boy

Chaim Soutine

Oil, 1930, 25¼" x 14¼"
Private collection, Paris

Born in a little Russian village near Minsk, Soutine was one of
eleven children in a wretchedly poor Jewish family. Childhood
poverty, emotional insecurity, persecution under the Tzar, and
then escape into freedom formed the pattern of his sentimental
education. He came to Paris in 1913 and entered a new and
more congenial atmosphere, where his racial background no
longer ostracized him and his talents guaranteed status. Soutine
was one of the many artists from Eastern Europe who uprooted
themselves and took up a new life in the cosmopolitan art
capital, contributing heavily to the culture of their time. The
rapidity of his liberation from social and emotional repression,
however, left its scars on this moody and embittered young
idealist. No artist willingly chooses poverty, squalor, and disorder, but Soutine seemed almost constitutionally predisposed
to live unhappily and even exulted in his wretched life. He
suffered painfully from stomach ulcers and frequent nervous
indisposition, and his life oscillated wildly between emotional
crises.

If Soutine suffered something beyond the normal from the
pangs of genius, he also knew how to transcend suffering in
art. Like the great Catholic mystics of the seventeenth century
and like El Greco, he discovered that pain need not be merely
a neurotic exercise; pain and sensuality could meet on a high
plane of spiritual gratification. He was a genuine *exalté*, but

very much in terms of the material world. His sensuality was that of a pure painter in love not with ethereal quantities but with physical reality. It is significant that his two greatest artistic admirations were Courbet and Rembrandt, the Rembrandt who painted weighty sides of beef in brilliant, jewelled color.

Soutine's intensity of emotion and melodramatic distortions mark him as an Expressionist. Unlike the German Expressionists active in his period, he explored no dark psychological depths and avoided sentimental or didactic content. His violence is Expressionistic, but the idiom is closest to the language of van Gogh and Rouault, an anguished expression modified by traditional French hedonism and respect for *la belle matière*. Rouault's sumptuous chromatics may have influenced Soutine directly. A phrase a critic coined for Rouault's rich compost of color would suit Soutine very well: "rotten with color." For the younger artist also pushed his chromatic expression to the point of surfeit.

Seated Choir Boy is one of a series of paintings of figures in sacerdotal garments, of page boys and of other studies in costume whose richness appealed to Soutine's lapidary eye. In great streaks of fat, shining pigment the artist has set down an impression of remarkable freshness and vividness, in a single, dramatic statement. The free, elliptical shorthand and the compactness of the statement give the painting its modern character, even though the artist's idiom is more traditional than most in his own time. Also modern is the emphatic vitality and almost independent esthetic function of the pigment, apart from any representational aims. The pure, disinterested paint matter has such a vivid life of its own that it threatens the very existence of the subject matter.

PLATE 43

The Old King

Georges Rouault

Oil, 1936, 30¼" x 21¼"
Carnegie Institute, Pittsburgh

For Rouault, 1903 was a year of spiritual crisis. He recovered
from a serious illness to find the paintings he had made under
the tutelage of Gustave Moreau empty and hollow. That year
his long friendship with the Catholic novelist Léon Bloy began,
and out of their meeting came Rouault's conversion to Catholi-
cism (he had been educated in Protestant schools as a boy) and
a fundamental change in his art. From the writing of Bloy and
perhaps that of another devout Catholic author, Ernest Hello,
the artist derived a new faith in the spiritual efficacy of art and
a tragic sense of human life. Hello had written: "Art must be
one of the forces that will cure the imagination; it must say
that evil is ugly . . . Religion and art live in the same atmosphere, both colored by the same far reflections, both dishonored
by the same turpitudes." In 1903 and 1904, Rouault began to
paint his remarkably powerful studies of prostitutes, cruelly
exposing the degradation of their lives.

Technically, Rouault was influenced first by the savage caricature of Goya, Forain, and Daumier, then by the new freedom
of expression that Matisse and the Fauves brought to art. In
1905 he joined the Fauves in their first joint exhibition, but
his murky blue washes and "overwriting" with an expressive
network of black lines were far removed from their blithe,
if vehement, hedonism. Rouault's somber mood and religious
preoccupations isolated him from the main currents of the art

of his time. He once declared: "I do not feel as though I belong to this modern life . . . my real life is back in the age of the cathedrals."

In 1907, Rouault launched another striking series, of judges in single portraits and group compositions. With these wolfish guardians of the law Rouault satirically noted the miscarriage of justice in human affairs. Soon afterward, he was attracted to one of his central and most moving themes, the clown; in magnificent color and with emotional force, he managed to express through the Pierrot his powerful feelings of man's tragic destiny. Color became enriched and his line more fuliginous and opaque until his canvases glowed with the brilliance of stained glass.

The Old King was probably begun in 1916, put aside during Rouault's print-making period, and completed in 1936. It is a more sumptuous and tranquil image than the early judges and prostitutes, but it still has an angular, unwelcoming quality, what James Johnson Sweeney has called a "Celtic unfriendliness." It represents a new language of pictorial invective, because the image suggests the subject's avarice and meanness of spirit, but the artist's savagery has softened somewhat in the direction of lyricism with his advancing age. *The Old King* vies with Soutine's creations for coloristic splendor, and the strangely disturbing and penetrating characterization bears the stamp of Rouault's very individual genius at its best.

PLATE 46

Night Fishing at Antibes

Pablo Picasso

Oil, 1939, 86" x 136"
Museum of Modern Art (Mrs. Simon Guggenheim Fund), New York

In *Masters of Modern Art* Alfred Barr describes this painting as "the largest and possibly the most important canvas painted by Picasso during the decade following the *Guernica* mural of 1937." Here Cubism has been resurrected not merely as a plastic discipline but to create a confusion and loss of identity. The figures and the world are turned inside out and upside down. The two fishermen at the center of the stage, one crouched anxiously over the water, the other with his head raised and the tines of his spear touching a rhomboid-shaped fish, are a series of superimposed anatomical cross-sections. At the right are two girls standing on cobblestones, one with a bicycle and ice cream cone. At the left a brown, faun-like figure is seen reflected in the water—or standing on its head. A yellow moon hangs in the sky, looking like a gay paper lantern; a lantern casts its reflections in the water, illuminating a rather angry, upside-down fish. In the background is a forbidding, angular pile of violet triangular forms that may be a rocky shore with rooftops.

The constant metamorphosis of forms gives the impression that in this topsy-turvy pictorial world figures, sky and water may be reversed and change places at any moment. The landscape treatment suggests the Byzantine and early Renaissance convention of the *paysage moralisé*, the shrunken moral landscape of faceted rocks through which saints and sinners gin-

gerly walked, as on a bed of cut glass, in their search for
heavenly consolation. The labyrinthine confusion of the locale
and the facility with which human figures assume the shape
of monstrous grotesques also suggests the more modern religious
fables of Franz Kafka. Picasso's extreme macabre humor has
definite Kafkan overtones of desperate gaiety; it makes a
mockery of normal vision, and fumbles man's identity. There
is no overt "religious" content in this humor or in the atavistic
and grotesque deformations of the human form. The violence
of our era has, metaphorically, split the human image asunder;
Picasso faithfully registers this fact, shows no signs of patching
up the damage, at least in his lifetime, and makes this situation
an occasion for a Dionysiac revel in this handsome nocturne.

Perhaps Picasso uses color indifferently here, and his Cubist
stylization is by now something of a stereotype. With all its
air of contrivance, however, the painting is full of formal invention, energy, and a quixotic humor that stimulates and awakens
the imagination. Even familiarity does not dull the edge of Picasso's wit or quite tame his monsters. We can recognize just
enough of ourselves in them to be uncomfortably fascinated.

PLATE 47

Homage to Richard I, Duke of Normandy

Georges Mathieu

Oil, 1954, 38" x 64"
Collection Richard B. Baker, New York

The royal blue in this painting by one of the livelier contemporary talents in Paris is not only an expressive esthetic quantity but part of a deliberate aristocratic pose assumed by the artist. Not the least of Mathieu's fascinations has been his identification with heroic moments of France's medieval past and his painstaking research in heraldry, all to the end of fashioning some sort of personal myth. Many of his recent paintings have been called "homages" to a variety of noble family names excavated from the bloodier days of the historic past; other titles have been taken from critical battles in French history.

In preparing to paint an immense canvas of 1954, *The Battle of Bouvines,* Mathieu and two friends—one of them a descendant of Toulouse-Lautrec's family—put on feudal aristocratic garb and prepared for imaginary battle, a grave magic rite designed to put the artist in the proper frame of mind for painting his work. Aside from the dubious publicity value of this fancy-dress party, it indicates the artist's genuine interest in heady moments of historical conflict and serves as a rich metaphor for his conception of the painting surface as a battlefield where dramatic pictorial incident explodes into action. It also suggests Baudelaire's cult of the dandy, a member of an artistic elite whose intense preoccupation with his own passions puts him above the morality of the common herd. The French critic M. Tapié de Céleyran whimsically declares that,

"Mathieu regards everything as totally absurd and shows this continually in his behavior, which is characterized by the most sovereign of dandyism."

If life and human behavior are "absurd"—a word popularized recently in the eloquent writing of the French novelist-philosopher Albert Camus—then almost any action or human decisions leading to action, anything that breaks the moral stranglehold of cynical and incapacitating apathy, could be considered valuable. To act at all becomes a triumphant expression of the human will, a solemn affirmation that choice and hence the human will still reign supreme in man's affairs. In the French postwar atmosphere of disenchantment and pessimism—after the humiliating experience of the German occupation and the moral ravages of war—French thought has been dominated by this somber scheme of values.

This mood of desperate and heroic scepticism, which challenges all human values, perhaps, but is also concerned with fundamental questions of freedom, has also affected French artists. For the sculptor Giacometti, expression through art is an onerous, painful act, and he has written that the distance between the nose and the chin of one of his sculptures opens up for him like a yawning "Sahara." For Mathieu, working in a charged and dramatic language of abstraction, painting starts with nothing and from nothing and tries to arrive at significant expression. The mere fact of a pictorial event, the exercise of pure nervous sensibility, the most rudimentary signs and ciphers placed on the canvas—all these can perhaps be taken as triumphant expressions of the modern European will-to-survive. Mathieu's paintings paraphrase the "Existential" human situation in France; they also suggest rather similar absolute aims in contemporary American paintings. By comparison with those of the so-called American Abstract Expressionists, however, Mathieu's effects are self-conscious and modish. He seems to have seized upon, and refined, the superficial aspects of a pictorial method whose radical implications he cannot wholly accept.

Part II:

Transformations
1886—1956

"We are experiencing in our epoch a fundamental transformation of art. It is not a change of sentiment but a new structure which is being born, therefore the aim is quite different. We have a new conception of both the form and the inner meaning. . . . People are more accustomed to life than to art; hence, the success of those works which give an appearance of life. The presentation of a work which rises above this appearance demands a very considerable change of habit. . . . I am talking of an art which is not descriptive. . . . The logic of a work of art is its structure. The moment the ensemble holds together and is balanced, it is logical. . . . Now what is this work about? About itself; everything in it has been done for the sake of the work itself."

—Pierre Reverdy, *Self-Defense* (1919)

Line Drawing: Henri Matisse. Head of Recumbent Figure. c. 1906-07 *Transfer Lithograph. 11⅛ x 10¾. Collection, The Museum of Modern Art, N. Y., Gift of Mrs. John D. Rockefeller, Jr.*

7

Fin de Siecle

"All these figures seem to be in an ideal pose of somnambulism; absorbed in a dream, they are unconscious of their movements and seem transported to another sphere."

—Gustave Moreau on Michelangelo

The history of nineteenth-century painting, as we have seen, was punctuated by crucial masterpieces, those major efforts which both summed up their epoch and set a new direction in painting. From Géricault's *Raft of the Medusa* flowed the great current of romanticism, given a new and freer interpretation by Delacroix in his *Massacre at Chios* and in his later *Liberty at the Barricades*. These in turn became seminal works for many of the Post-Impressionists both as provocative gestures of independence and for suggesting new ways to use color. Courbet's *Burial at Ornans* was a forthright declaration of naturalism; Manet's *The Luncheon on the Grass* demonstrated on a grand scale the operation of a revolutionary "modern" sensibility and introduced bold new technical innovations. Manet's hegemony was then disputed by the great Impressionist paintings of Monet, Pissarro, and Renoir. Seurat's *La Grande Jatte* became a center of controversy and it represented an effort to preserve, even while it was an almost unconscious denial of, the visual naturalism of the Impressionists.

Among the other Post-Impressionists it becomes more diffi-

cult to pick out single masterpieces as fountainheads for subsequent new artistic impulses. Gauguin's paintings in his Brittany period directly affected the Synthetist-Symbolist and Nabis
group that formed around him despite his disavowal of common aims. His huge canvas painted in the last years on Hiva-
Hoa, *Where Do We Come From? What Are We? Where Are
We Going?* was one of his most ambitious efforts and sums up
his style; in itself, however, it has only a speculative value as
a point of reference for certain aspects of twentieth-century
painting. Van Gogh's and Lautrec's whole work bore directly
on the painting that followed, and these artists created transcendent individual masterpieces, but it is an onerous task to
single out any one as the inspiration of a movement or school.
Cézanne's methods and example were more important than
any individual work, although his late *Bathers* (see plate 24)
was an important direct source for both Matisse and Picasso.

From the end of the nineteenth century to the present, isolating the crucial masterwork becomes a treacherous business.
Painting seems to move more quickly, the personalities are
more diversified, and the leisurely evolution of a style and its
crystallization in a single great painting are less common. The
sequence of painting, as it might be plotted on a graph, no
longer seems to develop in a clear, straight line with obvious
nodal points. Instead, painting advances on a series of fronts
at once and takes enormously variegated and unexpected forms.
The rapidity and variety of developments, the fragmentary
character of artistic productions (by comparison with the nineteenth-century past), have led to the characterization of the
twentieth-century period as "experimental." An apparently in-
nocuous word, it has unfortunately been exploited by philis-
tines and bigoted critics of modern art as a term of derogation.
It allows them to withhold recognition of merit or substance by
reserving judgment indefinitely, in the cold war that is waged
by a few bleak calvinistic spirits on any vital, exploratory manifestations of creative life. It recalls the dismal vigil of Manet's
critics, who patiently waited for him to cease his nonsense of
turning out "unfinished" paintings. These critics were full of
righteous approval when he finally exhibited the relatively conventional *Le Bon Bock* and were the more deeply offended when

he reverted immediately afterward to a bolder-than-ever Impressionism.

For social reasons art in the twentieth century presents a more restless, mobile surface. The rapidity of social change and the diffusion and extension of culture have accelerated the tempo of artistic change. Movements and counter-movements proliferate and decay, creating new formal expressions at an exciting rate. A single personality like Picasso, though his remarkable multiplicity of styles *is* unique, could only have happened in our century. He contains within himself the germ of many movements. Yet in all the multiple activity in painting there are, as there were in the earlier periods, a few main threads of pictorial logic discernible despite the many variations and mutations of styles. In the immediate historical background loom the figures of Paul Cézanne, Gauguin, and van Gogh. The injection of personal emotion and the liberation of form and color by Gauguin and van Gogh had their influence on groups as diverse as the Fauves, the German Expressionists, and the more inspirational abstract painters. Cézanne's formal researches were the direct inspiration of Cubism and of much twentieth-century abstract art of a geometric rather than "free-form" character. In addition, many new influences from remote and marginal cultures began to operate in the new century. Artists seemed to be open to all sorts of esthetic hints from the past and more ready to assimilate them.

The tempo of assimilation has been speeded up for one reason because the contemporary world has made communication across time and space more simple. Picasso could "discover" Negro sculpture because of the new encyclopedic museum just as Gauguin had found sympathetic primitive forms in it even before he went to Tahiti. The process of Westernizing alien cultures had begun with the rage of the Japanese print as early as the late 1850s. A new curiosity about all esthetic objects was abroad, and there was a growing sense of the family of art forms. In the modern world a piece of Negro sculpture, a Cycladic terracotta, a Fayum fresco, all seem to telegraph their esthetic message more quickly. The liberation of the artist from traditional subject matter, the slow extinction of the academic tradition have made him more susceptible to pure style in every manner of esthetic object.

Pablo Picasso more than any other single personality has by his stylistic virtuosity and prolific invention helped put the stamp of "universal culture" on our epoch. He above all determined, in Gauguin's phrase, to "dare everything" and in the process of doing so gave the temple of art its most thorough housecleaning so far. However, before Picasso could go delving into the attic and cellar of the house of art in the spirit of enlightened and creative archeology, another twentieth-century painter had already begun to break in the windows and let in light and air, making the job that much easier. He was Henri Matisse. An exquisitely sane and balanced Frenchman lacking Picasso's megalomania, Matisse did not insist on recasting art history all alone but left something for the future and showed a dutiful respect for the immediate past. Matisse was a twentieth-century phenomenon, but he also continued the great line of French *maîtres* in his work and life. He was perhaps the last of that line, bringing to a close one great epoch of French painting while Picasso opened another, an international era whose end is still not in view.

Henri Matisse's early career is characterized by a slow and conservative development which may be due to a relatively late start. Five years older than Lautrec, one year younger than Vuillard, and two years Bonnard's junior, Matisse was still doing school pieces when all these artists were making major contributions in the early nineties. He produced unequivocally revolutionary work and assumed the leadership of the new generation only in 1905, at the age of thirty-six. His late arrival was somewhat similar to that of Gauguin, who began to show a radical new style only around 1888, at the age of forty. And this was in contrast to the precocious development of artists like Seurat, Lautrec, and van Gogh. In one way the situation was more difficult for Matisse because he straddled two generations, the Post-Impressionist and the modern. In years he belonged to the past; by temperament, to the future. When his contribution is set against the belated Impressionism of Vuillard and Bonnard, its revolutionary character becomes sufficiently dramatic.

Matisse came to Paris in 1891 to study art after he had with difficulty dissuaded his father from forcing him into a career of law. There he enrolled in Bouguereau's studio. It is a little ironic that he should have chosen Bouguereau, who had been Cézanne's particular nightmare and life-long envy. Cézanne despised his slick academicism and yet longed for the official honors the Salon's darling reaped. In his moments of despair he wished for himself Bouguereau's completeness of realization although he could not, of course, abide the academic artist's immaculate, empty style. It was Bouguereau's student from Picardy, Henri Matisse, who was more than any one of his generation to fulfill the heritage of Cézanne and extend in his own way the great tradition of the Post-Impressionist master.

In Bouguereau's studio Matisse followed the injunction of the day, "to copy nature stupidly"; his academic exercises, however, could not have completely obscured his talent, for Matisse caught the eye of another Ecole des Beaux-Arts instructor, Gustave Moreau. Interested in the young artist's painting, in 1892 he invited Matisse to work with him informally. This was the beginning of Matisse's serious artistic education. Moreau was an odd artist for the Ecole, painting as he did in a tradition of the romantic "decadence." His lush, static visions were among the last attenuations of late nineteenth-century "estheticism" and grew out of the same literary and nostalgic dream-world that inspired the English Pre-Raphaelites. He loaded his canvas with jewel-like color until it was like a heavily encrusted, ornamental Eastern tapestry. His imagery was exotic; drawn from mythology and literature, it was oppressive in its ornateness and lack of vital force. Beauty for Moreau was a matter of attaining a "necessary richness" of surface and a trance-like inertia of forms.

Moreau's voluptuousness was cold, and he was primarily a decorator, just as his opposite, ascetic number in romanticism, the bloodless Puvis de Chavannes, was also a decorator. The inwardness and vague yearning for ecstasy which had inspired Gauguin to a bolder and genuinely barbaric art petered out in sterile decoration with these "decadent" painters. Paul Verlaine, the Symbolist poet and a close friend of Gauguin, had written the epitaph of the gilded style in his poem "Melancholy":

"I am the Empire at the completion of Decadence
Watching while the great white Barbarian horde advances,
Composing indolent, complex acrostics
In a golden style on which the languid sunlight dances."

To give this languishing exoticism a renewed vitality in the concrete physical terms of painting required another revolution in the language of painting. In that revolution, Matisse was to be the central figure.

Moreau's practices and theories of painting fortunately seem to have had little bearing on his activity as a teacher. He did not impose his style on his students but rather encouraged their independence, and the atmosphere of his studio was liberal and stimulating. His young charges were urged to go "down into the streets" and not merely slave at copying in the Louvre. Although Moreau's color was artificial, it may have influenced Matisse and his colleagues somewhat in their subsequent interest in the potentialities of expressive color. Among his students there were, besides Matisse, Rouault, Marquet, Manguin, and Camoin, all of whom some thirteen years later were to participate in the Fauve exhibitions. To his star pupil Henri Matisse, the tortuous and elaborate Moreau had the astonishing foresight to predict: "You are going to simplify painting." After his death in 1896 Cormon took over Moreau's studio and shortly thereafter expelled Matisse, his reason being that Matisse was over age. But he was probably disconcerted by the vital character of Matisse's painting. Matisse then worked briefly in an informal class with Carrière, where unconventional spirits like Puy and Derain, among others, had gathered. These too were later to join him as fellow-Fauves.

During his student days Matisse had begun to experiment rather tentatively, first with a dark, Courbet-like naturalism and then in an Impressionist technique. Urged by Moreau to try a major effort, in 1896 he painted a large Impressionist interior, *The Dinner Table;* it was exhibited in the spring of 1897 at the *Salon de la Nationale,* a recent offshoot of the official Salon. That spring the controversy over the Caillebotte Bequest of Impressionist paintings was at its height. The great collection had finally gone on view at the Luxembourg Museum, although a number of the more controversial paintings had been refused by the state. This event fed the bitter hostility of official and state art circles to Impressionism, and Matisse's loose technique in his entry to the Salon brought down the fury of the conservative Salon members on his head.

In terms of advanced painting of the time, *The Dinner Table* was relatively laggard, although it is a work of charm and distinction. It was closer to Fantin-Latour than to the contemporary, Impressionist-derived efforts of Bonnard and Vuillard. These artists employed the melting colors of Impressionism but heightened them and strengthened their surface patterns in line with Nabi precepts. They had also begun to use color more emotionally, following the example of Gauguin, and to give their scenes of everyday reality overtones of mystery; they never ventured as far afield as had Gauguin, however, in their pursuit of *le mystère* or the "pure joys of esotericism." Chromatically, the "Intimists," as Bonnard and Vuillard have become known, went beyond Impressionism and at moments achieved a pure, burning expression of color. Bonnard in particular managed to develop beyond merely charming taste and grace in his canvases after 1900. Curiously, his later simplifications of design, his feeling for large, color-saturated areas probably owed something to Matisse. Yet while Matisse in the nineties was proceeding laboriously by trial and error, Bonnard and Vuillard had reached a more radical formulation of color and design. It was only in 1905 that Matisse began to lead the way. After that date Vuillard's gentle art subsided to a mellow whisper of little consequence to the history of the modern decades, while Bonnard went on enlarging his style, achieving ever more voluptuous color effects.

There were a variety of styles other than Vuillard's and Bonnard's current during Matisse's student days. It has been pointed out in the preceding chapter that *Art Nouveau* had become an immensely popular decorative fashion in the applied arts and affected the fine arts as well. In the hands of the weaker Nabis it remained a decorative style, tied to nostalgic longings for past epochs of communal art and reflecting the *fin de siècle* malaise. The mingling of decadence and primitivism, of effete decoration and blunt expressive statements, went on throughout the period. Out of the ashes of *fin de siècle* morbidity sprouted both exotic blooms of fantasy and more simplified expressions which became extremely important to twentieth-century developments. The period saw the first manifestations of primitivism, of Expressionism, and of fantastic art as we now know it.

In 1886 the self-taught "primitive" Henri Rousseau, a retired customs collector, began to exhibit at the *Salons des Indépendants;* his monumental, archaic forms were arrived at intuitively without the benefit of excursions to a museum of ethnography or to Tahiti. In Northern Europe the impact of Impressionist and Post-Impressionist styles led to a free flowering of an intensely personal, visionary painting style. The Belgian Ensor in the late eighties began to paint tortured fantasies and grotesques, a feverish *bal masqué* mocking contemporary life from the point of view of a pessimistic, gothic temperament. He adopted the brilliant, sun-drenched colors of the Impressionists but used them to express highly charged, subjective emotion.

In France a less macabre fantasy was explored by Odilon Redon. Dedicated to "putting the logic of the visible to the service of the invisible," Redon derived his imagery from worlds of fancy, and his work anticipated the shocks, distortions, and dissociations of twentieth-century Surrealism (see plate 16). It is important to keep in mind that a proto-Surrealism was an underground force nourishing romantic and Symbolist literature throughout the latter half of the nineteenth century. The charms of irrationally inspired imagery had been discovered in the seventies by Rimbaud, and before him by Lautréamont (Isadore Ducasse), though it was not until 1925 that these poets were claimed by the official Surrealists as their high priests and given more than a marginal place in literary history. Rimbaud's often-expressed theory of *voyance* (vision) very appropriately fits the visionary art of Redon. "The poet," Rimbaud wrote, "makes himself a visionary by a long, immense, reasoned derangement of all his senses." That cultivation of disorder became the open sesame to Redon's gentle fantasies as it did for the more violent and grandiose visions of the modern Surrealists.

Redon's art also grew out of and reflected the whole turn-of-the-century climate. Despite many literary allusions, however, his paintings gave fantasy a plastic reality. He was interested in color and form as expressive ends in themselves, unlike Moreau, for example. Redon's passionate colors prepared the way for the opulent palette of Kandinsky and Klee in the twentieth century. As a sign of the times, the gnomic character of Redon's painting and his gorgeous chromatics were also present in Bonnard's and Vuillard's art. The "Intimists," however, never relinquished their grip on everyday reality. A world of Paris streets, parks, and domestic life engaged their eyes, but how often do their human images shrink away, lost in a pattern of wallpaper or dispersed by a glorious passage of iridescent color! Nineteenth-century naturalism eroded away in the poetic but artificial Impressionism of Bonnard and Vuillard.

Another development was the beginning of the style of painting that we know as Expressionism. Identified now with Teutonic sensibility, it was first anticipated by van Gogh and then more unequivocally expressed by a Norwegian artist, Edvard Munch. Munch came to Paris in 1889 and discovered van Gogh, Gauguin, and Lautrec. He developed a curvilinear style, in the spirit of *Art Nouveau,* and dark, gloomy themes. His paintings were haunted by a sense of death, as was so much of the minor art of the time. He used oils and woodcut, which he took up after Gauguin's example, to project fear, loneliness, hysteria, and human suffering. Munch created a convincing imagery of human somnambulists powerless in the hands of an evil destiny. A fugue from reality and the sense of the imprisoned individual soul became the substance of his powerful, melancholy northern art; Munch more than any other personality of his time inspired the more emotional expressions of twentieth-century painting. Thus did the *fin de siècle* mood of melancholy, foreboding, and disenchantment carry over like an extended romantic hangover, creating grotesque new forms of fancy. The radical contribution of Gauguin, Cézanne, and van Gogh was absorbed and largely nullified by these new fantastic expressions and even by such realists as Bonnard and Vuillard.

So strong was the mood of romantic discouragement when Picasso came to Paris in 1900 that it was quite proper he should contract the *fin de siècle* disease of despair. It was

Lautrec's disenchantment and mockery which attracted Picasso when he borrowed from the Parisian's style, not his linear energy or bold compositions. In Italy the new painters who in 1910 were to explode the bombshell of Futurism painted, around 1900, crepuscular, depressed works of a fantastic-Expressionist character. In general, the dynamic plastic elements of Post-Impressionism had all but faded from artistic memory. The new artist had to cast about considerably to find anything but evidence of enervation; there was a distinct danger that the main line of French tradition, of Impressionism and Post-Impressionism, would be lost sight of entirely. Art was desperately in need of an infusion of new blood and new vitality.

Many fascinating byways had been opened by the Nabis and by Bonnard and Vuillard, by Redon and by artists outside of France; and the Neo-Impressionists Signac and Cross carried on Seurat's pointillism, if in a spirit of orthodoxy and without his imagination or sensibility. The boldest inventions of Seurat, Cézanne, van Gogh, Gauguin, and Lautrec had been dissipated or distorted. Cézanne's Nabi admirers had robbed his forms of their force and their whole rationale, turning them into a decorative *cloisonnisme*. Cézanne's dynamic space and plastic color were ignored, and with the older Nabis, Denis and others, his influence was actually considerably less than Gauguin's.

It was in this atmosphere of irresolution and negativism that Henri Matisse worked. As many artists had done before him, he first recapitulated styles of the immediate past: naturalism, Impressionism, and Neo-Impressionism. On the whole, it is probably a sign of his artistic health that he could ignore the work of Bonnard and Vuillard even though theirs were the more advanced styles in the nineties. Only with the *Salon d'Automne* of 1905 did Matisse emerge as a radical spirit and assume the leadership of the important new movement of Fauvism. The movement lasted only three years, but it had time enough to jerk painting out of its heavy lethargy and renew the vital traditions bequeathed by the masters of Impressionism and Post-Impressionism. Under Matisse's leadership Fauvism unequivocally opened the door to the twentieth century.

8

Wild Beasts and Tame

"I transposed into an orchestration of pure colors all the feelings of which I was conscious. I was a barbarian, tender and full of violence. I translated by instinct, without any method, not merely an artistic truth but above all a human one. I crushed and botched the ultramarines and vermilions though they were very expensive and I had to buy them on credit."

—Maurice Vlaminck

In the early years of this century a number of great retrospective exhibitions of the Post-Impressionist masters were held in Paris and deeply stirred the new generation of painters. In 1901 the Bernheim-Jeune Gallery put on a sizable van Gogh show; van Gogh was shown again in a large exhibition at the *Salon des Indépendants* in 1905. In 1903 and 1906 Gauguin was honored with important exhibitions at the *Salon d'Automne* and the *Indépendants*. Cézanne's late rise in esteem had begun with Vollard's first retrospective in 1895, which so impressed the Nabis, and in 1904 and 1905 he was given larger salon shows that won an even more important following among the younger painters. That year Cézanne's name was more than any other on the tongues of the members of the *avant-garde*. The electrifying effect of the Post-Impressionists' exhibitions was not surprising, for the new painters had had no prior opportunity really to examine their works. Cézanne was something of a myth in his lifetime, a recluse in the south whom few of the young painters had ever seen and whose work was largely legend.

Van Gogh and Gauguin were known by the diluted derivatives of their paintings that the Nabis produced. None of these artists had been experienced at first hand by the neophyte painters, and, in fact, up to 1900 the most important and influential artistic event had been the 1896 exhibition of the Caillebotte Bequest at the Luxembourg; it had stirred Matisse and many other artists very deeply. In the following years the influence of Impressionism and of Neo-Impressionism, examples of which could still be seen regularly at the *Salon des Indépendants,* had been the most important. Yet the new painters soon exhausted Impressionist and Neo-Impressionist naturalism and felt themselves at an impasse. The bold colors and refined crudeness of Gauguin and van Gogh, and Cézanne's modeling with color as revelations to Matisse and his colleagues. Their discovery of these artists was the immediate inspiration of their daring new experiments and of the violent colors suddenly released in their painting.

Around 1899 Matisse had adopted Neo-Impressionist candy-stick color and technique and begun to apply pigment in pointillist dots. But immediately afterward he reverted to a darkish palette again, taking his cue from Courbet and the early Manet. In 1904 he met Signac and spent the summer near him at Saint-Tropez on the French Riviera. Again he began using the bright colors of Neo-Impressionism, but he loosened his forms and allowed color to function more freely, much to Signac's dismay. In the *Salon des Indépendants* held in the spring Matisse exhibited a large outdoor figure composition, *Luxe, Calme, et Volupté,* which was a rather free and personal adaption of Signac's methods. This was the painting which Raoul Dufy later recalled had freed him from a hackneyed Impressionist manner: ". . . Impressionist realism lost all its charm for me when I saw this miracle of the imagination at play, in drawing and color." Actually, despite Matisse's greater freedom, the painting was still derivative in character and relatively conservative.

In the fall, however, Matisse exhibited a new group of paintings whose assertive originality and violent independence could not be denied. Joining him in the exhibition at the celebrated *Salon d'Automne* were Derain, Manguin, Marquet, Puy, Valtat, Vlaminck, Friesz, and Rouault. Many of these artists had been fellow-students at Moreau's or Carrière's. Vlaminck, an outsider, was a fellow-townsman of Derain from Chatou, one of Renoir's former painting locales. Matisse had met him with Derain at the Bernheim-Jeune van Gogh exhibition in 1901, where he heard Vlaminck loudly and extravagantly singing the praises of van Gogh: "You see, you've got to paint with pure cobalts, pure vermilions, pure veronese." From Le Havre had come Othon Friesz, another charter member of the Fauves. In 1906 at their second exhibition, two more Havrois, Dufy and Braque, joined the group.

The label Fauve, or Wild Beast, was a term of derision coined by a journalist, Louis Vauxcelles. After seeing a small bronze in Renaissance style set in the midst of the gallery reserved for the young painting radicals, he remarked, *"Donatello au milieu des fauves"* (Donatello among the wild beasts). The phrase stuck, and afterwards the central gallery where Matisse and his friends were hung was jocularly referred to as the *cage centrale* or the *cage des fauves*.

The Fauve exhibition was as much a *succès de scandale* as the first Impressionist group show had been. Tired old epithets were dusted off and refurbished by glib philistine journalists: "pictorial aberration," "color madness," "unspeakable fantasies," "the barbaric and naïve sport of a child who plays with the box of colors he just got as a Christmas present." The new color and very free handling blinded critics to the Fauves' originality and, indeed, to their charm. The Fauves rendered landscapes, marines, city views, and holiday crowds with savage splashes of pure pigment, but their mood was sanguine and lyrical. The public made no mistake in sensing a genuine violence and a predatory character in Fauve color, brushwork, and distortions of form, but it confused means and ends. That violence—which by now, however, seems relatively tame—was part of an effort to breathe new life and vigor into painting by restoring the free play of instinct and spontaneous feeling.

The Fauves' outlook corresponded to a new, intoxicated rediscovery of natural life and feeling which had already been ex-

pressed in the closing years of the century by such books as
André Gide's *Les Nourritures Terrestres* and by the literary
movement of Naturism. As early as 1895, in his *Essai sur le
naturisme,* Maurice Le Blond had adumbrated the mounting
reaction of writers to the romantic decadence: "Our elders
preached the cult of unreality, the art of the dream, the search
for the new shudder. They loved venomous flowers, darkness
and ghosts, and they were incoherent spiritualists. As for ourselves, the Beyond does not move us, we profess a gigantic and
radiant pantheism." And the novelist Charles-Louis Philippe
had declared in a letter written in 1897: "What we need now is
barbarians. . . . one must have a vision of natural life. . . . Today begins the era of passion." Fauvism similarly grew out of
the new spirit of joyous, pagan affirmation, and it represented
a return to natural reality, after the romantic interregnum.

The Fauves did not wilfully distort reality for purposes of
sensationalism; they were intent on recapturing through new
strategies the nature that had begun again to elude the over-
subtle Neo-Impressionists and belated Impressionists. Matisse
and his associates meant to make Nature live again, just as in
their own time first Manet and then the Impressionists had made
it live again by new methods. They broadened their technique
and used juxtapositions of complementaries, but in wider
slashes, following their instinct rather than any reasoned or
"scientific" analysis. Above all they sought vividness and
whatever new combinations of pure pigment would give the
greatest possible luminosity.

Despite the vehemence of his expression and a high pitch
of emotion, Matisse was closer to the spirit of Cézanne than
to any other Post-Impressionist. While his first Fauve ventures
seemed not at all to emphasize structure, Matisse was conscious of using color to create form. His arbitrary splotches of
pigment conveyed vivid impressions of something actually
seen or felt in nature. He later spoke of "re-creating" color,
of finding a chromatic harmony that at once corresponded to
his sensations before nature and created a more intense, independent pictorial reality. By way of explanation of the liberties he took Matisse wrote in 1908: ". . . he [the artist] must
feel that he is copying nature—and even when he consciously

departs from nature, he must do it with the conviction that it is only the better to interpret her." In the case of many of the other Fauves, a Gauguin-derived academicism or the artificial colors of van Gogh were more apparent lines of influence. To Matisse, Cézanne was the most important factor, even though Matisse's exuberant pure color seems so remote from the relatively restrained and systematic palette of the nineteenth-century master. Georges Duthuit, the brilliant historian of the Fauve movement, asked Matisse how Cézanne influenced him and how it would be possible to associate Cézanne with "the idea of using pure colors." To this Matisse replied, "As to pure color, absolutely pure colors, no. But Cézanne constructed by means of relations of forces, even with black and white." For Matisse pure colors were plastic forces, too.

Among the paintings Matisse showed at the 1905 *Salon d'Automne* were a small landscape that he had painted the previous summer at Collioure under strong Mediterranean light, *Open Window,* and a portrait, *Woman with the Hat* (see plate 30). On the advice of Leo Stein, the first important Matisse collector, or perhaps at the urging of Mrs. Sarah Stein, his sister-in-law (accounts of the purchase differ), *Woman with the Hat* was obtained for the Stein family. It hung for many years in the celebrated apartment shared by Leo and Gertrude Stein on the rue de Fleurus, among the many superb early Matisses and Picassos that these dedicated patrons of twentieth-century art acquired. This painting had aroused considerable dismay in the press owing to the distortions of the human countenance and the liberties taken with compositions. Unlike either Cézanne or Gauguin, Matisse made no effort to set up a suave harmony of cool and warm tones; purples, greens, blues registered at fullest intensity, creating a wonderfully vivid, if discordant, effect against high-keyed oranges and yellows. The result was a new chromatic magnificence, but it irritated contemporary sensibilities, finally even those of Leo Stein, who took some time getting used to the new combinations of color and after 1907 was no longer able to accept Matisse's bold innovations.

With the offending color an extreme sketchiness of form was singled out for criticism. Contours were defined by changing, ragged patches of color; many areas were left thinly painted, almost untouched, as Cézanne had done, to take advantage of the luminous show-through of the white canvas. Oddly enough, in Matisse's two Fauve paintings, one feels behind the free, spontaneous expression the invisible armature of nature. The expressive attitude of the woman's head in *Woman with the Hat* is the result of careful observation, and *Open Window* actually suggests distance and space in the harbor vista. Even Matisse's most abandoned chromatic expression cannot disguise the operation of intelligence and a moderating good taste; there is always something exquisitely cerebral as well as a real impression of the external world in his art.

Of the criticism of the Fauve exhibition the most interesting was that of the old Nabi, Maurice Denis. Writing in *L'Ermitage,* he took a negative stand against what he saw as a new cult of novelty for its own sake and the fashion of the sketch, but he credited Matisse and his friends with vitality and force. His remarks unwittingly anticipated the abstract art Fauvism would soon lead to. "One feels completely in the realm of abstraction," he wrote. "Of course, as in the most extreme departures of van Gogh something still remains of the original feeling of nature. But here one finds, above all in the work of Matisse, the sense of the artificial . . . it is painting outside every contingency, painting in itself, the act of pure painting. . . . Here is in fact a search for the absolute. Yet, strange contradiction, this absolute is limited by the one thing in the world that is most relative: individual emotion. . . ."

The Fauves' lyrical release of emotions and their emphasis on "the act of pure painting" were to be major factors in the development of Expressionism and abstract painting. Almost immediately these experiments were taken up in Germany and elsewhere on the Continent. Indeed, the reverberations of the Fauve revolution were felt around the world, and from this short-lived movement dates the international character of modern art. In 1905 in Dresden a group of German painters, Kirchner, Heckel, and Schmidt-Rottluff, later joined by Nolde and Pechstein, exhibited under the name of *Die Brücke* (the Bridge). Between 1905 and 1913 these Germans painted under Fauve influence, floating bright lozenges of pure color on canvas and emphasizing rhythmically related shape and expressive, broken line. The group transferred its activities to Berlin after 1910. Under the impact of life in the great capital and an atmosphere of prewar tensions, perhaps, their painting became more strident and emotional, invaded by attenuated gothic forms and subjective fantasies. The First World War put an end to the Bridge and to their Fauve optimism and bouyant colors. The hysteria of the period produced in their later work the real beginnings of German Expressionist painting.

To the south in Munich the Fauve revolution was given a different direction largely by two Russian expatriates, Kandinsky and Jawlensky, with the cooperation of the Germans Marc, Mäcke, and Münter. Under the influence of the Fauves and *Die Brücke* they had begun to use brilliant and expressive color in the years after 1905. Later the impact of Cubism added geometric structure to their color, and in 1912 they formed a new group and exhibited together under the name of *Der Blaue Reiter* (The Blue Rider). That was also the year Kandinsky published his essay *On the Spiritual in Art,* which laid the foundations of his theories of abstract painting. During 1910 he had abandoned objective description entirely for a purely abstract, chromatic art whose greatest debt was still to the color and "pure painting" of the Fauves. It was Kandinsky who literally fulfilled Maurice Denis's prophecy that Fauvism would lead to a "search for the absolute."

In France the original Fauves showed no interest in carrying their experiments to such extremes; the excitation of their color sensations generally led them neither to anything resembling German Expressionism nor into realms of pure abstraction. (In 1912, however, a Frenchman, Delaunay, applied Fauve color exuberance to Cubist-derived abstraction in a style somewhat parallel to Kandinsky's. Delaunay's brilliant color disks and rhythms were more systematically ordered, and showed a Gallic reserve by comparison with Kandinsky's abstract-expressionist art.) The Fauves themselves were restrained by their hedonism and realism.

One artist, a former pupil of Moreau, who exhibited with the Fauves but never really shared their aims, proved the exception. Georges Rouault had participated in the Salon of 1905 but his work must have looked out of place despite the vigor of his expression. Rouault set his low-keyed colors in murky washes of blue, animated by a network of energetic black lines. There was an unusually somber mood to his entries. His style and imagery suggested Lautrec's, but his paintings were more crude in feeling and full of strong moral overtones. He painted professional entertainers and the underworld of Paris from the point of view of a stern evangelist loose in the fleshpots, yet he did it with a profound sense of human pathos. With forceful line and radical simplifications of form, Rouault created moral caricatures of remarkable power. Influenced by the Catholic mysticism of Léon Bloy, he intensified the religious character of his art in later years. His luminous paintings took their inspiration from medieval stained glass (he began his career as a stained-glass worker). On the whole, he stood apart from the great movements of his time, a solitary poet of exalted religious feeling.

The Fauve group held together for only three years. Individual personalities within it were too independent to sustain common aims, and all the members soon exhausted the high pitch of their feelings and were driven to find a more formal structure for painting. Even in the second joint exhibition in 1906 there had been a visible reaction against the informal character of their earliest painting. With its clean divisions of broad color areas, Matisse's portrait, *Madame Matisse,* for example, is a more compact and simple structure than the *Woman with the Hat* of the previous year. There is a certain sobriety and gravity in the mien; the blue-purplish mass of hair and the emphatic eyebrows throw the head into sharp relief, as if Matisse were reverting by means of pure color to the sharp value contrasts and more sculptured form of his earlier "dark" period. In a similar fashion, canvases by Dufy, Vlaminck, and Derain employed repeated linear accents to clarify and emphasize structure. In the next two years the renewal of interest in Cézanne and the emergence of Cubism, with its emphasis on formal doctrine, checked the more inspirational impulses of Fauvism. The movement had done its work, however. It had freed instinct and wiped out the lingering decorative trivialization of turn-of-the-century styles. Through the person of Matisse in particular, Fauve painting began ambitiously once again to address itself to some of the major traditional considerations of French painting.

In the years after 1908 the various participants in the Fauve exhibitions turned toward other goals and developed their own individual styles. Some of the most lawless Wild Beasts became tame and docile and were satisfied to work in minor modes, unable to sustain the grand inspiration of Fauvism. Of the more important figures in the group, Braque and Matisse alone went on to achieve major expressions and fulfilled all their early promise. With Picasso, Braque broke new ground when he formulated the geometric style of Cubism. On the other hand, Derain, Vlaminck, and Dufy developed less controversial and far less "difficult" solutions. Dufy passed through various influences, using each with a personal, decorative inflection. Around 1915 he began to develop his familiar style of using color "diffusions" and calligraphic line in those charming, playful decorations that have made him such a popular public entertainer. Vlaminck hit on a painting formula which dramatized the suburban Paris landscape by means of sonorous color chords, lavish paint application, and dramatic perspective. Like Dufy, he avoided the serious problems of painting in favor of pictorial stereotypes calculated to please a noncritical audience.

Derain held out somewhat longer before surrendering to popular taste. He felt the impact of Cubism, then evolved an austere "classical" manner, and finally after 1920 subsided into a mannered, modish style of brilliant but empty portraiture and landscape. Only Braque, under the stern discipline of Cubism, and Matisse, on his own terms, had the strength of artistic personality to continue making genuine pictorial researches and to use fully the momentous impulse Fauvism provided. Of the original group it was Matisse who showed the most consistent development and who was able to build constructively on the pure color expressions of his Fauve period.

9

Beyond the Pleasure Principle

"What I dream of is an art of balance, of purity and serenity devoid of troubling or depressing subject matter, an art which might be for every mental worker, be he businessman or writer, like an appeasing influence, like a mental soother, something like a good armchair in which to rest from physical fatigue."

—Henri Matisse

In 1905, even while *Woman with the Hat* was irritating Paris tempers, Matisse had begun a major composition that was to go well beyond his Fauve work. The painting *Joy of Life* (see plate 28) was completed for the spring *Salon des Indépendants*. Measuring nearly six by eight feet, this grand canvas showed a number of nudes sporting amorously in an Arcadian setting. The figures are flattened into two-dimensional shapes whose flowing contours form a series of rhythmic arabesques linked up to the arching trees in the wood clearing. Rhythmic line and flat design suggest *Art Nouveau*, as do the uniform, unbroken color areas, but these devices add up to a dynamic expression that goes beyond surface decoration and has none of the artificiality inspired by *Art Nouveau*. Color is distributed in broad planes so as to express space and movement; lines describe volumes while they organize a surface pattern. The artist had found a new stenographic shorthand of line and color which "re-created" in a flat design the complex sensations of mass and depth that we experience in the presence of nature.

The next year Matisse sent to the *Salon d'Automne* a figure composition which he called a sketch and which was even more stark in design: *Music*. It represented the beginning of a period of monumental painting culminating around 1910 in two great wall decorations, or rather oils designed for a wall surface. These were commissioned by Matisse's Russian patron Sergei Shchukin, who in time acquired thirty-seven of Matisse's paintings. In both these compositions the artist sought a more radical simplification of form and design, again emphasizing a sinuous arabesque of line and immense, uniform areas of pure color. Matisse himself understood that these simplifications were meant to intensify his sensations before nature and the human model. He had written how his methods differed from those of the Impressionists: "A rapid rendering of a landscape represents only one moment of its appearance. I prefer, by insisting on its essentials, to discover its more enduring character and content, even at the risk of sacrificing some of its pleasing qualities."

In an earlier version for the *Dance* that is now in the Walter P. Chrysler, Jr., Collection Matisse used a brilliant blue as a background for his terra-cotta red figures and green earth. These dazzling color combinations were apparently further intensified in the final version which Shchukin acquired and which now hangs in the Museum of Modern Western Art in Moscow. For the Paris editor Christian Zervos, Matisse summed up his color scheme in these words: ". . . for the sky, the bluest of blues (the surface was colored to saturation, that is to say, up to a point where the blue, the idea of absolute blue, appeared conclusively), and a like green for the earth and a vibrant vermilion for the bodies." Color saturation over an immense surface and "the idea of absolute blue," or some alternative "absolute" hue, became the keys to the artist's chromatic intention, rather than the ever-changing, broken, multicolored surfaces of his Fauve period.

A simpler polyphony of color, a ruder yet still elegant figuration (which more than anything else suggests the lively figures and moving line of Attic or Etruscan pottery painting) and a

decorative unity by means of rhythmic line, all on the grand
scale, were the radically new elements of Matisse's expression.
They were fused in a monumental style that combined powerful expressiveness and refinement, blunt directness and esthetic
subtlety. Matisse's monumental aspiration was echoed in Paris
only by Picasso and the Cubists. Not since the last great canvases of Gauguin and Lautrec had a French artist tried to
achieve such an ambitious expression or go so far beyond easel
painting. During the same period Matisse's powerful plastic
sense found expression in sculpture, too, in a series of small
figures and heads of remarkable vitality. On the sculpture of
this period rests his main claim as one of the fine, if occasional,
sculptors of our century.

Matisse went to Munich in 1910 to see a great exhibition of
Islamic art and made a careful study of the rugs, aquamiles,
textiles, and other Eastern *objets d'art*. The next winter he
went to Morocco and then repeated the trip in the winter of
1912-13. Like that of Delacroix and Renoir, his response to
the violent color, brilliant light, and lush nature of North Africa
was intense. In conjunction with his growing interest in the
ornamental and sophisticated art of the East, it led to stylistic
developments based on more emphatic decoration, and on a
more voluptuous feeling for color. In 1911, Matisse played alternately with loaded rococo decoration and simplified forms.
He painted four interiors in that year which show his new interests; flower-figured wall patterns in repeated curvilinear
accents and flat-perspective composition suggest Persian minia-
tures and Mohammedan art. The last version of these related
motifs, *The Red Studio* (see plate 29), in New York's Museum
of Modern Art, demonstrates again Matisse's admirable ability
to simplify ruthlessly, "even at the risk of sacrificing . . .
pleasing qualities." As in the *Dance,* he insists on a single color
statement, this time by saturating his canvas with a vibrant
brick red. Against this ground, he sets many small elements
of form and color: a twining green and yellow plant, the outlines of various studio objects and canvases hung on the wall
or resting on the floor, which contribute a variety of touches
of pink, green, and lemon yellow to the general harmony. Each
object is a suggestive cameo and an apparently isolated element,

yet each plays its part in the general decorative ensemble and subtly relieves with a new accent the over-all sonorous red tone.

This painting is extraordinary for many reasons. For one, it converts a decorative, miniaturist style into something grave and monumental. The painting is large (approximately six by eight feet) and gives a great feeling of breadth and spaciousness. Deliberate mental control is imposed on color sensibility limited to a narrow tonal scale, and space is simply diagrammed by bare outlines of form, but with no effect of monotony. A number of small compositional elements are scattered over the large surface, each intact and apparently unrelated. Yet in conjunction they make new patterns and a general movement. Gauguin's transitional style around 1888 suggests Matisse's methods, although Gauguin worked with less finesse and in a thicker impasto. Matisse has intellectualized and refined on Gauguin and yet avoided any rigid schematization. In fact, he seems to be trying to balance an apparently anarchic effect in his disposition of forms and color within a very calculated formal pattern. This was Matisse's way of still keeping alive his Fauve spontaneity and, to go further back in time, the "freedom" of Impressionist selection.

Matisse wished to be less synthetic than Gauguin and restore to painting instead the freer sensibility of the Impressionists by following the random dictates of his senses, but he also wished to avoid the excessive informality and objectivity of their painting. With extraordinary originality he was able to make a modern synthesis of these two contrary pulls, to organize the senses by the intelligence and to stimulate the mind by fresh perceptions based on nature. In *The Red Studio* all the little visual data of the room refresh the eye and keep it awake and moving from one pictorial element to another. There are two significant phrases which together might well define the tonic qualities of Matisse's art: *arrière pensée* and *l'imprévu*, calculation and the unexpected. Active intelligence and active sensibility ever susceptible to new impressions exist together harmoniously in the best of his paintings.

About 1914, Matisse's art began to change again. Under the influence of Cubism his palette became more sober; he made fewer concessions to decorative motifs and emphasized

instead blank, negative areas of space and linear structure. Repeated curves and small ornament gave way to broad vertical
and horizontal divisions of the canvas and a dramatically simple
massing of light and dark areas. Among the many fine paintings
of this semi-Cubist period is *Piano Lesson,* in the Museum of
Modern Art. The head of Matisse's son is seen over the black
scrolling of a piano's music rack. At the left is an open case-
ment window with a wrought iron grille, at the top right hangs
one of the painter's more austere canvases. Attenuated, vertical
divisions give a great sense of spaciousness and tranquillity.
There are a few broad planes of color—pink, orange, and a
wedge of green at the window—which make a grave, subdued,
harmony against the dominant gray ground. The child at the
piano and the figure in the painting are barely indicated, and the
child's features are erased by a slash of color. Only the curling
ornamentation of the window grille and the music rack provide
ornamental relief in this abstract composition whose grid-like
divisions suggest the art of Mondrian. The austerity of this phase
persisted until 1917, when Matisse's natural, decorative impulses took charge once again. In 1917 he began regularly to
spend his winters in Nice, and there he painted with renewed
sensuousness in a softer and more realistic style.

Matisse's extreme simplifications of the period around 1910
and the constructivist discipline of Cubism were now synthe-
sized with his own instinctive hedonism and resulted in a series
of monumental and opulent paintings. One of the strongest
and most charming was *The White Plumes* (see study for *The
White Plumes,* plate 37) of 1919, a portrait of a half-length
figure in a bizarre feathered hat. Here the artist combined
generous, leisurely curves and solid form with delighted attention to small repeated decorative elements in the hat and coiffure. The image of the young lady has gravity and richness, a
sensuous appeal and a quality of cool detachment. She joins
the company of Manet's magnificent barmaid at the Folies-
Bergère as another modern woman of mystery whose secret
is her creator's esthetic detachment.

Early in the twenties Matisse began to paint the exotic
odalisques with which he is perhaps most identified in the public mind. In some he used thin medium as transparent and

delicate as water color; in others he modeled form solidly and enriched his surface with fat pigment that stood out almost in relief. He sought a solution with both methods for the problem that had concerned the Post-Impressionists: a balance between the illusion of deep space and the flat painting surface. To this end he alternately emphasized elaborate rococo ornament in wallpaper patterns and in a variety of colorful pictorial accessories and then, by contrast, rudely simplified and generalized his models and their settings until they appeared as anonymous as the flat, blank oval of the child's head in *Piano Lesson*. Whichever direction Matisse's painting took, it was to the end of finding new plastic forms. His ability to create vital form was also reflected in renewed sculptural activity in the late twenties.

In the apt phrase of the critic Clement Greenberg, Matisse revealed himself during his "rococo" period as an excellent "connoisseur of feminine flesh." A playful eroticism has been a staple item of French sensibility from the great eighteenth-century decorators through Renoir. With Matisse, however, it is coupled with a resolute artistic detachment. He often eliminated the features of his model or reduced his figures to a bland, blank symmetry. The possible carnal attractions of his women were sublimated into pictorial values. Whatever his style, Matisse was always an exquisite master of color and compositional arrangement; he deflects our interest away from subject matter to pure pictorial considerations by his authoritative ways with pigment. As Cézanne had done before him, Matisse often all but eliminated the sex, individuality, or distinct human effluvia of his models, thus assuring himself that his esthetic taste would not be compromised by the sentiment or emotion the subject matter might provoke.

Monet had described his late, Impressionist *Nymphéas* as an island of tranquillity for the troubled modern, a decoration in whose presence "nerves strained by work would relax." In 1908, Matisse published "Notes of a Painter" in *La Grand Revue*, and there succinctly summed up and explained his artistic position. In the course of this essay appeared a statement of hedonism not dissimilar from Monet's describing Matisse's dream of "an art of balance, of purity and serenity . . .

something like a good armchair in which to rest from physical fatigue." During the following decades, when the world seemed about to be wrenched apart by destructive social forces, Matisse's statement acquired a somewhat ironic ring; he has often been attacked for merely giving pleasure while ignoring the moral and political issues of this time. His art is indeed remote from the agonies and dislocations of our period if it is compared with Picasso's, for example, but that is not necessarily a criticism of it. The operative words in the passage quoted above are "balance . . . purity and serenity." Those words define some of the absolute values of French painting tradition throughout history, values which have been independent of the character of external events in any particular period. To create an art appealing to both the mind and the senses, a highly civilized art, is also one way of preserving important human values in a time of crisis. Matisse was never a moralist in the sense that Rouault, Klee, and Picasso were, nor was he an escapist into a delightful dream world of romance, a sort of Moorish fairyland of odalisques and lavish, colorful settings, as some have imagined. His imagery was often exotic, but it was based on nature and the visible world. Out of what he saw he created a civilized artistic island just after a world war and in a period of general barbarism.

One might add that "serenity" has not always characterized Matisse's painting, certainly not in his Fauve period nor thereafter. Serenity was perhaps the ideal aim, but Matisse was determined to arrive at it dynamically; he continued to experiment restlessly, always avoiding the easy and pat solution. During the early thirties he abandoned the enriched surfaces and rococo decoration of the immediate past and boldly simplified once again. His pigment thinned, color was applied in even larger areas and often in clashing combinations, and his figuration became even more monumental.

In 1932 Albert Skira published *The Poems of Stéphane Mallarmé* with twenty-nine echings by Matisse. The etchings are without the descriptive light and shade or interior modeling of the artist's earlier graphic work. Everything is contained in an expressive cursive line which describes form in a nearly abstract fashion. Matisse's coiling arabesques still suggest the curvilinear style of *Art Nouveau,* but each stroke of the burin creates round volumes and a sense of space with remarkable compactness. The breadth and spaciousness of Matisse's late style are also well demonstrated by the murals he executed for Dr. Albert Barnes on commission and which were installed in Dr. Barnes's picture gallery in 1933. A frieze of dancing figures, treated quite abstractly, make a dynamic flowing rhythm of curved and angular shapes. Majesty and simplicity characterize the mural and this period in Matisse's art, and a sense of riches held in reserve.

In the late thirties and forties Matisse began to repeat himself in many still life and figure paintings, as if some inner tension had been lost. The elements in his compositions became even more outsize, immense females and huge palm fronds, still life objects, or patterned shapes. He seemed as productive as ever, yet his invention was possibly less exciting, his colors pleasing rather than bold, and somewhat diluted. The whole texture of his art seemed thinner. Many writers, however, have found this slackening more than compensated by the release of a new abstract lyricism. There is no denying, for example, the vitality and charm of the artist's *Jazz* cut-outs. *Jazz* was a book of illustrations, reproduced from stencils of colored paper paste-ups, and a series of remarks, *pensées,* and asides written by the artist in his own beautiful cursive handwriting. The illustrations are bright, suggestive silhouettes drawn from "memories of the circus, of popular tales or of travel." They have the bright scintillation and directness of children's art, and they are witty and wonderfully alive.

The *Jazz* cut-outs could be described as noble decoration. If they lack the depth and evocative power of the earlier collages of Braque and Picasso, it is because Matisse was simply trying to enchant the eye in obedience to the most unpremeditated impulses. He realized that enchantment must seem spontaneous and that fine decoration should delight rather than provoke "profound admiration." The same mood and similar esthetic aims animate the decorations that the artist completed in 1951 for the Dominican Chapel of the Rosary at Vence. Matisse designed murals, windows, furniture accessories, and even the chasubles worn by the priest for this "gay" chapel, as it was aptly described by one of the Dominicans.

Much of Matisse's artistic production during his career was channeled into wall decoration, tapestries, book illustration. Even more than the Nabis, Matisse realized the goal they had set themselves of going beyond easel painting toward a monumental decorative art and of breaking down the barrier between fine and decorative art. But he did so without creating an airless, artificial style. His forms fused traditional and modern tendencies. He went to nature for his impressions, but he found a more essential and succinct way of expressing his feelings, a form-language in tune with contemporary modes of feeling.

Matisse continued and extended Cézanne's effort to bring volume within the limits of color and flat design. To this problem he brought to bear his own special discoveries of new color harmonies and a natural feeling for linear decoration. He showed a remarkable courage throughout his career in his choices of the more difficult solution; at crucial points he decided in favor of crudeness and simplicity as against overrefinement. By constantly consulting nature and, until the very end of his life, emphasizing expressiveness rather than pleasing decoration even when it meant introducing a deliberate note of ugliness, Matisse kept in check a certain *mondain* taste and fluency. He might have been satisfied simply with sophisticated decoration as Dufy was, or with a repeated formula, as were his fellow-Fauves, Vlaminck and Derain.

Matisse was in the great line of French *maîtres* by reason of his sober and methodical living habits and his dignified, professorial attitude towards painting. He enjoyed a grand old age, and in the late autumn of his life a grand creative lyricism flowed again in the decorations at Vence. The question of his stature will probably not be settled in our generation. He was undoubtedly one of the two great figures of the first half of our century, the other being Picasso. Matisse renewed French tradition in a strictly twentieth-century idiom. He did not, however, open so many doors as did Picasso, the greatest modern inventor of forms, nor explore whole new depths of experience. It has been said that his gifts were his limitations: a civilized hedonism, his balance of expressiveness and taste, his steadfast refusal to depart entirely from reality; in short, the hallowed classical rationalism and balance of French tradition. Yet there is some question whether French tradition did limit Matisse's expression. There are few works of art in our century, including the most remarkable inventions of Cubism, that for grandeur and expressiveness can challenge his paintings of either 1910 or of the period 1915-17, such as *The Piano Lesson, Goldfish* (Samuel Marx Collection) or *The Moroccans*. It would seem that two equally valid courses are presented to the finest creative spirits: either to explore the innate possibilities of the language of painting, or to *use* that language in order to express ideas, states of mind or the life of the passions. Matisse chose the first course; Picasso is of the second order of artists.

10

The Assassins

"Real resemblance no longer has any importance, since everything is sacrificed by the artist to truth, to the necessities of a higher nature whose existence he assumes, but does not lay bare. . . .

"And then after all, since anatomy, for instance, no longer existed in art, he [Picasso] had to reinvent it, and carry out his own assassinations with the practiced and methodical hand of a great surgeon."

—Guillaume Apollinaire, *The Cubist Painters*

The years 1906 to 1908 were as critical to the development of twentieth-century styles as the early years of the 1880's were to the formation of Post-Impressionism. In both cases the stylistic cycle was from a free color expression toward firmer pictorial structure, a recall to order in terms of form. As we have seen, Renoir, Seurat, Cézanne, and, in the latter years of the decade, Gauguin, began to introduce more explicit design in their compositions and go beyond pure optical sensation. When in 1906 Matisse painted *Joy of Life*, the informality and inspirational character of Fauvism were superseded, just as a new formalism had previously supplanted Impressionism. This new tendency was complemented by the interest aroused by successive Cézanne exhibitions in 1905, 1906, and 1907. And in 1907 Cézanne's correspondence with Emile Bernard was published. His letters contained among other remarks the advice to "see in nature the cylinder, the sphere, the cone," an expression of formal principle that in a short time was to be adopted as a major premise by the members of the new Cubist movement.

Picasso had no doubt seen *Joy of Life* at the rue de Fleurus apartment of the Steins where it hung in the fall and winter of 1906, for he was a frequent visitor to those enlightened patrons of modernism during the period. In his monumental study of Matisse, *Matisse, His Art and His Public,* Alfred H. Barr, Jr., suggests that early in 1907 Picasso began to prepare a large composition as a challenge to Matisse's great canvas. This was to be *Les Demoiselles d'Avignon* (see plate 25). The title refers ironically to the inmates of a Spanish brothel on a street of that name in Picasso's native Barcelona. *Demoiselles* joins Matisse's major work to mark another great watershed in contemporary art. Picasso's Cubism emanated directly from this critical painting, and with this work Picasso took his first significant step towards assuming leadership of vanguard painting. In terms of his preceding styles *Demoiselles* represented a remarkable about-face and was the beginning of the pattern of the more violent stylistic changes that dramatically mark his career.

Picasso had been born in Malaga, on the Mediterranean coast of Spain, in 1881. The family moved to Barcelona in 1896, where Picasso's father, José Ruiz, an art teacher, became an instructor at the Academy of Fine Arts. (According to Spanish custom, Picasso was free to choose either of his parents' surnames, and he took his mother's.) Barcelona was a lively intellectual center, and Picasso's precocious artistic talent soon brought him into contact with the local poets and painters of progressive tendency, and in time stirred him to go to Paris. Between 1900 and 1904 he stayed for a number of lengthy periods in the international capital of art, and after 1904 he lived there permanently. On his first visit he had painted street and café scenes in alternately somber and vivid colors, with savage brush strokes and a disenchanted eye; these rather melodramatic paintings evoke Lautrec, Steinlen, and an exacerbated, disenchanted *fin de siècle* atmosphere.

Toward the end of 1901, Picasso began to use a pervasive "blue" tonality that seemed to have been siphoned off from a

Degas laundresses theme perhaps, or Gauguin's tropical jungles or Cézanne's Provençal skies. His subject matter of human derelicts, disreputables, and the oppressed poor of Paris also reflected his own economic distress, hunger, and personal state of soul at the time. By 1903, when he painted *The Old Guitarist* (now in the Art Institute of Chicago), he had achieved a number of remarkable works in a consistent style and full of brooding poetry. The lugubrious, bluish darkness of these canvases recalls the somber tonalities of Spanish painting; their motifs, Manet's more picturesque Parisian version of a Spanish subject matter of human pariahs, beggars, and blind men. To these sources Picasso added an El Greco-like attenuation and an almost excruciating sensitivity. In a period when he was engaged in intense experimentation with many influences, Picasso had also discovered Gauguin's archaic simplicity. His blues and ochres recalled the mysterious synthetic color of Gauguin's late paintings, and the large, flattened forms and hieratic profiles of his figures also suggested Gauguin. But Picasso fused these many elements into a highly personal style and used them to describe the sad human wreckage of the great modern city.

Around 1905 Picasso lightened his palette, relieving it with pink and rose, and restrained the more extravagant bathos of his "blue" period. He began to paint circus performers, harlequins, and mountebanks in a more airy and graceful manner, with extraordinary subtlety and sensibility. These touching, fugitive visions of a strange gypsy tribe of entertainers, half-mournful, half-heroic, are perhaps the most poetic visual creations of the modern period. In a sense, Picasso had revived a very special world of personages, even more so than Degas and Lautrec had done with their ballet and cabaret scenes. Yet Picasso's stoic old *saltimbanques* and emaciated young acrobats with reproachful eyes haunt us like a dream; they are the stuff of vision rather than reality. They are, in fact, something in the nature of a metaphor for Picasso's sense of his own artistic isolation. These figures eloquently express in dumb show the plight of the man of superior sensibility whose very gifts outlaw him from society and force him to wander, homeless, in a shadowy limbo of heroic but futile dreams. Throughout his career Picasso has shown a special affection for the melancholy lyricism of the clown, and even in his more abstract inventions he consistently uses fragment of figures of *commedia dell'arte* origin.

In Picasso's later "rose" period, pure, tremulous sensitivity gave way more and more to classicism. By 1905 and 1906 generalization and a greater breadth of style became evident in his figuration, suggesting the supple graces of Hellenic sculpture or Pompeian frescoes. The roses, red terra-cottas, and siennas of his palette summon up the warm colors of Roman wall decorations and the atmosphere of classical Mediterranean culture. Here was the first hint of another constant element in Picasso's art, lost and recovered again: a remarkable ability not only to imitate the mannerisms of classical figuration but to evoke the very atmosphere of the first dawn of Mediterranean humanism. It was soon to be disputed, both as spiritual tendency and as style, by the discordant, barbaric violence of primitivism. Out of the tension between these two elements, a classical humanism and primitivism, evolves the whole rich iconography of Picasso's art. Often he uses these two disparate styles and sources, metaphorically, to express certain states of mind and to suggest the curious discontinuities of modern culture.

The eruption of Picasso's primitivism, which in turn led to and was fused with a radical new formalism, began in 1906 during a summer spent at Gosol, a small town in the Spanish Pyrenees. At this time the precocious Picasso was only twenty-five years old; during the previous five years he had already produced over two hundred paintings and many hundreds of drawings, had developed a style of intense originality—two complementary styles, in fact—and had revealed exquisite poetic gifts. That achievement would have satisfied any but the most restive nature. Like Matisse, however, Picasso was driven to simplify, and even momentarily to brutalize his finer sensibilities, in order to arrive at a new and more vital artistic solution. At Gosol he began to express through his painting and drawing a new interest in archaic Iberian sculpture.

Before he left Paris, Picasso had been at work on a portrait of Gertrude Stein. Despite some eighty sittings, he had still been dissatisfied with the face and had left it unfinished. He returned in the fall and repainted the face in a completely different style, transforming it into a stiff but powerfully expressive mask. The soft, gentle style of his "rose" period was now a thing of the past. In subsequent paintings of 1906 and 1907, Picasso went on to create squat, angular, primitive-looking figures; heavily pigmented until the paint stood out in low relief, they were at once sculpturesque and intensely expressive of brute paint matter. It is worth pointing out the richness of the paint paste at this time in view of immediately following developments.

Throughout these two years Picasso was searching for new sources of vitality and for new certainties. One of the forms this search took after Gosol was a more emphatic emphasis on his *matière*. It does not matter that this new insistence on the physical reality of the pigmented surface was, during Cubism, coupled with "metaphysical" ambiguities, or that Cubist surfaces varied between opacities and transparencies. From the ethereal poetry of the "rose" period Picasso was moving to a more "materialistic" art. It is interesting that Guillaume Apollinaire wrote in 1913, in *The Cubist Painters:* "Cézanne's last paintings and his water-colors belong to Cubism, but Courbet is the father of the new painters. . . ." While Courbet's naturalism, as imitation, was found obsolete by the twentieth century, his materialism and feeling for some tangible, verifiable reality remained a vital, perhaps *the* vital force in painting. That quest for certainty had to be restated in valid, contemporary terms, and that is what Cubism set about doing. Cubism, and also Matisse's non-Cubist art of the same period, tested themselves against a new reality. This reality emerged as anti-naturalistic to all appearances, yet it still retained the structure, density, and rich physical presence which naturalism had sought. In the twentieth century, naturalism and the mood of intellectual enlightenment which produced it returned to painting, but in the guise of anti-naturalism. This puzzling paradox will perhaps become more clear with a further description of Cubist methods.

Cubism received its climactic impulse in 1907, with Picasso's *Les Demoiselles d'Avignon.* There are a number of preliminary studies for this painting which make an interesting commentary

on the evolution of Picasso's style and indicate progressing
stages of abstract formalization. From the beginning it is clear
that the painting had behind it as a general inspiration Cézanne's monumental late compositions of bathers, even as
Matisse's great work had had. (We know that a particularly
coveted painting in Matisse's private collection was a Cézanne
bather group acquired in 1899.) The architectural development
of nude figures within limits of a flat, rectangular pictorial
structure, then, directly inspired both works. Matisse, still
working somewhat in a lyrical landscape tradition, set his figures out-of-doors, allowing circulation of air and light; Picasso
placed his indoors, packing them into a cramped space, and yet
in some ways he is closer to the structural spirit of Cézanne,
since he has emphasized the piling up of flat planes and his
architectonic scheme is more compact and solid than Matissean
space. On the other hand, Picasso's very expressive color was
far more artificial. It did not describe, even by suggested anal-
ogy, natural space relations.

In the earliest studies for the painting Picasso introduced two
sailors into his brothel scene and even suggested some general
allegory by placing a skull in the hands of one. In the final version the clothed figures and all pictorial accessories except a
still life in the foreground were eliminated; the figures and the
setting are so generalized that one cannot draw any definite
conclusions about their sex or vocation. Five figures are in the
finished oil; the three at the left have mask-like faces in the
"Iberian" style of Gertrude Stein's portrait; their forms, their
draperies, and the curtains, which the nude furthest left pushes
aside, are sectioned off into broad, angular wedges and flat
planes which fuse background and frontal plane. Icy blue, rose,
white, maroon, and ochre make a cool color harmony, and the
splintering of the forms into flat triangular and curved shapes
makes the whole surface resemble somewhat a bed of broken
glass, reflecting a vari-colored light. The two right-hand figures
add startlingly dissonant notes to the general scheme. Their faces
are painted in the style of garish and rather frightening African
masks, violently treated in savage parallel strokes of orange,
deep blue, green, and red. The texture of pigment is rough, the
feelings aroused by the discordant, aggressive color are at odds

with the rather more suave forms and slick surface of the rest of the composition; and these figures at the right are also much more abstractly treated.

With *Demoiselles* a new formal and psychological sensibility erupted. Matisse or perhaps Derain—accounts vary—had introduced Picasso to Negro sculpture and to the flat masks of Congo or Ivory Coast art while *Demoiselles* was in progress, and the last two figures were apparently painted under this new influence. Their raucous and barbaric note surpassed the most violent color expression and form distortions of the Fauves, for Picasso had added a note of primitive, psychological terror to formal violence. The two leering masks anticipate the "Surrealist" imagery dredged up from the unconscious mind that appeared much later in Picasso's art.

A new movement towards primitivism was apparent in the other arts at the same time, most particularly in the music of Stravinsky. In 1910 he composed *The Firebird,* and two years later, *The Rites of Spring,* with its even more primitivistic, clashing sounds. A decade later T. S. Eliot wrote his classic, "The Wasteland," an elaborate allegory describing the plight of overcivilized modern man in search of spiritual rejuvenation with rich allusions to the fertility rites of a more primitive society. If we think of the overrefinements and what might be described as the romantic death-wish of the *fin de siècle* period, we can understand the violent search for new vitality and the reaction to oversophisticated art forms in the early twentieth century. It might be added as a pertinent social note that in 1900 Sigmund Freud had published his great work on dreams and had begun his exploration of the Unconscious, an investigation which indicated that the primitive past lurked not far beneath modern man's veneer of civilization.

During the rest of 1908 Picasso continued painting figures and heads within the simplified planes of African sculpture. Negro sculpture had not only been a psychological and emotional stimulus, but had also suggested that such radical simplifications of form might have new esthetic meaning. Picasso's enthusiasm for primitivism coincided with his discovery of the ingenuous painting of Henri Rousseau, *le douanier,* who had been taken up by Guillaume Apollinaire, the Steins, and other friends of Picasso. In 1908, Picasso bought for a few francs a large portrait by Rousseau which he found in a junk shop. To celebrate the purchase, Picasso gave for the artist a now celebrated studio party commonly referred to as *Le Banquet Rousseau*. The guests included Braque; Apollinaire and his mistress, Marie Laurencin; Leo and Gertrude Stein; Fernande Olivier, Picasso's mistress; and a number of *avant-garde* critics. The guileless Douanier was overwhelmed by speeches, toasts, and a poem which Apollinaire wrote for the occasion and recited. Picasso and the vanguard painters had "discovered" the obscure Rousseau, although he had been exhibiting regularly ever since 1886. In his naïve simplicity, his archaic forms and flat presentation, they found a sympathetic note, for the search for a new simplicity was the order of the day. It was some time, however, before Rousseau's inventions were paid the most solid tribute painters can accord another artist's work, that of imitation. A sober, rather timid *petit-bourgeois* in life, on canvas Rousseau projected pneumatic giants, giantesses, and exotic dreamlike settings which conveyed the powerful fantasy and the myth-making powers slumbering in the brain of Everyman. His untutored forms had the primitive authority of those strange, urgent shapes found on Romanesque capitals, yet his art was "popular" in character, as bright and gay as a "chromo." In the twenties Léger adapted to his own purposes Rousseau's robust forms, and in the forties Picasso directly consulted the more fantastic and mysterious side of Rousseau's genius.

Picasso's primitive or "Negro" period was combined with a renewed interest in the art of Cézanne and with an effort to construct compositions by flat planes. During 1908 and 1909, Picasso's palette shifted to more somber and resonant colors: first, reddish browns and greens and then khakis, beiges, and steel-grays. From a sculpturesque rendering of form and a solid masonry-like surface, he moved to abbreviations of form and a kind of visual shorthand of angular fragments, with still more sober color schemes, less opaque and weighty in tone. In 1909 the new style which Apollinaire later called "Analytical" Cubism crystallized. Braque had followed Picasso's experiments with interest and now joined him in exploring the new manner. Landscape, still life, and human figure motifs were reduced to an almost abstract arrangement of overlapping flat planes, wedges, and curves, quite as if natural appearances had been exploded and the artists were attempting to piece them together again.

Many analogies have been drawn between Cubism and modern science, between the "simultaneity" of vision (or shifting points of view) Picasso and Braque applied to nature, and space-time physics. The fact is that Cubism was simply a further development of Cézanne's structural approach to nature and his denial of Renaissance perspective, but with certain fundamental changes in intention. Cézanne had distorted form and introduced more than one visual point of view in order to bring volumes within the limits of color and the flat surface. But Cézanne, unlike Picasso and Braque, retained the spirit of natural space. Little variations in texture or color were employed to define a plane of an object or the space-interval between objects, which becomes equally important. In his more abstract compositions Cézanne gave almost as much emphasis to these intervals as he did to the objects. He weighted space with color so that we "feel," through oppositions and resistances, the forces objects exert even when they are not described literally, and we "know" that they are present even in Cézanne's most abstract transpositions. Yet within this tense, abstract equivalent of external space the artist retained the feeling of panoramic landscape, of a living, sensible atmosphere and, above all, intimations of nature's unfolding grandeur. In his celebrated statement that the artist should seek the cylinder, sphere, and cone in nature, Cézanne was far from suggesting that some cold, formal geometry be an end in itself. He wished rather to simplify and purify his almost religious feeling of wonder in the presence of nature. And nature was to him light, atmosphere, distance as well as abstract geometric form, the magnificent and inexhaustibly varied "spectacle that the *Pater Omnipotens Aeterne Deus* spreads before our eyes."

Picasso and Braque were by contrast very little interested in capturing the relationships of form or in the great spectacle of nature. They shifted painting's center of gravity, not wishing to create works of art that were an extension of natural space but rather trying to invent pure formal arrangements that were real on their own terms. This meant that painting had to have its own inherent, palpable, sensuous reality to relieve its abstract forms. There are few "impressions" of external nature of a descriptive character in their highly arbitrary inventions, but there are sensations of the concrete, physical reality of the painting-object. (It is significant that the word "concrete" was later used by Mondrian, Kandinsky, and Arp to describe their entirely non-objective art.)

In the first period of "analytical" Cubism, Picasso and Braque limited their palettes to grays, beiges, tans, and whites, almost as if they were conducting a laboratory in form and wished to limit the number of variables and hence better control their experiment. Never willing to abandon natural appearances completely, they introduced hints of geometrically schematized forms, fragments of anatomy, or their ubiquitous guitars and pipes. These suggestions of an original motif appeared more as "insignia" or "emblems" than subject matter as it had been traditionally conceived.

In the evolution of twentieth-century painting, Cubism was perhaps the most remarkable single achievement. It represents a high moment of artistic intelligence and reason. The Cubists found a new symbolic language of form having little or no connection with imitation or representation. They built up a vocabulary of signs and ciphers which could be used as pictorial substitutes for outward appearances, thus freeing them to concentrate principally on esthetic values. Their work was dominated by a lofty spirit of idealism and intellectual adventure. There is, indeed, a special sense of exaltation in the canvases of Picasso and Braque during the "analytical" phase of Cubism, as if they were aware that they were extending the frontiers of art.

The first taste of Cubist innovations came to the public at the *Salon des Indépendants* of 1908, where Braque showed a landscape in the new style. The critic Louis Vauxcelles took Braque to task; he "mistreats form," wrote Vauxcelles, "and reduces everything . . . to cubes." Later Guillaume Apollinaire officially adopted the term Cubism to describe the movement. In the immediately ensuing years, from 1910 to 1912, a host of young painters began to work in the new style: Jean Metzinger,

Albert Gleizes, Fernand Léger, Juan Gris, Francis Picabia, Roger de la Fresnaye, Jacques Villon, Marcel Duchamp, Robert Delaunay, Le Fauconnier. Some were content to work in an almost anonymous, impersonal style but not without distinction; others added their own distinct inflection, in some cases radically altering the character of Cubism. Cubism, in fact, became the most productive and influential movement of the period, and it directly inspired a variety of foreign derivatives such as Futurism in Italy and The Blue Rider movement in Germany.

Even as practiced by Picasso and Braque, Cubism was by no means a pure "visual music." There were "metaphysical" and psychological ambiguities in fluid Cubist space, and evocations of natural appearances, which suggested a concern with something other than pure design. Cubism was a formal scaffolding which could be alternately enriched from or purged of external reality. As early as 1909, Braque had painted a nail in at the top of his canvas, with its cast shadow, as if to emphasize by this bit of "illusionism" that the work was firmly planted on the wall. The next year both Picasso and Braque began to point up the ambiguities of their paintings by introducing fragments of hand-lettering, imitation wood grain, and naturalistic textures that looked real. By 1912 and 1913 they were pasting actual calling cards, bits of newsprint, chair caning, and rope strands to their canvases; they used fragments of illusionary, "eye-fooling" detail lifted bodily from actuality or painted facsimiles of the same. The Cubists continued to enrich their surfaces with new textures in these paste-ups or so-called collages during the next two years. Sometimes the drawing by the artist in a collage was limited to a few lines and the bits of pasted material predominated. At other times actual materials merely added a textural fillip to a richly painted surface.

The illusionism of the collage enhanced both the esthetic and psychological significance of the work of art. If a piece of paper were pasted on a surface, it bluntly forced the surface up into prominence and emphasized its flatness, checking movement in depth and immobilizing the multiple, shifting planes of Cubist structure. This was another way of accenting the materiality and the physical reality of a painting. And these sudden evocations of natural appearances in the midst of painting that seemed to have only decorative and plastic intent also had a considerable shock value. The collage challenged any reality other than that of the Cubists' painted world; and it indicated that even unartistic material could be given a non-utilitarian and esthetic meaning. In the paste-up it is the stuff of actuality—the imitation wood grains, the real newsprint—that seems quite out of place and unreal; and the painting paradoxically becomes more intensely real by contrast. Gertrude Stein reported that in the company of Picasso she saw wooden cannons drawn along the streets of Paris during the war and the delighted Picasso commented, "We are the fellows who invented that." The implication was that a facsimile would in some situations be perfectly adequate. For the Cubists the facsimile reproduced just enough of the story of natural appearances to provide a connecting link to the external world, but it did not compromise the esthetic standards of the creator.

The collage also implied an attack on the traditional integrity of medium and on the academic sanctity of painting. As Alfred Barr has put it, the Cubists seem to be saying and not without some arrogance, "Look, we can make works of art out of the contents of waste baskets." In 1919 in Germany Kurt Schwitters brought to the collage a degree of refinement that was nothing short of uncanny in view of its limitations as a medium (see plate 33). He also, by implication, became a commentator through the collage on a shredded and disintegrated postwar society which he interpreted from a profoundly disenchanted point of view. In Italy, in the immediately preceding period, on the other hand, Carrà, a Futurist, used the collage with didactic intent as a plea for action and for Italian intervention in the war. He arranged his bits of paper in centrifugal designs that emphasized dynamic movement.

When the English writer and painter Wyndham Lewis wrote his brilliant, wrong-headed intellectual history of modernism, *Time and Western Man,* he singled out Cubist painting and the collage for special condemnation. To Lewis these paintings were an admission that the modern artist was a victim of emotional impotence and that vital impulse had been replaced by a synthetic "materialism." The gross, undigested matter of the collage was nothing more than the last "stale pumpings" of nineteenth-century naturalism, the incorporation of Victorian wallpaper into painting and a symptom merely of ennui and spiritual decay. Lewis's complicated brief against the modern mind and sensibility (his sweeping indictment included a variety of artists: Picasso, Proust, Joyce, Gertrude Stein, Anita Loos, and Charlie Chaplin) is based on the specious premise that non-representational expressions are necessarily "dehumanized" or mechanistic. It also supposes that intellectual passion and artistic vitality are antithetical.

There is no question that the Cubists intellectualized, but being cerebral and being mechanical or uninspired are two different matters. Picasso's and Braque's formalism was animated by a noble ideal of beauty, an ideal which they were able to endow with sensuous meaning and translate into concrete, material effects. As for the paintings of the "impure" Cubists, Duchamp, Picabia, and the Futurists, Mr. Lewis is simply too solemn about their work. Their art did, indeed, reflect a mechanized world, but that did not necessarily mean that their sensibilities were brutalized or vitiated by that world. They assimilated a new industrial environment and then expelled it, just as Charlie Chaplin did in his film, *Modern Times,* with his brilliant pantomime on man's fears of the monstrous machine. Duchamp and Chaplin were honest enough to recognize and accept the comical horrors of the machine age, but they were far from being its victims. On the contrary, in both cases human resourcefulness and high jinks triumphed over a deterministic, mechanized order of things. Duchamp threw a monkey wrench into his mechano-set forms by introducing sudden puns and elaborate pictorial conceits. (One should also remember that as early as 1886 a "mechanical" figuration reflecting at least in part the new interest in Victorian gadgets and in industrial life was employed by Seurat with droll effect.) Perhaps the most intelligent formulation of the problem is not that twentieth-century artists dehumanized man but that they assimilated and thereby "humanized" the machine. Modern artists learned both to laugh at the machine and to turn it to serious esthetic purpose.

As far as Mr. Lewis's Victorian wallpaper is concerned, the makers of the collage brilliantly demonstrated that unartistic material, including wallpaper, was grist for their mill and could be given distinction and esthetic meaning. Schwitters and Carrà indicated that abstract art in the form of waste basket pastings might even illuminate and pass eloquent comment on the condition of contemporary society.

In 1913 and 1914, Picasso and Braque began to enrich their surfaces with brilliant color and to replace collage pastings with varied painted textures. Using stippled touches that suggested Neo-Impressionist technique and loading their canvases with ornamental motifs, they seemed, indeed, to be richly recapitulating preceding naturalist movements. In 1912, Delaunay fused the spectrum colors of Fauvism with Cubist design and created a pure-color abstract art which Apollinaire later called Orphism. At the same time Kandinsky was also moving toward a free-color lyricism. Picabia, Duchamp, and Léger began to draw their own conclusions from Cubism. While Picasso and Braque had seen the Cubist painting as an autonomous esthetic object, these more recent converts now transformed it into a "machine." Their forms began to look like the cogs, flywheels, and other appurtenances of machinery, and they sought an esthetic equivalent for the smooth, efficient functioning of the machine. Léger had worked in a Cubist-inspired style as early as 1910; in subsequent years he intensified his palette, though limiting it mainly to brilliant primaries, and created masterfully composed arrangements of smoothly beveled, machine-like forms. Léger's are among the very handsomest of modern paintings.

In Italy a faith in the lyrical possibilities of industrialism and a concomittant assault on academic canons of beauty were violently expressed by the first Futurist manifesto of 1910, signed by Balla, Boccioni, Carrà, Russolo, and Severini. Most of these artists had just previously been painting in a morbid and sentimental *fin de siècle* manner, out of van Gogh by way of Munch. After 1910 their art took its formal cue from Cubism, became dynamic, aggressive, and charged with a new excitement. Out of Cubism's shifting planes they made an art responsive to violent movement. The Futurists exulted in the modern delirium of speed and in the dynamism of industrial life. Boccioni, the most powerful figure in the group, created paintings and highly imaginative, streamlined sculpture which were as mobile in form as stroboscopic photography. There were certain hysterical elements in Futurism, however, one of which was the gratuitous violence growing out of a naked worship of the new landscape of power ("The roaring motor car," the Futurists declared, "is more beautiful than the Winged Victory"). Some may find in Futurist boast and stridency a prophecy of fascism. In any case, their emphasis on kinetic sensation and the programmatic character of their art were far removed from French Cubists' conception of the painting as an object of esthetic contemplation.

While these variations and divagations were taking painting further and further from Cubism's original intent, Braque and Picasso insisted all the more on the material reality of the painting-object. They intensified their contact with the external world and almost vengefully loaded their paintings with a surfeit of brilliant, rococo detail. When they stepped up both the "material" impact and the abstract character of their painting, cracks and fissures appeared in their art. Through these cracks peeped a curious new and psychologically suggestive imagery. In among the shifting transparencies of Cubist structure phantoms and chimeras began to take shape. Picasso's circles and sharp angles, rents, tears, and roughened textures seemed to acquire Freudian overtones and a new spirit of mockery. But just as the "illusionism" of the collage was about to give way to a hallucinatory, abstract imagery and mock-sinister overtones, Picasso, around 1915, suddenly reversed his style. He began to draw and soon after to paint in a meticulously representational style. At the end of the war and in the immediate postwar period a return to "humanism" competed with a vigorous spirit of enlightened disenchantment for hegemony in painting.

11

Doctrine and Magic

"We shall have dictatorship of thought without any control being exercised by reason, and it shall be outside the scope of esthetics and morality."

—André Breton, *First Manifesto of Surrealism,* 1924

"Whatever springs from the combination of magic with a denial of reality is essentially ethical."

—Louis Aragon

"Every time I begin a picture, I feel as though I were throwing myself into the void."

—Pablo Picasso

In the hands of Picasso, Cubism became a vehicle of both pure esthetic contemplation and "magical" pictorial incident. During its first and purest phase Cubism was primarily a means of plastic expression. As it became enriched, or adulterated, with undigested matter from external reality, it acquired added psychological depths and meanings. A "metaphysical" question was posed by the collage as to the nature of reality. Which was more real, the internal structure of the work of art or the fragment of the external world incorporated in it? The poet Paul Valéry had declared that "a work of art is always a forgery." Picasso and his friends carried this esthetic scepticism, and with it the belief in the creative personality as a supreme artificer, to a point where they used art to challenge the reality of the world about them.

A postwar climate of disillusion and negativism spurred them on to more esthetic mischief until, indeed, the notion of the art object as an esthetic and psychological booby-trap became a positive doctrine and acquired an elaborate program.

The inspiration of these developments which took form in the movements known as Dadaism and, later, Surrealism was partly political and partly artistic. From the period of French romanticism and from the time of Delacroix and Baudelaire, the artificial cultivation of "disorder" had been an acceptable way of liberating artistic sensibility from the restraints of reason and logic. A new and more intense consciousness of the creative process and of its inherent mysteries turned romantic and Symbolist poets and some of the artists of their period into traffickers with the occult and the magical. The spell of the exotic and the barbaric, on both an actual and an imaginative plane, held Gauguin in thrall. In the twentieth century the exotic was brought down to earth and localized in daily life; a whole new technique for extracting mysterious associations from the commonplace visual material of the ordinary world came into play. This could not have happened, however, without both the precedent of past romantic tradition and the impact of the First World War.

The war destroyed any lingering Victorian optimism or faith in progress that had not already been routed by the dislocations of a rapidly changing industrial society. Rational and "scientific" faith had been the inspiration of the great revolutions in modern painting, but by 1916 they had been replaced by an atmosphere of extreme scepticism. The age of the machine and the age of mass destruction produced varying reactions among modern artists. In the case of Matisse there was little apparent direct evidence of our convulsive era in his cool and determined hedonism. In the case of Picasso, there was an extreme reaction; indeed, it would be tempting to adopt the language of psychoanalysis and view some of the later phases of his art as the crystallization of some huge traumatic shock experienced in our social life. And the dualism of his style, the dispute between primitivist and Hellenic sources in his art, could even be shown as part of an effort to preserve the hallowed western traditions of artistic language against the menace of barbarism. Picasso's intricate artistic personality, however, will become more clear against the background of other artistic movements. It is safe to say that social forces precipitated or at least speeded up the timetable of the twentieth-century abstract art movements, Dadaism and Surrealism.

Cubism had demonstrated that abstract art could lend itself to a multiplicity of meanings. Léger and Picabia used it to pass comment on "the machine." Marcel Duchamp, somewhat in the manner of the Futurists, adopted the language of Cubism to express movement and the dynamism of the modern world, drawing on extra-pictorial associations. He also introduced new elements of wit and pictorial punning into an abstract form-language as he gave his works progressively more elaborate descriptive titles, titles which seemed only remotely connected with any recognizable content in the works themselves. In time Duchamp abandoned painting altogether and created constructions of a mechanical nature which metamorphosed inanimate forms into something psychologically meaningful, humorous and yet disquieting. Like images in a dream his utilitarian forms took on entirely new magical properties in a secret drama ruled by the logic or illogic of the subconscious. By playing on incongruities of chance associations, Duchamp ingeniously injected an atmosphere of mock-scandal and mock-anxiety into art. His constructions were "teasers" which gripped the mind and yet defied normal processes of reason.

Duchamp also wished to express his contempt for the "esthetic" and for nineteenth-century canons of beauty. His "ready-mades," non-esthetic contraptions which could be assembled from a hardware store counter, were in a sense allied to the primitivism that reared its head first in the art of Gauguin. They represented another more violent wrench away from the hollow conventions of the academy. By 1920, however, Duchamp had carried his rebellion to the point of purely iconoclastic punning, painting that year his celebrated mustache on a reproduction of the *Mona Lisa*. The attack on authority even compromised some of the most precious idols of modernists, or rather, the exalted popular image of these idols; Picabia in 1920 put a toy monkey in a frame and called it a portrait of Cézanne. Despite such gratuitous, playful sarcasms, however, both artists showed a basic respect for non-artistic material, just as Picasso and Braque had done in their collages. In fact, the more incongruous the material, the more the artist felt challenged to make out of it a plastic construction that "worked" in esthetic terms.

The protest and spirit of defiance of Duchamp and Picabia crystallized in 1916 in the artistic and literary Dada movement. Dada originated in Zurich but its guiding spirits soon transferred their activities to Paris. The word Dada, which was chosen at random from a French dictionary by one of the founders, the Rumanian artist Tristan Tzara, means "hobby horse." It is as meaningless and nonsensical as the movement itself deliberately set out to be. Dada was a desperate, systematic negation of contemporary esthetic and moral belief, part of an effort to meet the wartime destruction of human values in kind, by making art too seem preposterous. A world at war made no sense, therefore art would make no sense, reasoned the Dadaists. Dada was also conceived as an attack on the militant Futurist program of war intervention. Dada disdained progress, "the machine," and attacked wartime chauvinism.

In *Alice in Wonderland* and in the poems of Edward Lear the dividing line between sense and nonsense is a subtle thing. So in Dada there was a method in the madness of Tzara, Arp, Ball, Hülsenbeck, and the other originators of the movement. Dadists wrote and recited gibberish poems simultaneously, held demonstrations in which bewildered innocents in the audience were suddenly called upon to function as chairmen, drowned out their own speeches at mass meetings with deafening music. "What is beautiful?" asked a Dadaist, George Ribemont-Dessaignes. "What is ugly? What is great, strong, weak? What is Carpentier, Renan, Foch? Don't know. What is myself? Don't know. Don't know, don't know, don't know."

Dada lived by slogans which were parodies of the hollow exhortations and high-sounding declarations of European statesmen and politicians in the war and postwar periods. The utter anarchy and irresponsibility of Dada defeated itself in the end, and the movement was short-lived. It was important because it attacked excessive solemnity and pomposity in art and in life, and because it provided a point of view, albeit a negative one, for a number of important artists who either participated directly in the movement or expressed sympathy with its aims. Arp, Paul Klee, and George Grosz were artists who made something of lasting significance out of it. And Dada in time led to the formation of the Surrealist movement.

Picasso was perhaps the first modern artist of stature to show elements of Dada and later of Surrealism in his painting. In some of his wooden constructions and many of his collages done around the period of 1912-1913 there were deliberate inanities, nullities, and nonsense effects that were quite in the spirit of Dada: forms that looked like rather lunatic distortions of the human figure or a head but were simply happy "accidents." During the later phases of Cubism a fantastic and grotesque character asserted itself. Picasso played up the expressive possibilities of his material to accent this character, while Braque, on the other hand, restrained any latent associations and emphasized the pure esthetic quality of his arrangements.

In 1917, Picasso's playful Dada spirit was given free range when he designed the set and costumes for a new Diaghilev ballet, *Parade*. His costume for a character in the production known as "The Manager from New York" was an inspired piece of Dada fantasy. The "Manager" was dressed in a contraption that included cowboy boots, pipes, corrugated paper, a megaphone, and an attached cardboard, Cubist skyscraper. The ballet music implemented this free fantasy on high-speed American culture and dynamism with a pandemonium of modern sound effects: a dynamo, a siren, a telegraph key, an airplane, and a typewriter. Conceived by Jean Cocteau, choreographed by Massine to Erik Satie's musical score, the work was described by Cocteau as a *ballet réaliste* and was meant as a burlesque on contemporary music hall vaudeville. It is interesting that the term realist was associated with such a free interpretation of modern visual and sound effects. Picasso's inventive and abstract "Manager" was in contrast to his curtain painting for the ballet, executed in a charming, mannered style of realism and depicting a group of acrobats, harlequins, and circus characters. It was in reference to this ballet that Apollinaire apparently later used the term Surrealism which was to gain such wide currency in the succeeding years.

The dualism in Picasso's work of a realistic figurative style (see plate 36) and an abstract manner with Dada overtones continued throughout the early 1920's. While he pushed Cubism to new heights of monumental decoration, which perhaps reached a peak in 1921 with two impressive compositions on the same theme entitled *Three Musicians,* he was also working in a neo-classic style. His realistic compositions of figures on a beach, of sleeping peasants, and of nudes modeled after classical gods and goddesses and his portraits in a similar manner grew more and more gigantic in scale. They also became curiously pneumatic and static. There was a flavor of Roman or Egyptian decadence in Picasso's classicism, in his colossal, nerveless torsos and stuffed and lifeless heads.

Picasso's painting in this new style is complex in its motivation. In one way, he seemed to wish to re-establish contact with tradition, providing himself with a kind of humanist ballast against his more extreme conjuring tricks and flights of imagination. On the other hand, he was too honest and faithful to his own age to be able to profess through art a real belief in classical figuration. So he actually devitalized his forms and turned them into dummies, as if to demonstrate that Hellenic tradition really *was* "dead." Tradition in the conventional sense and "neo-humanism" was the business of the archeologist and not the living artist, Picasso seemed to say. The nostalgia for a golden age of classicism and the dream of order, harmony, and antique beauty had already been given a new modern turn in the "metaphysical" creations (see plate 32) of Giorgio de Chirico, whom Picasso had met shortly after the Italian artist's arrival in Paris in 1911. De Chirico worked in Paris for four years and his dreaming reveries on the monuments of the past, among which were set incongruous modern images such as locomotives and mannikins, laid the groundwork for Surrealist inventions of the next decade. For Picasso, the Italian's art may have indicated that the Greco-Roman tradition was an idol with feet of clay.

Picasso's return, for whatever reasons, to a "humanist" style was also part of a general *détente* that took place after the First World War. The tempo of modern art momentarily slackened, and the excesses of Fauvism, Cubism, and Dadaism were frowned upon. Matisse, for example, was at the time entering his "Nice" period, and his style had temporarily become more pleasing than adventurous. In classicism Picasso found respite and refreshment, but he learned too how to inject his own irrepressible atavism into the new manner. The sheer inertia and exaggerated scale of his neo-classical figures soon began to transform them into monstrous parodies of themselves. Around 1923 he introduced violent distortions and dramatic foreshortening in his figures, and by the end of the decade he had replaced these huge, stolid figures by sculpturesque, abstract forms entirely. He painted these forms so that they might suggest grotesquely immense monuments set in a natural environment, against a wide blue Mediterranean sky or a stretch of sea. Picasso's prior exercises in classical figuration had challenged his virtuoso powers. He proved that he could inject sentiment and prettiness in a realistic image and yet protect himself against banality by the cunning artifice of style. Classicism, however, provided scant refuge from the violent dissociations of modern life, and in Picasso's hands it soon produced puzzling chimeras once again, just as his concurrent style of Cubism was producing discontinuities, "Dada" yawps, and curious breaks in texture.

As he has done so often in his career, Picasso abandoned a fecund style to break new ground just when his manner had begun to catch on with other artists and inspire a movement. The protean Spaniard's influence may be felt, if somewhat obliquely, in the emergence in 1926 of a group of "neo-humanists," or "Neo-Romantics," as they were called. Pavel Tchelitchew, Eugène Berman, his brother Leonid, Kristians Tonny, and Christian Bérard held a joint exhibition that year, and although their styles varied considerably, they were allied in their reaction to the architectonic trend of Cubism and in their efforts to insert nostalgic, human sentiment into painting. They revived classical feeling in the spirit of nostalgia for a golden age or a classical landscape remote in time. Bérard's haunted portraits and Tchelitchew's emaciated harlequins seemed brave and tattered Paris bohemians wishing themselves into the romantic garb of some resplendent lost age. Berman revived a New Picturesque of architecture, drawing for inspiration on the old stones of Greek and Italian classical civilization. And Leonid gave the scenic a new meaning, taking his inspiration from the gentle, humanist reveries of Corot and Louis le Nain. Yet all these touching dreams were overcast by melancholy and marred by discontinuities and Surrealist dissociations. In the art of Tchelitchew, the great virtuoso of the group, figures soon began to metamorphose, Surrealist fashion, into monsters and parts of their anatomy were lost in "lap dissolves" against murky, ambiguous backgrounds.

In Picasso's art similar discontinuities had already emerged with a vengeance a few years earlier, in 1924 and 1925. About that date Picasso more or less relegated his figurative style to the graphic media, and his painting manner became unified once again around the solid core of decorative Cubism. His oils were convulsed by new Expressionist violence. He used barbaric color, aggressive forms that suggested anxiety or hostility, and actual figurative images of a disturbing, fantastic character. Typical is *Seated Woman* of 1927, a jigsaw arrangement of flat, curved shapes which make a brilliant, succinct design *and* a complex of profiles, each a bit more spectral than the last. One profile is in the shape of an axe blade; another looks like a voodoo mask; these intersect and fuse in a resultant white profile with a mean gimlet eye which is the image of fear itself. Yet convulsive content is elusive, for it is primarily a design pattern that the eye takes in, and the play of shapes distracts us from tracking down the more ominous *gestalts* of fear and fancy. Picasso's strict, ornamental form allowed him to concentrate and intensify his sense of terror, for terror was achieved within decorum and hence its dramatic impact was enhanced.

There is a certain Spanish cruelty in these phantasmagoria, and the more tender sensibilities are apt to get bruised on Picasso's highly expressive forms and colors. In 1926 the artist made a collage of a rectangle of sackcloth, newspaper, and a handful of nails with their points out. A circular hole in the cloth and two parallel lines drawn down across it suggest that the subject is another "guitar" theme. The sharp edges of the nails are extremely forbidding.

Official Surrealism was born in Paris in 1924 under the leadership of the poet-painter, André Breton, and the first manifesto was issued then. The movement reflected the same tendency toward convulsive content that had begun to appear in Picasso's art. Although there were many elements of Surrealism in late Cubism and even in Picasso's neo-classical style, and although the Surrealists at one time or another claimed him, Picasso never was directly allied with the movement. The Surrealists themselves were not merely nihilistic and destructive as the Dadaists had been; they were also deliberate romancers. They enlisted free association, fantasy, and every sort of mental subterfuge to free inspiration. They wished to replace logical order by a more highly charged flow of imagery mustered from the Unconscious, imagery that would shock and transport the spectator into a land of arcane marvels and revelations. The Surrealists declared their belief in "the omnipotence of the dream" and held that "nothing but the astonishing is beautiful."

Two styles mainly dominated the field. One was typified by Dali's creations (see plate 41), an academic manner which meticulously "illustrated" improbably marvelous or frightening visions in "hand-painted dream photographs." The other, exemplified by Breton and Masson, was a non-figurative form of "automatic" writing in which suggestive lines and abstract forms proliferated and the nervous sensibility of the creator was everything. Max Ernst worked alternately in each style. Like every other twentieth-century movement, Surrealism was only as important as the individual artists it formed or influenced. The most significant of these was the Spanish painter Joan Miró, who created an exotic fairyland of suggestive forms in a most personal style. Miró's world has the gaiety and liveliness of an animated cartoon; the deceptive simplicity of a child's drawing; and a Surrealist talent for unearthing a fierce and fearsome fantasy that vies in expressive power with that of Hieronymus Bosch. He is also one of the most powerful modern composers. His fertile invention and plastic authority triumph over a small style, just as they did in the case of another modern giant in an essentially "little" style, the great Swiss artist, Paul Klee.

Although Surrealism has perhaps formed only one important

new artist in the past two decades, the Chilean Matta Echaurren, it has been and still remains a most potent factor in the general evolution of twentieth-century art. In its emphasis on personal liberty even to the point of anarchism it took up Dada's attitudes of protest. On the other hand, despite their declarations and polemics, the Surrealists differed from the Dadaists in that they wished to subvert only contemporary authority and not art itself. As a movement it was not conscientiously "anti-artistic," and indeed many of its foremost artists like Dali and Tanguy willingly embraced the licked surfaces and finish of academic art. Where Surrealist inspiration has been associated with a genuine plastic sense as in the case of Picasso, Miró, and Klee, it has led to the formulation of new esthetic truths in a stimulating and novel fashion. The modern artists who have borrowed something from Surrealism are legion. There are suggestions of "automatic" writing and of some substratum of phantom imagery even in Braque, and Léger's efficient-looking pneumatic figures have a touch of dream and somnambulism about them. Of the great moderns only Matisse alone has resolutely stood his ground and refused to indulge in Surrealist fantasy.

A good deal of the confusing Surrealist strategy of mystification in its relations with the public may be understood as part of the modern artist's insistence on his prerogative to paint according to his own lights. When Dali declares that he aims to "discredit reality," he might clear his ambiguous statement up somewhat by adding that he does so in order to heighten the reality of the world of his own artistic imagination. Despite his air of romantic mystery, Dali's purpose is not dissimilar from Picasso's and Braque's when they began to challenge natural appearances with the eye-fooling tricks of the collage. Dali, Ernst, Tanguy, and the orthodox Surrealists discovered that their fantasy life not only could be used to defend artistic *laissez faire* but also yielded a heady sense of power. In the realm of the imagination the artist could be all-powerful and effective, no matter how ineffectual he might be in controlling the real world for the sake of his happiness. The Surrealist artist converted his frustrations in reality into an inner position of strength. By real or feigned techniques of mental self-intoxication, by the cultivation of disorder, he was able to feel he could shape his own destiny once again. Over the inner world of vision he reigned supreme, half sorcerer and half victim of his own creative fever, able to assume a variety of poses and capable of finding an "infernal grandeur" even in intimations of catastrophe and degradation. The Surrealists reminded themselves that Rimbaud's protean vision gave the artist many lives and many roles, as "the great invalid, the great criminal, the condemned man, and the supreme seer," because the artist had reached the fountainhead of *"voyance"* and the mysterious "Unknown."

The art of Surrealism and of artists who worked at one time or another under its inspiration had at least one thing in common: a half-playful, half-serious taste for the catastrophic. (Painting that was entirely dedicated to the catastrophic usually took the more solemn form of Expressionism.) As Clement Greenberg has pointed out in his excellent book on Miró this new sense of hazard grew out of a postwar mood of pessimism which came "on the downslope of the age that rose so hopefully in 1900." The First World War shattered the high hopes and the spirit of intellectual adventure that Fauvism and Cubism both reflected, and Dada and Surrealist art ushered in a new age of disenchantment and anxiety. Man's confidence in his powers to master the world were badly shaken, and the artist was distracted by external events from pursuing those purely hedonist aims which had ruled French painting from the time of Manet and the Impressionists. In the postwar period the sovereignty of innocent esthetic pleasure in contemporary painting was disputed by elements of the grotesque and the macabre. Miró's pictorial puns and humor were one way of alleviating and releasing the artist's fears. Yet there remained an unexorcised grotesque content in his art that pays a hostile and menacing world its due.

In the art of Picasso the macabre, as we have seen, also played a larger role after 1925 when he began interpolating in his Cubist diagrams those half-human, half-inhuman forms which are seen in dreams. During the closing years of the twenties the grimly playful side of Picasso's temperament took on a new artistic character. In place of his grotesquely inflated classical figures and flat-patterned Cubist shapes, Picasso substituted "bone" figures: potent abstract forms which created new, expressive anatomies, human and inhuman. Picasso's fecund invention in painting was matched by a series of alternately representational, though violently distorted, and abstract constructions in sculpture. The congeries of forms in these paintings and constructions often had overt or implied libidinous content; even in a world of phantasms Picasso's virility expressed itself with ease. The savage, destructive force of these skeletal structures alternated with a more representative, classical imagery in the graphic media, themes of girls with flowers in their hair, sleeping nudes and supermen drawn from mythology. There seems to be in Picasso's art always that rhythmic movement between paroxysms of violence and release in peacefulness and meditation, between barbaric invention and classical memories.

One of Picasso's many wonderful drawings of the period shows a hoary, bearded classical head eyeing a seated woman. The head is in Picasso's mytho-poetic, humanist style; the woman is one of his abstract anatomies, yet the two unrelated styles of figuration coexist harmoniously on the same sheet of paper. This drawing and many like it also suggest one of Picasso's continuing preoccupations, the relationship of the creator to his work and most particularly to the female model. In some drawings Picasso's creative demiurge is identified with a humanist image, an ancient god or satyr, and the model is a fantastic, monstrous creature. In others the relationship is reversed, and a strange, abstract anatomy observes a classical vision of female loveliness. We may take these creations as part of his personal myth of the artist-creator who casts himself in multiple, metamorphic images as alternatively an ancient God, superman, and monster. Throughout his career Picasso has alternated in modes, on the one hand prolifically fabricating chimeras, and at the same time creating ideal visions of grace and beauty based on classical models.

After 1930 Picasso began to explore intensively a symbolism of the bull and tauromachy, themes which had played such an important role in Goya's art. The bull became a projection of his deepest atavistic impulses and in the next years an even more precise moral symbol of the forces of darkness which fascism had loosed in Europe. In 1935, Picasso did one of his greatest etchings, *Minotauromachy* (plate 44), based on this symbolism. A half-human minotaur reaches out a horny hand to extinguish, or to ward off, a candle that a little girl holds. Between them writhes an agonized horse with a dead and torn female matador on its back, still futilely clutching her sword. On a ladder at one side is a bearded Christ-like figure, sadly observing the scene. At a window above are two gentle girls with pigeons. As an allegory the scene does not explicitly declare its meaning, but in terms of Picasso's whole development one can discern a familiar play of forces, of harmonious against convulsive images. The exact dramatic meaning is confused by the interchangeableness of roles; for example, the minotaur appears to have slain the matador with his own sword; and the Christ-like figure looks rather like a more humanized version of the minotaur. Hence the relationship of good and evil becomes bewildering and extremely complex. In any case, the little girl standing stiffly with her handful of flowers and tiny candle unequivocally suggests the innocent child-victims of Picasso's acrobat paintings. Her innocence and purity, however, are here more positively expressed and seem to irradiate the scene. Whether the great slavering beast will manage to extinguish her little candle, we do not know. The issue is left in doubt. The scene is dramatic, pregnant with mystery, and it makes superb theater. This same cast of characters, with variations, made its appearance again in 1937 in one of Picasso's greatest creations, *Guernica* (plate 45), a painting inspired by the fascist bombing of a Basque town during the Spanish civil war.

Picasso was a Loyalist partisan in the civil war and accepted from the Republican government an appointment as director of the Prado, although he was never able to go to Spain to assume any official duties. He fought his personal war against fascism, however, in pictures which were the most eloquent indictments of organized brutality in modern times. In 1937 he did a series of etchings, *The Dream and Lie of Franco,* and wrote a violent Surrealist poem to accompany the sequence of plates. Franco is described as "an evil-omened polyp . . . his mouth full of the cinch-bug jelly of his words," and he emerges in the drawings as a hairy, three-pronged turnip with carious teeth and a paper-hat crown. The rape of Spain is shown in an episodic sequence of scenes and images: a dead horse, human cadavers, women fleeing with dead children. Franco the "polyp" turns into a horse in one episode and is disembowled by an avenging bull. In another the majestic head of a bull confronts Franco's animal-vegetable incarnation and seems to dazzle and shrivel it by its presence.

In the same year Picasso painted his tragic mural, *Guernica,* a huge canvas (11½ feet by nearly 26 feet). The wartime agony of death and senseless destruction is emphasized by the stark black, white, and gray composition; there is no color. A broken, mangled form of a warrior at the base of the composition with his features askew; a woman with a dead child; a disembowled horse at the center with a spear-point tongue; another woman whose breast nipples have become bolts and who is crazed and cross-eyed with pain and grief—all these images and the expressive distortions suggest cruel affliction. Two forms dominate the composition, the fierce bull and the dying horse. From the right, out of a window, flows the fearful face of a woman and a long arm like a hallucination. She holds a candle over the scene, and it seems to be a symbol of the conscience of a horrified humanity.

Picasso explained the symbolism of the work simply, declaring that the bull "is brutality and darkness . . . the horse represents the people." The painting has the impact of a nightmare, the melodrama and simplicity of presentation of the comic strip, and extreme psychological subtlety. By his strict decorative form and strong figurative conventions Picasso has managed to intensify the emotions he wished to convey. *Guernica* has been criticized on the ground that its conventions are too private to excite general public emotion. If that is true, it is not so much Picasso's fault as our own and is a measure of the depletion of our artistic frame of reference. Picasso, in fact, has both deliberately simplified familiar classical figurative conventions and tried to fuse them with the convention of the comic strip to increase their clarity and legibility. The broken warrior at the bottom of the panel is a combination of a Greek hero derived from a classical bust and Kilroy or L'il Abner. Picasso multiplies terror by achieving it within decorum; his formalization gives horror the stark lineaments of classical tragedy. We may better appreciate the power and purity of Picasso's drama if we compare it to the hysteria and sentimentalism of German Expressionists who have treated similar themes.

Much of *Guernica's* force derives from the significant and cruel distortions of the predatory bull, the stricken horse, and the scarecrow human figures. In these forms Picasso found a subjective equivalent for public chaos and aggression. By disorganizing and dissociating the anatomies of his protagonists he expressed some of our deepest fears and terrors. Many writers have pointed out the resemblance of drawings and paintings of the insane to some of Picasso's inventions: the disorganized anatomy, the double-profile, the aggressive, compulsive repetition of ornamental pattern. One of the profoundly tragic meanings of *Guernica* is the projection, by controlled symbolism, of a kind of mass insanity and in the language almost of psychotic drawing. Goya, in his *Caprices,* had written as a note to one of his etchings that "the dream of reason produces monsters." Picasso added an up-to-date, clinical postscript to Goya's vision of man's inhumanity to man.

Few in the modern generation rose to the heights of expression and feeling attained by Picasso in the *Guernica* period. To achieve these heights Picasso gambled recklessly with the esthetic harmony and hedonistic intent of oil painting. For the sake of expression and as a criticism of the life of his time, he pushed art to an extreme point of human disenchantment, to a point almost of no return. It has been a measure of his greatness that he could sustain such an extreme point of view with no loss of either coherence or quality. In art, perhaps only Goya has confronted the dark and predatory forces in man so unequivocally; in poetry, Swift and Baudelaire wrote as supremely disenchanted spirits but paid a heavy price with the loss of their sanity.

If no one could equal Picasso's expressive power in his own time, there were many who created a more balanced and harmonious art: Matisse, Braque, and possibly Léger and Miró.

How Picasso's form language could be used for purely esthetic ends was enchantingly demonstrated by Georges Braque, who has perhaps been closest to the Spanish master over the years, at least in terms of the superficial appearance of his paintings. The development of Braque's style in the post-Cubist period makes interesting parallels and contrasts to Picasso's. Even during analytical Cubism, Braque asserted his individuality and distinction, although his paintings are often mistaken for Picasso's. Picasso's works of 1910-1912 are stamped with his individual temperament and have their own distinct and expressive accents; Braque's are more serene and harmonious, dedicated to pure esthetic contemplation (commentary, plate 31, pp. 137-8). Braque was probably the first to use foreign matter in his Cubist work, mixing his pigment with sand and imitating or actually incorporating green and gray marbleized surfaces. In Braque's collages, however, there are rarely disquieting psychological overtones. His compositions are a triumph of refinement, and an indefinable nobility of sentiment subdues gross matter. Braque's textures do not irritate or excite the nervous sensibility of the observer as do Picasso's; they are always subordinated to exquisite taste.

On the other hand, his purpose in the collage is never merely decorative either, but like Picasso's represents an effort to achieve a new certainty. Positivist in spirit, the collage belongs to a period of scientific and philosophical enlightenment, a period whose confidence in the powers of rationalism had not yet been shaken by the barbarism of a world war. For Braque the collage was a means of verifying through observable facts the truth of Cubist "space." He wrote: "The painter who wished to make a circle would only draw a curve. Its appearance might satisfy him, but he would doubt it. The compass would give him certitude. The pasted papers [*papiers collés*] in my drawings also gave me certitude. . . . The pasted papers, the imitation wood—and other elements of a similar kind—which I use in my drawing, also succeed through the simplicity of the facts; this has caused them to be confused with *trompe l'oeil*, of which they are the exact opposite. They are also simple facts, but are *created by the mind*, and are one of the justifications for a new form in space."

Around 1914, Braque's designs increased in scale and spaciousness, and he tentatively began to use a free curve and meandering line as a counterpoint to the more rigid angles of orthodox Cubism. With this free curve Braque anticipated the organic shapes of Arp and Miró. However, he never used these devices to express any pointed Dada or Surrealist content. After serving heroically in the war (he was wounded and received two citations for bravery), Braque returned to Paris and resumed painting more or less where he had left off. In the transition from analytical Cubism to the more decorative forms that both Braque and Picasso began to employ after 1914, the art of Juan Gris was an important factor. Both artists have indicated that Gris was perhaps the only other Cubist who very much interested them. Now, in 1917, they found a solution to the amorphism and fluidity of their earlier forms in Gris's more explicit and ornamental shapes and in his interlocking structure of form. Over the next eight years Braque and Picasso reached the summit of the Synthetic Cubist style in a series of monumental canvases. Using free curves, slow zigzags, and organic shapes, Braque kept pace with Picasso's sharper-edged forms and more brilliant color. He may have lacked Picasso's intensity and dramatic invention, and he was obviously very much influenced by the Spaniard's formal innovations. But Braque never merely imitated Picasso. He created form on his own terms. And for sheer decorative elegance and balance his art is perhaps the more satisfying in this period.

Around 1922, Braque made a tentative return to natural appearances just as Picasso and Matisse had done before him. His forms became even freer and less schematized, his descriptive content more particularized. He translated into subtle tonal harmonies the sensuous properties of objects taken from nature. Against low-keyed backgrounds of beige-gray, apple green, and brown he painted in the most delicate tones the "dark purple of a grape, the bloom of a peach, the yellow brown of a pear," as Henry Hope described these effects in his first-rate monograph on the painter. Then, contemporaneous with Picasso's neo-classic figures, Braque began to paint large, semi-draped female figures of classical inspiration, his so-called basket carriers. They vaguely suggested Renoir's late, "strawberry" nudes in their ample proportions and loose modeling, but they were of course schematized as flat, semi-abstract forms. From 1927 to 1930, Braque again seemed to take his cue from Picasso and experimented briefly with a more severe style, as if he suddenly mistrusted the elegance and ease of his preceding decorative manner.

During the early thirties Braque made a number of sketches, prints, plaques, and sculptures of nymphs and classical figures, utilizing a flowing, calligraphic line. And in the late years of the decade his direction in oil painting paralleled Picasso's once more as he began to play off dramatically illuminated areas against deep shadow and out of these contrasts to create a pictorial world of serene and gentle phantoms. Again the resemblances of his forms to Picasso's is striking but only superficial, for his expressive purpose is entirely different. Braque's phantoms, disembodied shadows, and reflections evoke no terrors nor do they have any particular psychological import. They suggest only a serene lyricism and esthetic detachment, as if the world were seen tremulously through some distorting medium, through a rippling stream perhaps. In this illusive atmosphere Braque's images undergo unnatural distortions, bending, merging, drifting apart in a grave, measured formal dance.

In the years since he painted *Guernica*, Picasso, on the other hand, has explored, with infinite and inexhaustible variations, the themes of features-askew portraits and figures, ever intensifying their Expressionist violence. At the same time he has continued to draw and make prints in a dreaming classical spirit. In fact, Picasso has become a kind of master thief who is able to transmute influence and style from almost any period of culture and make them his own. Behind his stylistic virtuosity is a conviction that all art styles are simultaneous and form one continuous living present. "To me there is no past or future in art," he has written. "If a work of art cannot live always in the present, it must not be considered at all. The art of the Greeks, of the Egyptians, of the great painters who lived in other times, is not an art of the past; perhaps it is more alive today than it ever was." In a sense, Picasso is a "universal" mind in the grand style of Delacroix, with a vast artistic culture at his beck and call. On his own admission Picasso starts from a "void," with the kind of ascetic exaltation of the romantic and Symbolist poets, and then discovers a teeming world of form. In this jungle-growth of imagery he sets himself the task of eliminating the inessential. "In my case," he has written, "a picture is a sum of destructions."

Picasso now lives in Vallauris, a small hill town above Cannes which his activity in ceramics-making has turned into a thriving pottery center. In recent years the artist has enjoyed a happy and congenial family life with a new young wife who has borne him a child. Perhaps as a result, a lyrical mood has suffused his art. The grave notes of the somber, haunted still life and double-profile figures he produced during and just after the last war have given way to more cheerful effects. His forms have been purged of violent content. The alarming congeries of images is still there, chimeras stalk about on canvas, but the effect is more *buffo* than macabre. Picasso's sweetened mood has drugged his monsters into an impassive, statuesque sleep or converted them into impotent clowns. His themes and dramatis personnae survive intact from the convulsive past, but he now presides over them in a benign, autumnal mood. Like Prospero in Shakespeare's lyrical late play, "The Tempest," he can banish his dragons and devils with a wave of the magic wand of his art. They may appear on stage, but no excessive dramatic disturbances will be tolerated.

The change from a dramatic to a lyrical art has also meant a certain thinness, a reduction in the emotional intensity that produced the potent imagery of *Guernica*. Emotion is now diffused by the general mood of benevolence and no longer pinpointed in sharp, searching forms. And it also seems that Picasso is less and less interested in testing himself in an ambitious painting. His recent effort to turn the symbolism of *Guernica* against American participation in the Korean war took the form of a huge mural painting, *War and Peace*, exhibited in Rome in 1953. Picasso is a Communist party member, but for all his anti-Americanism the didacticism in this painting was but a feeble imitation of his own past and failed to sustain intensity.

But Picasso is still immense, if not in the single, large work then in the grand design of the whole corpus of his art. The disjointed fragments he produces have an immense master scheme behind them, a frame of reference that embraces all artistic periods and stylistic vocabularies. His varied artistic essays in many media have the scope and multiple levels of meaning of Joyce's *Ulysses* or *Finnegans Wake*. Picasso is undoubtedly our greatest modern myth-maker. For the past three decades he has been excavating in the art of the past and converting it into an art of the present. He has drawn from the Hellenic mainstream of humanist culture, from peripheral Mediterranean civilizations, and from the barbaric imagery of primitive peoples. His imagery shuttles back and forth between the warring inspiration of Greco-Roman tradition and primitive art, and it strikes fire from their opposition. The bland, ideal beauty of Greek or Fayum heads may be recaptured in a lithograph; in a ceramic or a bronze, Cycladic, Etruscan, or Negro sculpture will be the inspiration, filtered through the sieve of Cubism. Often the two sources fuse in a painting or a drawing, establishing that characteristic psychological *frisson* between the civilized outer man and the atavism that lurks not far beneath the surface.

What gives significance to Picasso's erudition and recondite insights is pure artistic temperament. Temperament and sensibility vitalize every material and medium he touches, in prints, drawing, painting or sculpture. In recent informal sculpture his immense vitality is as marked as ever. Among the gayest and most inspired sculptures have been a series of wonderfully droll and expressive owls, some of which have an uncanny resemblance to the artist himself. Painted with gay, Mardi Gras colors, they have been assembled from shovel parts, bolts, nails, screws, all embedded in plaster which has then been cast in bronze. They have the expressive vitality and spontaneity of a child's plasticene modeling. It is impossible to say why they are such passionate creations. From them one can only conclude that Picasso is a law unto himself. He goes on indefatigably creating plastic marvels, behaving at the age of seventy-five as if his art were at a new beginning. Picasso's genius disarms criticism entirely; one can only marvel at his continuing vitality.

12

Painting Now

"... the cycle of great personalities is over. There remains good painting."

—Giorgio di San Lazzaro, *Painting in France*, 1951

"Yesterday is not quite out of sight; tomorrow is not yet clear in view. But the atmosphere of vitality is unquestionable. A new visual idiom seems to be taking shape. . . . Perhaps the situation today has its closest resemblance with one just half a century ago in 1903."

—James Johnson Sweeney. Introduction to the catalogue, "Younger European Painters," 1954

After the Second World War the cry went up in America: "Where are the younger French painters?" The war had cut America off from the artistic activity of Europe, and it was with the most intense curiosity that Americans set themselves to appraising the new artistic productions from Paris. The first results were disappointing. As it turned out, France's "younger" painters appeared to be young neither in years nor in spirit. Like children who have been deprived of personality by powerful parents, the most discussed painters of France lived uncomfortably in the shadow of the giants of modern painting: Picasso, Miró, Braque, Léger, Matisse, and Bonnard. In fact, it seemed that the most vital and adventurous artists, the *avant-garde,* indeed, were still the venerable pioneers of modernism.

An interesting new discovery in the older generation was the occasional painting and drawing of the sculptor Alberto Giacometti, who had formerly been a Surrealist. After the war Giacometti began to draw and paint figures and portraits of immateriality and sketchiness, lost in a web of line and hatchings. His images were diminished almost to the point of unreality and seen as if through the wrong end of a telescope. These impoverished forms, complementing new and very remarkable, attenuated sculptures, suggested a poetry of despair and provided perhaps the most original and convincing picture of the postwar mood to emanate from Paris.

The so-called "younger" painters, or older young painters (for the most part they were at least in their forties) were thoroughly under the spell of either Picasso's or Matisse's figure formulas or the hot, sensuous color of Bonnard. These many gifted eclectics worked in a figurative semi-idiom and employed color that reflected the "good taste" of the so-called *Ecole de Paris* (School of Paris). Among them were Estève, La Picque, Tal Coat, Tailleux, Pignon, Borès, Gischia. Typical and perhaps the most charming is Pignon, who just after the war painted very professional and agreeable semi-abstract landscapes and figures in ingratiating warm color. In recent years Pignon, following the fashion of the times, has become increasingly abstract; in either style, however, his work appears simply too polite, tidy and cautious and lacks temperament or some distinct point of view. Pignon is a "natural" painter as many of the other members of the post-war group have been, with a typically French feeling for *belle peinture.* But like so many of the other members of his generation who were in touch with and yet did not directly participate in the great movements of Fauvism, Cubism, and abstract art and Surrealism, he has produced only second-hand memories of the great moments of the modern past. "Tradition," a French writer has declared, "can only be preserved by revolution." The intermediate generation of Paris painters, robbed of potency by their elders, have been incapable of making any profound visual revolution; they have relied instead upon good manners, taste, and a temperate hedonism to sustain them.

These particular qualities of taste and hedonism have often been identified with the School of Paris, which embraces a disparate group of painters, all of considerable stature but none central to the greatest developments of twentieth-century painting. Modigliani, Soutine, Pascin, Utrillo, and sometimes Chagall have been linked as members of this school. They have in common the fact that none has been a great innovator, that they have all stood outside the great movements of their time, and that they all wished to inject more sentiment into painting. In a period of movements and counter-movements, they remained somewhat apart, and their individualism proved a limitation. They were all romantic, either in their lives or their art, and all but Chagall, perhaps, shared a fatal enchantment with *la vie Bohéme* of Montmartre and Montparnasse.

The legend of Paris Bohemia began innocently enough with the Impressionists and was later given a more sinister twist by Lautrec. (In both cases the favorite haunts of Paris Bohemia were in the Montmartre quarter on the Right Bank; in the early years of the century the Left Bank Latin Quarter supplanted it.) Lautrec had painted Montmartre in the full incandescence of its first bloom both as an artistic *quartier* and a gaudy district of nocturnal pleasures. Utrillo painted the same sector as a ruin of its former self, burned out and dying. He injected into the decaying walls and façades and tortuous streets of the "hill" —the famous Butte of Montmartre—a melancholy poetry with his almost compulsively repeated motifs. This monody of bleak walls, impoverished foliage, and leaden skies, particularly during Utrillo's so-called "white" period between 1909 and 1914, represents the last twinge of a romantic nineteenth-century Impressionism. The touching lyricism of these early paintings and their feeling of emptiness and fatalism are also reflected in the unhappy story of his life. The neglected, illegitimate son of Suzanne Valadon, an alcoholic in his teens, trading pictures for wine and food and lodging, Utrillo grew up like a rank weed in a sunless, unwholesome atmosphere. The pathos of his painting is at least in part the unhappy story of the depressed fringe of Paris Bohemian life.

The same tragic-sensitive mood was also projected but with

more esthetic merit in the painting of Jules Pascin, who came to Paris from Middle Europe and committed suicide there in 1930 at the age of forty-five. His delicate and touching paintings of prostitutes and degraded adolescents are remarkable works of pure nervous sensibility, though he never made any startling technical discoveries and was limited by his subject matter.

A more virile spirit was Chaim Soutine, born in Lithuania, also something of a painter of despair. In the early twenties Soutine developed a powerful Expressionist style, using excruciatingly brilliant color and loading his pigment on canvas until it stood out in low relief. His tormented cataclysmic landscapes and violent figure pieces, all set down with breathtaking color, added a new richness and emotionalism to School of Paris painting. The freedom and fury of his manipulation of paint, his pure delight in pigment matter apart from representational aims put him in close contact with certain modes of contemporary abstract painting, especially in America. Another of the *peintres maudits*, Soutine lived out a wretched and unhappy life in the cafés of Montmartre and Montparnasse and died during the Second World War of a sickness brought on at least in part by nervous instability and exhaustion.

The greatest waste, perhaps, in recent artistic history was the untimely death from tuberculosis of Amedeo Modigliani in 1920 at the age of thirty-six. Modigliani's death was hastened by his disorderly living habits, his dissipations and poverty, and a wild indifference to the general state of his body. He came to Paris from Italy in the early years of the century and was affected by the art of Cézanne, by Cubism, and by the fashion of Negro sculpture. Out of these influences, which he perhaps never explored very profoundly in formal terms, he fashioned an aristocratic and mannered figure style. Elegantly linear, his stylized, mask-like heads with their columnar necks and ravishing, rich color are among the most enchanting portraits in modern painting. He left behind a gallery of many of the most celebrated figures of Paris Bohemia, Jean Cocteau, the dealer Zborowsky, and others, and some of the splendid nudes of the century. In all his work there is a fine balance between touching poetic sentiment and stylistic dignity, between romantic vision and some sad, cold reality.

Romance, pushed to the point of fantasy, played a large role in the paintings of Marc Chagall, who came to Paris from Russia early in the century and for a time painted in a Cubist manner, though introducing personal and emotional color. Chagall's imagery, an engaging topsy-turvy world of rabbinical figures, village steeples, brides, bouquets, and clocks, was derived from memories of Russian-Jewish life and folklore (see plate 40). During his Cubist period he demonstrated a mastery of design and an ability to inject anecdote and romantic sentiment into an abstract painting vocabulary that was unique in France. In later years he sufficiently pleased himself with a simpler, sentimental romanticism. Like so many of the School of Paris painters, Chagall found a satisfying pictorial formula and doggedly stuck with it, becoming a sometimes repetitious performer, but an undeniable popular success.

In addition to a certain romantic sentiment, all the members of the School of Paris had in common their taste and an ability to paint lyrically and charmingly. Now ordinarily taste would seem to be a commendable quality, but sometimes it can result in timid conservatism. The new generation that appeared after the Second World War suffered from their "taste"; unlike the original School of Paris artists, they were unable to go beyond mere taste and achieve a significant personal statement.

In very recent years, however, have come signs of new vitality; there has been a concerted assault on mere "taste" by a number of quite literally young painters who work largely in abstract idioms. Their painting indicates common aims, but they are not officially associated with each other. Their immediate inspiration has been the work of members of the older generation: Hans Hartung, Fautrier and Wols. These new young painters work on a large mural scale and with increasing energy and ambitiousness. In fact, their paintings show the discernible influence of that large-scale abstract art which has become the most serious and vital new development in postwar American painting. Four of the most interesting of this group are Mathieu, Soulages, de Staël, and Riopelle, a Canadian working in Paris. De Staël died last year at the age of forty-one; the others are all between thirty-two and thirty-six years old. This group of artists paint with more energy and conviction and on a grander scale than any of their contemporaries, in an effort, like that of so many of the braver spirits of the past generation to go beyond easel painting. Their art is muscular and sensitive, automatic and highly controlled, crude and refined, by turns. The pure act of painting, the energetic application of pigment to canvas, counts for a good deal, yet out of what might appear as automatic and "accidental" effects they achieve often enchanting harmonies of color and a plastic meaning, the conquest of a large pictorial space.

In this, as well as in their use of a free, cursive calligraphy they are close in mood to the interesting and significant contemporary American painting and have often shown their awareness of it. If an invidious distinction may be made, American painting of a similar character, in the art, for example, of Jackson Pollock, Wilhelm de Kooning, Adolph Gottlieb, Clifford Still and Franz Kline, perhaps demonstrates more dynamism and is more immediately physical in its impact. On the other hand, traditional French taste has muted the violence of these new French painters and given their work a refinement, a poise, and an elegance that makes it very handsome indeed. Whether they will be able to pursue the more radical implications of the new abstraction rather than mere handsomeness remains to be seen. In the most recent examples by Mathieu and Soulages shown in New York it seemed that something of their original fine inspiration had been lost; the cosy, Klee-like pictorial effects that have dogged so many of the smaller contemporary French talents such as Maneissier and Bazaine also dominated these paintings. In any case, Mathieu, Soulages and Riopelle seem to be very much the French painters of the day and comprise that long-sought, mislaid "younger" generation; they are contributing the most heavily to whatever contemporary atmosphere of vitality may now be discerned in French painting. It is interesting that once again, as had been the case earlier in the century, the most significant contemporary French painting is couched in an international style.

In Paris today, in America, and in every other part of the globe it is an abstract painting idiom that still inspires modern artists to their most exalted efforts. (Two painters who derive from Surrealism, Francis Bacon in England and Matta Echaurren in Paris, but the character of whose work is very much determined by its execution, are the exceptions.) This does not however, mean that there is not a good deal of sound and estimable, if perhaps outmoded, painting being done in other styles. Two painters in eccentric manner who are perhaps out of touch with their time but who are most original are Bernard Buffet and Jean Dubuffet. Buffet is a minor stylist, a connoisseur of emaciated human flesh and still life, and impoverished interiors. His mannered elongations of form are often tiresome, and he has been overpraised; but there is a flavor of authentic experience behind his mournful scenes, and his leaden, soiled surfaces and graphite scratchings have an undeniable nervous vitality.

Dubuffet is fifty-four, paints in thick paint paste mixed with sand and sometimes ashes, gouging out or blackening in heavy outlines of faces and figures—raw images of a child-like simplicity (see plate 48); despite the ferocity of technique, his work at its best has a whimsical charm as well as intense vitality. He commands a genuine violence and an original expressiveness. Dubuffet has collected L'Art Brut, the art of the untutored, of prisoners, mediums, clairvoyants and the insane, as he has described it. One of his fascinating collections is now the property of an American artist-collector, Alfonso Ossorio, and the crude and curiously vital fantasies of its artists suggest the derivations of Dubuffet's art. Despite his conscious and conscientious primitivism and his efforts to épater, however, Dubuffet is a subtle and sophisticated manipulator of texture and color. In a statement for the Museum of Modern Art's show of contemporary European painting last year, the artist tersely set forth his own lively if irreverent views of art: "Too highly honored, art is rarely nowadays a free celebration (to which one would rush even if it were forbidden). It has become, instead, a game of ceremonies which leads it far into alien terrain. Its true and only terrain is rapture and delirium. . . . To help art regain its place, it should, I believe, be stripped of all tinsel, laurels and buskins. . . . Once disencumbered, it will doubtless begin again to function—to dance and yell like a madman, which is its function, and stop putting on pretentious airs from its professor's chair."

Another whole group of artists, young and old, paint under the leadership of Alberto Magnelli, a close friend of the late Mondrian. They work in the doctrinaire spirit of geometric abstraction, where so often lines and uniform color areas seem to have been meticulously measured and drawn with compass and ruler. The "nonfigurative" painting of Magnelli, by now an old-time Paris resident, has distinction, but also a certain sterility. The more purist varieties of abstract painting have shown no signs of adding anything more than minor refinements to the lofty achievement of Mondrian or the Constructivists.

What the future holds in store for Paris painting it is impossible to say. Although there has been much talk of a return to realism and to more recognizable figuration, no such reaction was evident after the Second World War. On the contrary, the reaction was much more toward an adventurous and experimental art than had been the temporary "humanist" *détente* which occurred after the First World War. One of the charges brought against abstract painting—a term which must include painting as "concrete" as Arp's collages and as full of poetic, symbolic content as Miró's canvases—has been of puritanism and overintellectualization. If anything, the painting of recent years in France represents an effort to inject more emotion into modern painting.

On the evidence this aim has been accomplished more vitally and with more originality in America, and perhaps, too, in England and Italy. It is curious that the countries with the least secure modern traditions have now been able to produce the most vigorous contemporary art. Perhaps it is precisely because the artists of these countries have been more free to ignore the immediate past, which has now become a seductive trap for the French, and pit themselves against the present, seeking authority within themselves alone. Until a short time ago the habit of painting and public acceptance of, and pride in, artistic activity were almost uniquely French; and this cultural circumstance nourished the artist and sustained him. Now this very fact may actually militate against him, make him relax, fatally, into the arms of French tradition and be satisfied with an art that is little more than pleasant decoration.

However, the French artistic mind is notoriously resilient and alive to every sort of esthetic current. The situation of tension and crisis that has somehow provoked American artists into a burst of vital expression is no longer peculiar to America but is world-wide. France, moreover, is still bathed in the aureole of artistic greatness and is still the home of most of the great modern masters. The cycle of great personalities is perhaps at an end, but out of good painting another cycle may begin anew without warning. Perhaps it is already stirring in the art of Mathieu, Soulages, Riopelle, and others. No one can accurately predict what form the new idiom will take, but when it emerges, we shall know it on sight for what it is, an original expression, authentic in terms of its own time. And the future heroes and martyrs of modern art who embrace the new and the "difficult" will undoubtedly bring down on their heads the wrath of the pundits of our great metropolitan newspapers and magazines, just as Manet, the Impressionists, Cézanne, Matisse and Picasso did before them. By the degree of antipathy their works excite we shall no doubt be able to recognize them as the painters of tomorrow.

Chronology Part 1 (1855 — 1895)

1855   Courbet organizes a private *Pavillon du Réalisme* at Paris World's Fair which includes his *Burial at Ornans;* exhibition impresses Pissarro, Manet, Degas, shocks general public; Delacroix observes it with mixed feelings.

1856   Manet leaves studio of Thomas Couture to paint independently.

The engraver Bracquemond, a friend of Degas, discovers the Japanese print, soon to become an important factor in the art of many of the Impressionists and Post-Impressionists.

1858   Monet meets Boudin at Le Havre, is guided by his methods of painting out-of-doors.

1859   Manet is rejected at the Salon.

Pissarro exhibits Corot-influenced landscape at the Salon.

Pissarro meets Monet, who has just come to Paris for the first time, at Suisse Academy.

Birth of Georges Seurat, Paris.

1861   Manet's debut at the Salon with *Portrait of the Artist's Parents* and *Spanish Guitar Player;* his paintings are howled down in the press but inspire a group of young painters, including Fantin-Latour, to call and pay their respects. Manet subsequently meets Duranty and other realist critics, and Baudelaire.

Cézanne makes his first trip to Paris, at the insistent urging of his boyhood friend, Emile Zola; meets Pissarro.

1862   Manet and Degas meet at the Louvre.

Monet is demobilized and returns to Le Havre to paint with Boudin and Jongkind. Goes to Paris and enrolls at Gleyre's studio, where he meets Renoir, Sisley, Bazille.

Baudelaire praises Manet in a published article.

Degas paints *The Bellelli Family* in Florence, in a new realistic manner.

Degas paints first racing pictures at Longchamps,

seeking a "contemporary" subject matter.

1863   Death of Delacroix.

Baudelaire publishes eulogy on Delacroix.

Salon des Refusés instituted by Emperor after protests at Salon jury's autocratic behavior in rejecting new painters; Manet shows *The Luncheon on the Grass* at this new Salon; it is reviled in the press but acclaimed by younger painters, who begin to look to Manet for leadership.

1865   Manet's *Olympia* shown at regular Salon and violently attacked by critics. Manet repairs to Spain disturbed by public hostility to his art; meets Theodore Duret in Madrid.

Monet works on large out-of-door *Luncheon on the Grass* in the Fontainebleau forest at Chailly; Renoir and Sisley paint at nearby Marlotte; Monet also works with Courbet along Normandy coast.

1866   Manet and his friends begin to foregather at the Café Guerbois; Emile Zola begins defense of Manet and new painters in the press; he writes in *L'Evénement* that Manet's work will one day grace the Louvre, and is discharged from newspaper shortly after.

Renoir's paintings made at Fontainebleau are strongly influenced by Courbet.

Pissarro has disagreement with Corot, settles at Pontoise just outside Paris.

1867   Manet and Courbet hold special one-man shows at Paris World's Fair in defiance of Salon.

Monet, Renoir, Pissarro, Sisley, Bazille, Cézanne rejected by Salon jury.

Death of Baudelaire.

Birth of Pierre Bonnard, at Fontenay-aux-Roses.

1868   Poverty drives Monet to suicide attempt.

Renoir, in his correspondence, notes he is too poor to buy paints; his *Lise* accepted by Salon jury and praised in the press.

Degas paints his first theatrical subject, *Mlle Fiocre*.

1869   Monet and Renoir work in Bougival, at La Grenouillère; they begin to use the divided color and paint dabs of Impressionist technique.

Henri Matisse born at Le Cateau, in Picardy.

1870   Franco-Prussian War drives Monet, Sisley, Pissarro to England, where they are impressed by the paintings of Constable and Turner.

Bazille is killed in the war.

1871   Courbet exiled for participation in Commune.

1872   Cézanne paints with Pissarro at Pontoise.

Monet settles at Argenteuil on the Seine after travels in Holland; Renoir frequently joins him there.

Dealer Durand-Ruel buys block of twenty-nine paintings from Manet for 40,000 francs (about $8000).

1873   Manet's *Le Bon Bock* attains great popular success at the Salon; he joins Monet and Renoir at Argenteuil; they paint in more brilliant color, developing mature Impressionist technique.

Degas returns from trip to New Orleans; resumes studies of orchestra, ballet class subjects which he had begun at Paris Opéra in 1872.

1874   First group exhibition of the Impressionists at Nadar's studio, Boulevard des Capucines: one hundred sixty-five pictures, thirty artists, among them Monet, Renoir, Sisley, Degas, Pissarro, Cézanne, Berthe Morisot.

Critic coins the label Impressionist as a derisive term, inspired by one of Monet's entries, *Impression: Sunrise*.

1875   Manet's Impressionist work, *Boating at Argenteuil*, shown at Salon and brings down wrath of conservative critics.

First auction sale of Impressionist painting at Hôtel Drouot; paintings sold at average price of 144 francs.

Cézanne at Pontoise with Pissarro once again.

Death of Corot.

1876   Second group exhibition of Impressionists; Duranty publishes *La Nouvelle Peinture,* first full-dress appreciation of the Impressionists.

Cézanne has quarrel with Monet, retires to L'Estaque, near Marseilles.

Renoir paints one of the great classics of Impressionist period, *Le Moulin de la Galette*.

Gauguin exhibits landscape at Salon; meets Pissarro and begins to collect Impressionist painting.

1879 Fourth group show; through good offices of Degas, American Mary Cassatt exhibits with Impressionists. Renoir shows *Mme Charpentier and Her Children* at the Salon and it proves a public favorite.

1881 Sixth group exhibition; Monet ceases sending to the Salon entirely.

Renoir travels in Italy, expresses discontent with Impressionist methods and is impressed by Italian and antique painting classics.

Cézanne paints with Pissarro and Gauguin at Pontoise, then retires to Aix-en-Provence; his paintings emphasize structure and solidity, deny flimsy design and evanescent effects of Impressionist work.

Lautrec comes to Paris to study.

Birth of Picasso, Malaga, Spain.

1883 Manet's death.

Renoir paints *Dance at Bougival,* emphasizing line and drier color.

Seurat exhibits large charcoal-drawing portrait of his friend Aman-Jean at the Salon; it is praised by Claude-Roger Marx; Seurat paints *Une Baignade—Asnières.*

1884 Redon, Seurat, Signac, Cross, and other artists found *Salon des Indépendants;* Seurat exhibits his *Baignade* there, announcing new manner of Neo-Impressionism.

Gauguin abandons commercial career for painting.

1886 Eighth and last Impressionist group show; Monet, Renoir, Sisley refuse to participate, objecting to Neo-Impressionist entries.

Seurat shows *A Sunday Afternoon on the Island of la Grande Jatte;* Pissarro adopts pointillist technique of Seurat and Signac.

First large American exhibition of Impressionist work staged in New York by Durand-Ruel, with moderate success.

Henri Rousseau exhibits at *Salon des Indépendants* for first time.

Degas exhibits group of paintings and pastels focusing on females at their ablutions, at last Impressionist show; his art becomes more energetic, his style freer.

Cézanne works in silence and isolation in the South; using thinner medium, he continues his formal investigation, modeling with little planes of color.

Gauguin goes to Pont-Aven in Brittany, meets Emile Bernard.

Moréas and Gustave Kahn found the literary review, *Le Symboliste;* Symbolist movement attracts more writers and leading poet, Mallarmé, who later becomes a friend and admirer of Gauguin.

1888   Belgian James Ensor uses brilliant Impressionist palette to create large-scale fantasy, *Entrance of Christ into Brussels.*

Gauguin's second stay at Pont-Aven. Formation of Symbolist-Synthetist painting group around him. Gauguin joins van Gogh at Arles in the fall and leaves after violent quarrel and Vincent's breakdown.

Bonnard, Vuillard, Denis, Sérusier meet at Julian Academy. Sérusier visits Gauguin in Brittany; returns to expound Symbolist-Synthetist theory to Julian Academy friends.

1889   Gauguin and Symbolist painters exhibit at Café Volpini during Paris World's Fair.

Denis, Sérusier, Bonnard, Vuillard band together under name of Nabis.

Lautrec exhibits for the first time at *Indépendants.*

Van Gogh enters sanitarium at Saint-Rémy.

1890   Death of van Gogh by suicide.

Pissarro abandons pointillist technique.

1891   Van Gogh retrospective at *Salon des Indépendants.*

Lautrec's first posters of Montmartre music hall subjects.

Matisse studies painting in Paris in Bouguereau's studio.

The Nabis hold their first joint exhibition; the Natanson brothers launch *La Revue Blanche,* to which many of the Nabis contribute prints.

Monet begins his *Haystack* series, to be followed the next year by *The Poplars* and *Rouen Cathedral.*

Cézanne at work on some of his greatest compositions: *The Cardplayers, Bathers, Mont Sainte-Victoire*.

Gauguin and Paul Verlaine are given a Symbolist evening by Mallarmé and others; sale and exhibition of Gauguin's paintings held to finance a trip to Tahiti. First trip to Tahiti.

Death of Seurat.

1892   Architect Victor Horta anticipates style of *Art Nouveau* with decoration for house at 12 rue de Turin, Brussels.

1893   Matisse works at Gustave Moreau's studio; meets Rouault, Marquet there.

Gauguin returns from Tahiti, holds exhibition at Durand-Ruel.

1894   The great Caillebotte collection of Impressionist painting is provisionally rejected by Luxembourg Museum.

1895   After nearly twenty years of obscurity, Cézanne is exhibited in a large retrospective by the new dealer Vollard; show acclaimed by Renoir, Degas, Pissarro; has a profound effect on Bernard, Denis, Bonnard, Vuillard, and the Nabis, as a rejection of Impressionism.

Gauguin returns to Tahiti.

1896	Matisse has success at *Salon de la Nationale* with two paintings.
1897	Caillebotte Bequest accepted in large part by the state despite severe public criticism. Matisse shows Impressionist-inspired work, *The Dinner Table,* at the *Nationale;* it meets with intense opposition from Salon jury members. Bing's *Art Nouveau* Gallery opens in Paris, exhibits proto-Expressionist painting of Norwegian Edvard Munch. Gauguin paints large *Where Do We Come From? What Are We? Where Are We Going?* in Marquesas Islands; unsuccessfully attempts suicide.
1899	Matisse meets Derain and Puy at Carrière's Academy. Nabis hold large group exhibition at Durand-Ruel in homage to Odilon Redon. Derain and Vlaminck meet at Chatou. Sisley dies.
1900	Large Seurat show at *Revue Blanche*. Picasso's first trip to Paris; influenced by the art of Lautrec and Steinlen.
1901	Large van Gogh retrospective at Bernheim-Jeune Gallery; it stirs younger painters; Derain introduces Matisse to Vlaminck at show. Picasso begins painting beggars, human derelicts in pervasive and melancholy "blue" tonalities. Lautrec dies.
1903	Rouault, Marquet, and others found *Salon d'Automne;* Rouault meets Léon Bloy, his style begins to change. Gauguin exhibition in Paris. Death of Gauguin, Pissarro, Whistler.
1904	Rouault shows somber-hued paintings, pastels, water colors of prostitute subjects in savage, caricature style at *Salon d'Automne*. Matisse paints with Signac at Saint-Tropez in vivid, Neo-Impressionist manner.

Picasso settles in Paris. Braque comes to Paris from Le Havre.

1905   *Salon des Indépendants* holds important Seurat and van Gogh shows.

Matisse shows large Neo-Impressionist *Luxe, Calme et Volupté* at *Indépendants* in the spring, a painting which inspires Dufy to change his style.

At the *Salon d'Automne*, Matisse, Derain, Marquet, Rouault, Puy, Manguin, Camoin, and others show new paintings in bold colors; they are labeled Fauves (Wild Beasts) by the critic Vauxcelles; their painting stirs violent controversy. The Steins buy two Matisse paintings from the exhibition.

In Dresden, Germany, Heckel, Schmidt-Rottluff, Nolde, Kirchner, and Pechstein organize *Die Brücke* (The Bridge) group along Fauve lines.

Beginning of Picasso's "rose" period; Leo Stein collects Picasso.

1906   Second Fauve exhibition and a large Gauguin show at the *Salon d'Automne;* Dufy and Braque join the Fauves.

Matisse shows *Joy of Life* at *Salon des Indépendants,* evidence of a new formal synthesis; Steins purchase the painting. Matisse meets Picasso at the Stein apartment in the rue de Fleurus.

Picasso returns from summer at Gosol in the Pyrenees to repaint his portrait of Gertrude Stein in a more primitive manner; Matisse buys first Negro sculpture and is probably responsible for introducing Picasso to African art.

Death of Cézanne.

Modigliani comes to Paris.

1907   Picasso, under the influence of Negro art and Cézanne, paints his revolutionary *Demoiselles d'Avignon* in proto-Cubist style.

Large memorial exhibition of Cézanne at the *Salon d'Automne* and publication of his letters to Emile Bernard.

1908   Braque, following Picasso's lead, paints landscape in the south in severe geometrical style, limiting colors to ochres, tans, greens; exhibits paintings in new style at Paris Salon; critic Vauxcelles accuses Braque of reducing everything arbitrarily to "cubes."

1909   Picasso and Braque develop Cubism towards a higher degree of abstraction.

Utrillo enters his "white" period, painting moody impressions of the Paris suburbs.

1910   Boccioni, Balla, Carrà, Severini, and Russolo sign first Futurist Manifesto in Milan; adopt formalization of Cubism to create sensation of movement and more dynamic effects.

Léger, de la Fresnaye, Marcel Duchamp, Marcoussis, Delaunay, Le Fauconnier, Herbin, Jacques Villon, and others paint in Cubist manner.

Matisse sees large exhibition of Islamic art in Munich; exhibits *Dance* and *Music* at *Salon d'Automne,* commissioned by his Russian patron, Sergei Shchukin.

Wassily Kandinsky paints first abstractions in Munich. Chagall, Mondrian come to Paris.

1911   Picasso and Braque introduce facsimiles of hand lettering and eye-fooling textures into their Cubist painting.

First Cubist group exhibitions at *Indépendants* and *Salon d'Automne.* Chagall paints under Cubist discipline, but uses bright colors and explores fantastic content.

Matisse travels in North Africa; under Cubist influence begins to emphasize more sober color and schematic design.

De Chirico comes to Paris, paints romantic fantasies that anticipate his later "metaphysical" period and Surrealism.

The term "Expressionism" is first used in Munich to describe German painting by Nolde and others.

1912   Delaunay, Picasso, Léger, Metzinger, Le Fauconnier exhibit with the Futurists in Paris. Juan Gris joins the Villon brothers and Metzinger in the *Section d'Or* group and exhibits Cubist-inspired paintings with them.

Gleizes and Metzinger publish *Du Cubisme.*

Picasso and Braque begin to make collages.

Picabia and Marcel Duchamp give their paintings exasperating, far-fetched titles; their forms become more mechanical in character as they make an effort to undermine formal purity of Cubism.

Delaunay paints lyrical, pure-color abstractions in brilliant hues; his new style labeled "Orphism" by Guillaume Apollinaire.

Kandinsky publishes *On the Spiritual in Art*, suggesting an approach to abstract painting as a kind of visual music with its own laws of harmony and counterpoint.

Kandinsky, Klee, Marc, Mäcke, Münter form Blue Rider group in Munich and exhibit together.

Mondrian, living in Paris, paints along Cubist lines.

1913   Guillaume Apollinaire publishes the very important appreciation of Cubism, *The Cubist Painters*.

Picasso and Braque use vivid colors and decorative shapes with ambiguous overtones: Synthetic Cubism.

1914   Marcel Duchamp's first "ready-mades."

1915   De Chirico returns to Italy; with Carrà, and later Morandi, paints in "metaphysical" manner.

Picasso begins a series of realistic drawings and portraits, but also continues to work in Synthetic Cubist manner.

1916   Tzara, Arp, Ball, Hülsenbeck found Dada movement in Zurich; first manifesto and publications.

Rouault devotes himself almost exclusively to prints for the publisher Vollard.

1917   Picasso's "neo-classic" style takes definite form; he does sets and costumes for Diaghilev ballet "Parade"; Apollinaire describes Picasso decorations as "Surrealist."

At Nice, Matisse paints in a softer and more anecdotal manner, reviving bright, sensuous color.

Mondrian paints pure abstractions in rigid, geometric forms and the primary colors; Mondrian, van Doesburg, van der Leck, and others launch *de Stijl* movement at Leyden, Holland.

1918   Death of Apollinaire from head wound suffered in

war. Degas dies.

Braque's postwar paintings in Cubist manner are softer and show more interest in natural appearances.

1919   Léger works in his own personal style of decorative Cubism, using vivid primary colors; he is influenced by machine forms.

Ozenfant and Jeanneret (Le Corbusier) start Purism.

Kurt Schwitters makes first Dada *Merz* collages.

Renoir dies.

1920   First public demonstration of Dada in Paris.

Miró settles in Paris, meets Picasso.

Mondrian in Paris publishes *Neo-Plasticism*, a defense of geometric abstraction.

Matisse begins painting nudes and odalisques against decorative "rococo" background.

Death of Modigliani.

1921   Picasso paints *Three Musicians*, Léger paints *Three Women (Le Grand Déjeuner)* in monumental Cubist style.

1922   Miró completes *The Farm*, both summing up past descriptive style and indicating a new abstract direction.

Large Dada exhibition in Paris at the Montaigne Gallery.

1924   Breton issues first Surrealist Manifesto; defines Surrealism as "pure psychic automatism."

Braque paints first of his large, semi-draped basket carriers, figures of classical inspiration.

Léger is in direct contact with Mondrian and the *de Stijl* group.

1925   Miró exhibits with Surrealists in first group show; also included, Picasso, Arp, Klee, Masson, Ernst, de Chirico, Man Ray. Picasso introduces convulsive, Surrealist elements into his Cubist compositions.

Matisse paints odalisques with richer pigmentation, loaded ornament and more sculpturesque distortions.

1927   Death of Juan Gris.

1928   Picasso paints and does sculpture in an abstract, constructivist style; in painting, beginning of his so-called "bone" period.

1929   Second Surrealist Manifesto; Dali joins the group.

Braque paints in a more severe style, possibly under Picasso's influence.

1931   Braque works in a neo-classical style, emphasizing linear calligraphy.

1932   Matisse works on monumental Barnes mural decoration, *The Dance;* etchings to "Poems of Stéphane Mallarmé" published by Albert Skira.

1937   Picasso paints tragic mural *Guernica* for Spanish Pavilion at Paris World's Fair. More Expressionist and Surrealist violence in his "double-profile" paintings of the period.

Braque also uses multiple profiles and dramatic dark and light patterns in Cubist figure compositions, but without the disquieting overtones of Picasso's.

1940   Death of Klee and Vuillard.

1941   Léger, in America, paints acrobats, cyclists.

1944   Death of Mondrian, Kandinsky.

1946   Picasso works at pottery and at lithographs inspired by classical mythology at Antibes and Vallauris.

Emergence of French postwar painters of varying tendencies: Pignon, Estève, Maneissier, Buffet, Dubuffet, Bazaine, Soulages.

1947   Death of Bonnard.

1948   Léger executes mosaics for façade of church at Assy.

1949   First Paris one-man show for Georges Mathieu.

1951   Matisse completes Vence chapel decorations.

Death of Dufy.

1954   Exhibition of "Younger European Painters," Solomon R. Guggenheim Museum, New York.

Death of Derain.

Death of Matisse.

1955   Exhibition, "The New Decade: 22 European Painters and Sculptors," Museum of Modern Art, New York.

Death of Léger.

Glossary

Abstract Art

Painting or sculpture without representational intentions, having little or no resemblance to natural appearances. Kandinsky from 1910 and Mondrian after 1917 developed the most "pure" abstract styles in modern painting, but the term is often used to refer to work by the Cubists, Miró, and others even when there are some suggestions or evocations of nature. Manet began the process of "abstracting" from nature when he reduced the visible world to flat shapes and silhouettes; Cézanne went further by radically simplifying forms into an interlocking system of basic, geometric shapes. In the twentieth century abstract idioms have dominated painting.

Art Nouveau

Also called the *Jungendstil* in Germany. A style of architectural decoration based on curvilinear forms, originating in Belgium in the early nineties under the leadership of Henry van de Velde. Its stylistic vocabulary was derived from the paintings of the French Post-Impressionists. The style of *Art Nouveau* was romantic and perhaps "decadent," but its social aims and esthetic anticipated the functionalism of modern architecture.

Belle Peinture

The traditional hedonism of French painting. Chardin, Manet, and Braque are all excellent examples. In each case there would seem to be a characteristically French love of medium and a natural delight in its sensuous possibilities. *Belle peinture* also implies the intimacy of easel painting.

Blaue Reiter, Der (The Blue Rider)

A group of German painters who began to exhibit together in Munich in 1912: Klee, Kandinsky, Marc, Mäcke, and Münter. Their work combined the intense color of Fauvism and Cubist geometry of form.

Brücke, Die (The Bridge)

The German derivative of the Fauve movement, organized in Dresden in 1905 by Heckel, Schmidt-Rottluff, Nolde, Kirchner, and Pechstein. In later years these painters moved to Berlin, their art became more subjective and "gothic" and acquired a convulsive, Expressionist character.

Cubism

A movement in painting originated in 1908 by Picasso and Braque which transposed natural forms into abstract arrangements of overlapping or transparent planes. It was based on Cézanne's late work and came as a more formal, architectonic reaction to the spontaneous effects of the preceding Fauvist painters. It has probably been the most important and generative single movement in twentieth-century art.

Dadaism

An experimental movement in painting and literature originated in Zurich by Tristan Tzara, Hugo Ball, and others in 1916. It grew out of war and postwar disillusionment; its fantasy, "shock" tactics and use of normally unartistic material anticipated Surrealism. Dada was a modern form of protest against the sacred cows of art tradition. Out of Dada's exasperation, disparagements, and perversity flowed many entertaining and in some cases permanently significant works of art.

Divisionism

A method of applying unmixed, pure color in contrasting dabs, used intuitively by the Impressionists and more systematically and self-consciously by the Neo-Impressionists. Where there was a single tone (orange, for example) these artists "divided" it into its separate, constituent hues (red and yellow) for the purposes of obtaining the greater intensity of an "optical" mixture.

Expressionism

The emphasis on "inner" worlds of subjective feeling rather than on descriptions of the objective world, usually projecting "extreme" states of mind. It describes much of twentieth-century German art, including the work of Nolde (after 1910), Kokoschka, and Beckmann, but also some aspects of Picasso's painting. Its spiritual fathers in the nineteenth century were van Gogh, Ensor, and Munch.

Fauvism

Led by Henri Matisse in 1905, the Fauve painters freely distorted form and used vivid, spontaneous color effects in an effort to liberate the painter's instincts. For all their violence, they were also inspired by a traditionally French decorative hedonism. Matisse, Derain, Braque, Vlaminck, Rouault, Dufy and others exhibited together as Fauves. The movement lasted only three years, but its influence has been international and of lasting significance.

Futurism

An Italian movement based on Cubist formalism which attempted to capture movement and the dynamism of the modern industrial world; Futurism spurned tradition. Its animators were Boccioni (a fine sculptor as well as a painter), Severini, Carrà, Balla, and Russolo.

Impasto

Paint paste when applied to the canvas so that it stands out in opaque relief.

Impressionism

Originated by Monet, Renoir, Pissarro, Sisley around 1874, a method of painting with small, vibrant dabs of pure color. By this technique the Impressionists thus showed the movement and scintillation of light in nature, and the spontaneity of their own feelings.

Law of Simultaneous Contrasts

In the middle of the nineteenth century the French physicist Chevreul had discovered that colors create around themselves an aureole which is their complementary. Following Chevreul's lead Seurat and the Neo-Impressionists learned to enhance the brilliance of their color schemes by implementing this optical effect. They added intensity and luminosity to their surfaces by painting in complementaries and by applying pigment in contrasting dabs of pure color.

The Nabis

Sérusier, Denis, Valloton, Bonnard, Vuillard were some of the members of this group inspired by Gauguin's Pont-Aven painting; they took their name from the Hebrew word "prophet." Active between 1890 and 1900, the Nabis adhered to Gauguin's practice of using "symbolic" color and strongly outlined surface patterns but varied widely both in style and in their choice of subject matter. Bonnard and Vuillard applied the new theories of decoration to subjects of everyday life; esthetically, they were the most significant of the group.

Naturalism

A literary and artistic movement in the middle and later half of the nineteenth century whose aim was to depict life by a documentary realism. In the novels of Emile Zola these aims were combined with a reforming zeal and a spirit of "muckraking." Only Courbet, perhaps, shared that spirit, if somewhat obliquely, as demonstrated in the deliberate coarseness of some of his peasant themes. The realism of Manet, Degas, and Lautrec in particular was conditioned by the new candor of the more orthodox literary naturalists. In painting, naturalism is also used as a general term for any style descriptive of the natural appearance of things.

Neo-Impressionism

A movement founded by Seurat and Signac about 1885 in an effort to systematize and "scientize" Impressionism. These artists employed the primary and intermediate colors in contrasting dots, giving their surfaces a confetti-like appearance; they based their color researches on the optical theories and demonstrations of Chevreul, O. N. Rood, and other scientists.

Optical Mixture

Delacroix in his late paintings broke tones down into their constituent hues and allowed the eye to mix or synthesize them. Rood demonstrated that such optical mixtures are more brilliant than premixed color taken from the tube. The Impressionists depended on optical mixing for their vivid effects; the Neo-Impressionists made a meticulous study of the physical laws of color and light, applying them in their art.

Pointillism

The Neo-Impressionist technique of painting in little contrasting dots of pure color, which a critic of the period once unkindly referred to as "colored fleas." A modified, low-keyed pointillism was used by some of the Cubists and Futurists to animate their surfaces.

Post-Impressionism

The reaction to the emphasis of the Impressionists on the literal truth of their visual sensations and to their formless compositions. Cézanne, Seurat, Gauguin, van Gogh were in their various styles all Post-Impressionist painters.

Primitivism

In modern art this term may include the bloodless Pre-Raphaelite style of Puvis de Chavannes as well as Picasso's powerful "Negro" period. Any painting is primitive that seeks a new rapport with archaic forms, whether that search is nostalgic, a conscious effort to be quaint, or stems from a genuine atavism. Gauguin was the first conscious modern "primitive" when he tried to paint "like children" during his stay in Brittany.

Salon des Refusés (Salon of the Rejected)

In 1863 Emperor Napoleon III permitted the artists whose work had been rejected by the high-handed jury of the official Salon to hold a counter-exhibition. Although he had been shown at the regular Salon two years before, it was at the *Salon des Refusés* that Manet emerged as the first revolutionary artist of the modern period in France.

Stijl, De (The Style)

A movement formed in Leyden, Holland, in 1917 by Mondrian, Vantongerloo, and other artists, designers, and architects; it was dedicated to applying principles of abstract geometrical design to all the arts, fine and applied.

Surrealism

A movement in literature and art founded officially by the poet-painter André Breton in Paris in 1924. The Surrealist painters emphasized "the omnipotence of the dream" and the chance associations of the subconscious mind. They were indebted to Dada and to the "metaphysical" paintings of de Chirico. Breton, Masson, Miró adopted manners in which nervous sensibility and automatism were most important; Dali, Tanguy, and others painted fantastic and hallucinatory works in a harder, more illustrative convention.

Symbolism and Synthetism

These terms were used interchangeably and together to describe the style that Gauguin and his followers developed in Brittany from 1888 to 1890. Their paintings were synthetic (or "Synthetist") in that they followed a broader principle of using strongly patterned colors and lines. This principle was opposed to the more literal observations of Impressionist realism. Gauguin and his friends thought of their paintings as "symbolic" rather than realistic, as dreams "in the presence of nature" rather than copies of the visible world.

Bibliography

GENERAL

Apollinaire, Guillaume. *The Cubist Painters*. New York, 1949

Arp, Hans and others. *The Dada Painters and Poets*. Edited by Robert Motherwell. New York, 1951

Barr, Alfred H., Jr. *Cubism and Abstract Art*. New York, 1936
Fantastic Art, Dada, Surrealism. New York, 1937
What is Modern Painting? New York, 1943

Baudelaire, Charles. *Intimate Journals*. Translated by Christopher Isherwood, with an introduction by T. S. Eliot. London, 1930

Baudelaire, Charles. *The Mirror of Art*. Critical Studies. Edited by Jonathan Mayne. London, 1955

Bell, Clive. *Since Cézanne*. London, 1923

Cézanne, Paul. *Letters*. Edited by John Rewald. London, 1941

Cooper, Douglas. *The Courtauld Collection, A Catalogue and Introduction*. London, 1954

Degas, Edgar. *Letters*. Edited by Marcel Guérin. New York, 1948

Delacroix, Eugene. *Journals*. Edited by Walter Pach. New York, 1937

Duret, Théodore. *Manet and the French Impressionists*. Philadelphia, 1910

Duthuit, Georges. *The Fauvist Painters*. New York, 1950

Fry, Roger. *Transformations*. New York, 1926

Gascoyne, David. *A Short Survey of Surrealism*. London, 1936

Gauguin, Paul. *Intimate Journals*. New York, 1936

Goldwater, Robert. *Primitivism in Modern Painting*. New York, 1938

Goldwater, Robert, and Marco Treves. *Artists on Art*. New York, 1945

Kandinsky, Wassily. *Concerning the Spiritual in Art*. New York, 1947

Lewis, Wyndham. *Time and Western Man*. New York, 1947

Mondrian, Piet. *Plastic and Pure Art*. New York, 1947

Moore, George. *Confessions of a Young Man*. London, 1888

Pevsner, Nikolaus. *Pioneers of the Modern Movement*. New York, 1937

Pissarro, Camille. *Letters to His Son Lucien*. Edited by John
    Rewald. New York, 1943
Praz, Mario. *The Romantic Agony*. London, 1933
Raynal, Maurice and others. *History of Modern Painting*,
    Vols. 1-3. Geneva, 1950
Read, Herbert. *Art Now*. London, 1948
Rewald, John. *The History of Impressionism*. New York, 1943
Sachs, Paul. *Modern Prints and Drawings*. New York, 1954
San Lazzaro, G. di. *Painting in France, 1895-1949*. New York,
    1949
Soby, James Thrall. *After Picasso*. New York, 1935
    Contemporary Painters. New York, 1948
Stein, Gertrude. *The Autobiography of Alice B. Toklas*. New
    York, 1933
Stein, Leo. *Appreciation: Painting, Poetry and Prose*. New
    York, 1947
Sweeney, James Johnson. *Plastic Redirections in Twentieth-
    Century Painting*. Chicago, 1934
Uhde, Wilhelm. *The Impressionists*. New York, 1937
Van Gogh, Vincent. *The Letters of Vincent van Gogh to His
    Brother, 1872-1886*. Boston, 1929
    *Further Letters of Vincent van Gogh to His Brother,
    1886-1890*. Boston, 1929
Venturi, Lionello. *Impressionists and Symbolists*. New York,
    1950
Wilenski, R. H. *Modern French Painters*. London, 1949

SELECTED MONOGRAPHS

ART NOUVEAU. *The Art Nouveau*. Henry F. Lenning. The
    Hague, 1951
BONNARD. *Pierre Bonnard*. John Rewald. New York, 1948
BRAQUE. *Georges Braque*. Henry R. Hope. New York, 1949
CÉZANNE. *Cézanne, A Study of His Development*. Roger Fry.
    New York, 1952
    Paul Cézanne. Gerstle Mack. New York, 1935
CHAGALL. *Marc Chagall*. James Johnson Sweeney. New York,
    1948
CHIRICO. *Giorgio de Chirico*. James Thrall Soby. New York,
    1955.

[249]

COURBET. *Courbet*. Marcel Zahar. New York, 1950

DALI. *Salvador Dali*. James Thrall Soby. New York, 1941

DEGAS. *Degas*. Daniel C. Rich. New York, 1951

DELACROIX. *Eugene Delacroix, His Life and Work*. Charles Baudelaire. New York, 1947

GAUGUIN. *Gauguin*. John Rewald, London, 1939

GRIS. *Juan Gris, His Life and Work*. Daniel H. Kahnweiler. New York, 1947

GUYS. *The Painter of Victorian Life*. Edited by C. Geoffrey Holme with a translation of Baudelaire's *Peintre de la Vie Moderne*. London, 1930

KLEE. *Paul Klee*. Will Grohmann. New York, 1954

LÉGER. *Léger*. Katherine Kuh. Chicago, 1953

MANET. *Manet*. S. Lane Faison. New York, 1953

MATISSE. *Henri Matisse, His Art and His Public*. Alfred H. Barr, Jr. New York, 1951
Henri Matisse. Roger Fry. New York, 1930
Matisse. Clement Greenberg. New York, 1953

MIRÓ. *Joan Miró*. Clement Greenberg, New York, 1948
Joan Miró. James Johnson Sweeney. New York, 1941

MODIGLIANI. *Modigliani*. James Thrall Soby. New York, 1951

PICASSO. *Picasso: Fifty Years of His Art*. Alfred H. Barr, Jr. New York, 1946
Picasso. Jaime Sabartés and Wilhelm Boeck. New York, 1955
Picasso, Master of the Phantom. Robert Melville. London, 1939

RENOIR. *Renoir, An Intimate Record*. Ambroise Vollard. Paris, 1925

ROUAULT. *Georges Rouault: Painting and Prints*. James Thrall Soby and Carl O. Schniewind. New York, 1947

ROUSSEAU. *Henri Rousseau*. Daniel C. Rich. New York, 1946

SEURAT. *Georges Seurat*. John Rewald. New York, 1946

SOUTINE. *Chaim Soutine*. Monroe Wheeler. New York, 1950

TOULOUSE-LAUTREC. *Toulouse-Lautrec*. Douglas Cooper. New York, 1952

VAN GOGH. *Van Gogh*. Meyer Schapiro. New York, 1950

VUILLARD. *Edouard Vuillard*. Andrew C. Ritchie. New York, 1954

Index